The Wisdom of the Dream

A C.G. Jung Foundation Book

The C. G. Jung Foundation for Analytical Psychology is dedicated to helping men and women grow in conscious awareness of the psychological realities in themselves and society, find healing and meaning in their lives and greater depth in their relationships, and live in response to their discovered sense of purpose. It welcomes the public to attend its lectures, seminars, films, symposia, and workshops and offers a wide selection of books for sale through its bookstore. The Foundation also publishes *Quadrant*, a semiannual journal, and books on Analytical Psychology and related subjects. For information about Foundation programs or membership, please write to the C. G. Jung Foundation, 28 East 39th Street, New York, NY 10016.

The Wisdom of the Dream

The World of C. G. Jung

Stephen Segaller and Merrill Berger

Shambhala

Boston

1989

Shambhala Publications, Inc.
Horticultural Hall
300 Massachusetts Avenue
Boston, Massachusetts 02115

9 8 7 6 5 4 3 2 1

First Shambhala Edition
Printed in the United States of America on acid-free paper
Distributed in the United States by Random House and in Canada by
Random House of Canada Ltd.

The photographs in this book were kindly supplied by the following: the authors 3, 4, 5, 6, 16, 18, 19, 20, 21, 22, 23, 26, 28; ABC–Capital Cities Inc. 30; Cornelia Brunner 14; Cliff Goddard 24; Robert Hinshaw 10, 11; the Jung family 1, 14; Mary Evans Picture Library 2; Metropolitan Museum of Art, New York 8, 9; NASA, Pasadena 29; Eric Scott Parker 12, 13, 15, 27; Martha Suazo 15; Swiss National Tourist Office 7; Joe and Jane Wheelwright 25; and Wheelwright Museum of the American Indian, Santa Fe 17.

Library of Congress Cataloging-in-Publication Data

Segaller, Stephen.
  Wisdom of the dream.

  Based on a three-part British television series.
  Bibliography: p.
  Includes index.
  1. Psychoanalysis. 2. Jung, C. G. (Carl Gustav),
1875–1961. 1. Berger, Merrill. II. Title.
BF173.S443 1989   150.19'54   89-42632
ISBN 0-87773-512-3

for Adam and Catherine

THERE WAS ONCE a man who was born in a land of mountains, where the people are self-sufficient and live close to the earth. All his life he dreamed and investigated his own dreams and other people's. He dreamed of places he had never visited; of people he had never met; of stories he had never heard, but which other people had known. He became a doctor, and patients came to him, to try to understand *the wisdom of the dream*. He was a successful psychiatrist who suffered his own emotional turmoil; a scientist and researcher who never refrained from speaking of the soul, of mythology, and of God. He was a story-teller and a stone-cutter; a scholar and a traveller; a painter, a healer and always a dreamer. His dreams have changed our ideas. When he grew old, he was honoured as a wise old man – but he said 'I am also an old fool.' Before he died, he said 'My work will be continued by those who suffer.' His name was Carl Gustav Jung.

Contents

Acknowledgements

It has been our privilege to spend more than two years pursuing *our* Jung, and listening to what Jung's friends, pupils and followers, say about him, his work, and their commitment to both. There are many people to thank for their different contributions to this process, sometimes as long as ten years ago.

Jim Graham of Border Television and John Ranelagh of Channel 4 made the film series happen. Paul Corley of Border and Gwynn Pritchard of Channel 4 supervised its birth. The Border TV film crew – Eric Scott-Parker, Cliff Goddard and Alan Moir – demonstrated considerable stamina and many other virtues in our efforts to pursue Jungian analysts onto mountain-tops, into deserts and across lakes. Richard Gibb performed splendid camera work at the end of the production schedule. The series production team of associate producer Gill Fickling, researcher Stephen Lowenstein and production manager Jean Nunn brought a mixture of invaluable talent; film editor John Hackney and his assistant Chris Nixon somehow made sense and kept track of the rushes; and our assistants Kimberley Harris and Clare Moberley and our nanny Sally Cardy kept everyone and everything in the right places.

We thank every analyst who talked to us to help us to understand Jung's thought; and especially those who gave us interviews, despite great age, ill health or reluctance. In particular, we should mention Andrew Samuels, Robert Hinshaw, Michael Edwards, Aryeh Maidenbaum, Bani Shorter, John Beebe, Aniela Jaffe, Robert Johnson and Joe and Jane Wheelwright for their particular help, patience or hospitality – and Dr Richard Evans of the University of Houston, a pioneer of psychology on film. Ann Baynes and Diana Crockford, members of the Baynes family in England, kindly lent photographs, family home-movies, and private diaries.

In Zurich we were treated with immense courtesy by Franz Jung, whose co-operation was invaluable, by his son Lorenz Jung, and another grandson, Dieter Baumann; and with kindness and co-operation by the staff of the Jung Institute in Kusnacht, as by Frau Cornelia Brunner, past President of the Analytical Psychology Club of Zurich, and Monsted Foto of Zurich, whose permission to reproduce photographs of Jung is gratefully acknowledged. We recognize the co-operation of the *Erbengemeinschaft Jung* (Jung's heirs) for permission to quote extensively from various works; of Routledge & Kegan Paul, for permission to quote from the *Collected Works*; of William Collins plc, for permission to quote from *Memories, Dreams, Reflections*; of Thames and Hudson, for permission to quote from *C. G. Jung Speaking*; and of the Wheelwright Museum of the American Indian, Sante Fe, New Mexico, for permission to reproduce their pictures of sand-paintings. The Jung Institutes of New York, Los Angeles and San Francisco, and their staffs, all welcomed us and gave us whatever assistance we needed; and the administrators of St Elizabeth's Hospital in Washington DC, and Barry Spodak in particular, allowed us to follow in Jung's footsteps into the psychiatric wards.

On reflection, this project in some ways became possible because of the kindness and influence of Lore Zeller, Harriet Friedman and Richard Friedman, Richard Auger and Jeannine Auger – all in Los Angeles. Whilst we express our gratitude to so many people and groups for their help in achieving whatever merits the film series and this book may have, the faults remain ours.

Finally, we should thank two people who travelled with us on every mile of this venture, in good humour and with patience which rarely deserted them. They were four years old, and a few months old, when it began. Only to our children could this book be dedicated.

The World of C. G. Jung

This book accompanies a television series about the supposedly difficult subject of psychology – the science of the human mind. In describing this work to our friends, colleagues and acquaintances, we detect an anxious reaction. For the recognition that life consists of more than the everyday practicalities is unsettling. But to those who are drawn to the possibility of an insight into the psyche, Jung is invaluable. His fascination with the mind went far beyond where most psychology stops. He was perfectly ready to discuss dreams, the human soul and religious belief. Yet his psychology is in today's terms 'user-friendly'. He was not an abstract theorist, but a doctor who liked to discover what was good for his patients, and not just to seek evidence for his assumptions.

In 1957 a young clinical psychologist named Richard Evans wrote a hopeful letter from his university office in Houston, Texas, to the famous Swiss psychologist. Would Dr Jung give a filmed interview in order to explain his lifetime's work to students in American universities? Jung, to Dr Evans's considerable surprise, agreed and a fee and date were set. Despite Jung's age – he was then eighty-two – and a slight illness, he submitted to the interview procedure for four consecutive afternoons.

To see the films today, almost thirty years after Jung's death, is extraordinary; this was the most distinguished living practitioner of the science of psychoanalysis, invented before the turn of the century; he was probably the most famous citizen of Switzerland, certainly outside the country; he was old, and he spoke in English. Yet the interview communicates an immense warmth and humour. There is no grand theory or condescension, merely a relish for the fascination of his life's work, of investigating human psychology. He peppers his observations with anecdotes, and often refers to his changes of mind and his astonishment when faced with the things patients said to him. Above all he communicates a love of people – a love which was clearly reciprocated.

In the making of the series *The Wisdom of the Dream* many letters were sent off to Zurich and further afield, asking for interviews. Many of those who agreed, often reluctantly, were as old as Jung himself was in 1957, or even older. But generously, and out of a commitment to do Jung justice with their own memories, these people all agreed to our requests – every single one of them. Therefore, in addition to our task of trying to communicate Jung and his work by the medium of film, we have a story to tell of how those individuals came to Jung, usually out of need rather than any professional plan, and how his attitude to the inner life changed them.

Most good psychological theory describes the way people actually do feel, behave and suffer, and it usually makes its point by telling stories that we both understand and feel to be true. At the practical level, this book is a longer exposition of the material gathered for the series, which of course is cut and edited until only a tiny fraction of the original material remains. But beyond that, it is the task of this book to communicate a sense of the deep connection that Jung and his followers feel between the outer world of everyday busy life, and an inner world where dreams and the sort of person any one of us is makes a difference to the way we live our life, to the people we like or fall in love with, and to our ability to live in harmony with the world around us. Our contributors were happy to share their life stories and material from their analyses with Jung as testament to his clinical method.

Both the Channel 4 television series and this book only serve to introduce the interested reader or viewer to Jung and his tradition. People who discover Jung very often say the same thing about his work and attitude to psychological life: 'When I first read that book, it was as if I was reading something I had always known, but had never put into words. I always felt that, but I didn't realize anybody else felt the same way.'

One American analyst, whose first career was in the obscure field of Oriental code-breaking for US Naval intelligence, first heard of Jung at a lecture intended to broaden the education of men leaving the armed services and starting to pursue civilian life. 'The lecturer simply said that Jung was a man who thought that the *cause* of things which happen in our lives was far less important than their *meaning*. I simply had to find out more about him.' It is beyond doubt that Jung's work changed people's lives. It is essential therefore to outline his life – though the occasional references to biographical detail here ought to whet many readers' appetites for his extraordinary and charming autobiography, *Memories, Dreams, Reflections*.

Carl Gustav Jung was born in 1875, the son of a Protestant minister, Paul Jung. At that time the family lived on Lake Constance, in the north-east of Switzerland. During his childhood the Jungs moved to a village on the outskirts of Basel, which was his mother's original home – her house stood a few paces from the main doors of Basel Cathedral. Jung was an only child, and a lonely one. In later life, he remembered how dreams and fantasies consoled him, and in many ways replaced the companionship of other children:

> I played alone, daydreamed or strolled in the woods alone, and had a secret world of my own.... The pattern of my relationship to the world was already prefigured: today as then I am a solitary, because I know things and must hint at things which other people do not know, and usually do not want to know. [*Memories, Dreams, Reflections*, pp. 48, 41]

Carl was an excellent student, with a talent both for arts and languages and scientific subjects. His dreams decided him upon science and he went to medical school at Basel University, where he duly discovered his vocation in psychiatry. In 1900, at the age of twenty-five, he took up his first hospital post at the Burgholzli clinic in Zurich – an established and traditional institution. By now, Jung was fascinated by the psyche and what it meant; but he found that the hospital policy was to treat the mentally ill simply as mad. *He* wanted to find out what was happening in the patient's inner life.

> The years at the Burgholzli were my years of apprenticeship. Dominating my interests and research was the burning question: 'What actually takes place inside the mentally ill?' That was something which I did not understand then, nor had any of my colleagues concerned themselves with such problems. Psychiatry teachers were not interested in what patients had to say, but rather in how to make a diagnosis or how to describe symptoms and to compile statistics.... The psychology of the mental patient played no role whatever. [*Memories, Dreams, Reflections*, p. 114]

Jung changed the direction of thinking in psychiatry. He did not subscribe to the essentially nineteenth century philosophical point of view – which fuelled the scientific progress of the industrial revolution – that human life could be reduced to an understanding of material facts. Jung spent more time studying and interpreting dreams than any individual before him had done. And as he evolved ideas about the existence of the unconscious, so he found a way of detecting how it differed from the conscious ego – the part of our psychological life where we know what we are doing or what we are thinking, and why. In his mental patients he saw vestiges of sanity – and deduced that there were two levels or aspects to every personality.

> Much of what we had hitherto regarded as senseless was not as crazy as it seemed. More than once I have seen that even with such patients there remains in the background a personality which must be called normal. It stands looking on, so to speak. Occasionally, too, this personality – usually by way of voices or dreams – can make altogether sensible remarks and objections. [*Memories, Dreams, Reflections*, p. 126]

Jung's word-association test was the experimental means of establishing the existence of the separate 'voice' of the unconscious. It was also his first major work to be published and recognized. Alongside his hospital work, Jung developed a private practice, seeing patients at the large house he and his wife Emma built in 1907, on the lakeside at Kusnacht, near Zurich. During the course of his career, Jung published enough books and papers to fill nineteen volumes of his *Collected Works*. He travelled widely from 1909 onwards, and his travels helped to confirm another of his great discoveries – what he called the 'collective unconscious'. This is to be understood as a further level of unconscious functioning in our psyche, which expresses the essential shared experience of what it is to be a human being, irrespective of culture or location. Jung explored every conceivable religious, mythological and artistic source, and the repetition of themes, of narrative stories, of symbols and patterns of behaviour, which he called the 'archetypes', convinced him that the collective unconscious was real. They are, as one analyst has said, 'the building blocks out of which human reality is made'.

During his life, in pursuit of psychological truth, Jung studied religion, mythology, philosophy and mysticism in a dozen languages. He travelled in Europe, Africa, North America and India. He painted, sculpted, carved in wood and stone, and designed the Tower which he had built further up Lake Zurich at Bollingen, a place of pilgrimage for those to whom Jung means a great deal. Among his more esoteric interests were alchemy, Gnosticism, astrology and UFOs; and he was absorbed by the boundaries of scientific knowledge, which at the end of his life were beginning to reach the point where the physical met the metaphysical. Jung liked to say that his ideas were never going to be proved by psychologists, but there was a chance that they might be, by physicists.

Intellectually, Jung represents a bridge between the nineteenth century and the twenty-first century: born in 1875, he lived long enough to witness the first stages of the programmes which sent man into space – and he had views on the psychological meaning of such a quest.

As a doctor observing his patients, Jung noticed that for many in the second half of life, the essential psychological problem could be described as religious; and he became more and more clear in his view that personal religion, and a sense of meaning, was an undeniable aspect of the human psyche. But he was not a theologian in any way; he did not wish to discuss the actual existence of God, and always referred to the 'God-image' instead. What he saw, however, was the reality of the religious experience. If patients felt, or lacked, a religious impulse, then that in itself was a real experience.

Jung coined the word 'individuation' to indicate the fruitful combination of the conscious and the unconscious psyche: both the world of ego, daily life, work, duties, practicalities and goals; and the world of dreams, of images, of playing and fantasising. Individuation is a process, rather than a goal – one works towards it, rather than expecting to achieve it. One analyst defines it neatly in a few words:

'Individuation is becoming that which it is in one fully to become.'

From childhood to the end of his life, Jung considered the soul – a word which has almost gone out of use – to be real. When he died, on 6 June 1961, and was buried in the well-concealed family grave in the corner of the Protestant churchyard in Kusnacht, the minister declared that 'He had given man the courage to have a soul again'. Jung's task had been immense. He wanted to understand the whole psyche, not just how to treat the symptoms of its imperfections. He wanted to revalue the very idea of psychological instability, or pain, as a potentially creative process – for us to recognize that depression, dreams and conflict all tell us something important which we need to hear. And he felt it important to identify the dangers inherent in the psyche, which were neglected at our collective peril. In his interview of 1957, he made a comment that has stuck in the minds of many who heard it, and remains a relevant warning in the age of hyper-technology:

> Nowadays particularly, you see, the world hangs on a thin thread, and that is the psyche of man. *We* are the great danger. The psyche is the great danger. What if something goes wrong with the psyche?

Jung was too important a figure not to attract speculation and controversy about his personal and professional life. In full-length biographies and in the pages of professional journals, accusations and defences have been exhaustively presented. Like the allegation that Freud was addicted to cocaine, the accusations that Jung failed to take a strong enough stand against Nazism and that he had a long-standing affair with a colleague (Toni Wolff) have no substantive bearing on the great body of his work, particularly in an introduction to Jung's psychology such as this. Even within the field, his very eclecticism continues to raise doubts about his professional standing. As Richard Evans wrote:

> Like many American psychologists, I had long respected and been interested in Jung as an important pioneer and historical figure in the history of psychology. It was equally true, however, at that time, that I shared some of the scepticism, abundantly in evidence, that surrounded many of Jung's fundamental notions. On the whole, American psychologists found Jung's work too mystical and philosophical to satisfy their criteria for sound, scientific research. In fact, it is interesting to note that at that time, Jung's ideas were more characteristically heralded by members of philosophy and English departments in universities than by the inhabitants of psychology departments.

Despite his remarkable achievements, the fact that *The Wisdom of the Dream* is the first international documentary series made about Jung reflects the fact that Jungian psychology has remained something of a closed world. This is an extraordinary paradox, because many of the psychological terms that are in everyday use today are those either invented or popularized by Jung. One needs to know very little 'psychology' to know what kind of person is an introvert or an extrovert; or to understand what is meant by someone's professional or stage 'persona'.

We all discuss our 'complexes', and we often attribute memories or feelings to the 'unconscious'. If only because of a song by The Police, 'synchronicity' has become a familiar word – it has something to do with coincidences not being mere chance.

All of these terms are Jung's legacy, and they point to Jung's central task, and his achievement. He was a doctor who only valued or wrote about the ideas or methods which he found worked for the assistance of his patients. On the other hand, psychology is accepted only to a very limited degree in the 'real life' of the majority of Western nations. As Jung found in his travels, supposedly less primitive cultures are far more 'psychological' in their outlook. Tribal societies understand the connection between their inner life, of ritual and mythology, and the outer life, in the battle with the elements or the need to preserve traditional religion in the face of invasion, colonization, conversion and repression. Jung investigated and observed all of this, and found his ideas more in tune with Masai tribesmen and Pueblo Indian elders than with the sophisticated culture of early twentieth-century Europe.

All Jung's thinking, and the language he used to express it, is summed up in the phrase 'the reality of the psyche'. He made an intellectual leap which in the history of thought will be seen to have been a major development. It is a very simple proposition: firstly, there is a psyche – something which contributes to our mental and emotional life other than merely responding to the physical surroundings. Secondly, the products of this psyche are real experiences. One analyst told us an amazing story about a man who survived the physical deprivation and inhumane torment of a concentration camp, by dreaming about eating sugar-noodles every night. The unconscious compensated for his outward circumstances, and enabled him to hold out until liberation.

Jungian, or analytical, psychology is a way of seeing the world. No one claims that it is the only way of seeing the world. For many people, the way life, or society, works is best explained by economic theory; other people prefer to see life as the execution of God's will; some believe in destiny while others think that politics provides both explanation and solutions. The connection between who we are inside and what we do, seems almost too obvious to be discussed. But there are relatively few people spending any real effort on making the connection.

Over the last fifty years, Jungian analysts have been trained in most

European countries and all over the USA and Canada, and this form of psychology is reaching more people, whether those who seek out an analyst or psychotherapist because of need, or those who read the more accessible works of analysts and authors like those quoted in the series and later in this book. Nevertheless, Jung's reputation remains distinctly less substantial than that of his early mentor Sigmund Freud, and Jung's work is scarcely taught in mainstream medical education at all.

The task of both the film series and the book is to introduce Jung's work to a new and wider audience. Psychology may seem an abstract subject to the layman, but its sphere of reference is basic. Why do we get angry involuntarily, why do we fall in love, and with whom? Why are some people competent at finding their way to a new place, whilst others get lost? Why do some works of art, some music, some poetry, speak to people of almost every race? Why does mythology survive? Why do we design buildings differently today from the way we did ten years ago? Why are people who live in mountains or on sea-shores of a different temperament from those who live on prairies, or on islands? Jung's psychology has some answers for many such questions.

The best means for presenting the material is to take an extended journey around the far-flung community of analysts, therapists and writers who follow Jung, with varying degrees of loyalty. It is a community, despite the distances: there are 1,200 Jungian analysts around the world, of whom the largest number is in the USA, where Jung's reputation grew fastest and secured its most prominent position. There are about equal numbers of men and women, and in almost every one of the studies where they work one finds a snapshot of Jung's Tower at Bollingen; one finds a photograph of Jung himself, usually the introspective portraits of the 'wise old man' in his last year, by either Cartier-Bresson or Karsh; one finds a small collection of artefacts of Greek, Egyptian, or tribal culture; one finds reproductions of Chagall, the artist who, they all agree, 'paints straight from the unconscious'.

Many of them were interviewed for the film series, but often appear only briefly; and in the pages that follow the space is available for a more substantial account of their ideas and interpretation. Like Jung himself, these too are doctors and therapists who devote their lives to helping others to overcome emotional suffering of various kinds. What is important is the nature of the tools for the job – and this is a uniquely exciting and stimulating therapeutic proposition: they help their patients to understand their suffering, integrate good and bad feelings, and overcome their troubles, using the resources that the patients' own inner life provides. The Jungian therapist who is worth his salt understands the potential in both his own and his patient's psyche for both sickness and health.

Analysts today partly follow Jung's lead, in fields of study which he himself embraced, and partly divert into new and unexpected areas. They study (as he did) religion, mythology, anthropology, culture, art, fairy-tales, legends, ritual, non-pharmaceutical healing methods, alchemy, relationships and alcoholism. They also study (as he did not) movies and movie stars, senility, science fiction, architecture, landscape, AIDS, the financial world, the Vietnam War, wilderness, ecology and babies. Some people differentiate between three distinct generations of Jungian analysts and followers: the first generation, who were definitely 'disciples'; the second, who might be thought of as 'revisionists', questioning many of the tenets of Jung, and 'modernizing' them; and the third, the 'New Agers' who take Jung as a broad starting point for the holistic examination of psyche in the world.

Among the claims made for Jung is that he was 'on the available evidence, the most conscious man who ever lived' or that he is 'the psychologist of the twenty-first century'. The 'New Age' movement, which is mainly confined to the USA, claims Jung among others as a mainstream thinker. There is some danger that 'Jungianism' can become an obsession or a clique, like any other 'ism', or that it becomes merely a fashionable recreational form of twentieth century *Angst*. Jung himself, apparently sincerely, said that he did not recognize the term 'Jungian', and he at least didn't wish to be one. He made no overwhelming claims for his work, or the assumptions which guided him, other than that they were natural and apparently truthful. He himself liked to say ironically that the unconscious was at least on the same level as the flea, or the earwig, or some such lowly creature – and these after all at least 'enjoyed the honest interest of the entomologist'.

On his eightieth birthday, Jung was honoured with birthday greetings, a huge family party which included a ferry-boat cruise on Lake Zurich, and the recognition of his life's work in tributes from around the world. One of his former patients, the German poet and novelist Hermann Hesse, wrote a short poem of tribute:

> The soul bends down and rises
> Breathing infinity
> Weaving itself from broken threads
> A fair new garment of God.

Honorary doctorates were conferred by Harvard, Oxford, and the Federal Technical Institute, the university-level academy in Zurich where Jung had taught psychology for thirty years becoming titular professor in 1935. The Zurich citation described him as:

... the rediscoverer of the totality and polarity of the human psyche and its striving for unity; the diagnostician of the crisis of man in the age of science and technology; the interpreter of the primeval symbolism and of the individuation process of mankind.

This accolade formed the backbone of our efforts to make a series of films about the essence of Jung's work. Firstly, the idea that the conscious and unconscious psyche form a unity; secondly, the idea that the psyche plays an important role in matters of the outer world; and thirdly, that we can only understand ourselves today if we see that we have inherited an evolved psychological life, just as the physical organs in our bodies have evolved – and that fact has influence upon the way we live and feel in the modern world.

In the vast range of acknowledgements to Jung's contribution to modern thinking, one most important point should not be forgotten. He was not a trained classicist or art critic, indeed not a theorist at all. He was a psychiatrist and therapist. The London analyst Andrew Samuels is concerned that the positive aspects of Jung's reputation have obscured the practical work he did as a doctor dealing with emotional and psychological distress.

You know, it's possible to watch films on Jung, to read books on Jung, and not know about his contribution as a therapist, as what I am very happy to call a shrink. People just don't want to know about the conventional aspect of Jung's work, even though Jung said 'I'm just, and have always been, a psychiatrist'. He was interested in psychopathology. He had something to say about depression. He had something to say about schizophrenia. He had something to say about hysteria. People should know that Jung was a very great therapist, it was the bedrock of everything he did, and I think his contributions to the art and practice of psychotherapy are immense.

Jung worked in an unusually open-minded way. He spoke of his psychological concepts as hypotheses, which were to be replaced if better ones emerged. It was Jung's work and reputation as a therapist which brought him patients. Many of his early patients became his pupils, and their conviction in the value of his approach was simple, because they had experienced his attitude first-hand, and it had transformed their own lives. From the 1930s onward, these men and women moved on and away from Switzerland with a strong sense of mission, to bring Jung's work of 'analytical psychology' to those who needed it in Britain, America and beyond. But what came first was their own need.

Edward Edinger: I was a couple of years out of medical school, and I was realizing that physical medicine, internal medicine, which I thought I was going to go into, wasn't for me – and I really felt quite lost psychologically. In fact, I had a lot of dreams at that time of driving with a frosted wind-shield, and I couldn't see out of the wind-shield, and I tried to peer out of the window to see where I was going. It was a typical circumstance of danger fostering the rescuing power, so to speak. It was in that circumstance that I came across Jung in the course of my reading.

Dr Joe Wheelwright: I got into this business because I wanted to go into analysis. I mean in those days nobody woke up in the morning and rolled over and said 'You know, my dear, I've just made a decision, I'm going to be a psychiatrist.' Or 'I'm going to be an analyst.' We didn't choose our profession. Our profession chose us. But what we knew was that we were neurotic as hell, and we'd better run, not walk, to the nearest analyst. In those days nobody went into analysis with the thoughts of becoming an analyst themselves – or virtually nobody.

Dr Marie-Louise von Franz: I was eighteen years old so I thought he was a Methuselah, an old bear or something. But I was very deeply impressed. I hestitated for half a year and then I went to his lecture and one day I wrote him a letter and asked him to take me in analysis. I read one of his books and I thought: I cannot judge what this man says without having experience myself. He's talking about inner facts and if you don't know the facts, you can't learn it by theory. He said laughingly 'So you want a teaching analysis.' I didn't know what that was so I said anxiously 'No, I'm crazy enough for the real thing.'

Joe and Jane Wheelwright originally met Jung in 1932, and both later became analysts. According to Jane, his approach was far from dogmatic, and was based on his simple human concern for the patient.

If they got better then there must be something in it. If they didn't, he'd have to think about it again or look it over some more. And he was very experimental, that was one of the good things about him. For someone who was as intuitive and imaginative and all the rest, he was extremely experimental.

Yet Jung was a fully-fledged medical doctor and trained psychiatrist. What made him different was that he applied the methods of science to the supposedly incomprehensible or indescribable activities and products of the psyche. The psychiatrist and analyst Jeffrey Satinover and the theologian Don Cupitt portray the balance between his priorities:

Satinover: Jung really started out with a very sharp scientific focus, and he certainly wanted to be thought of as a scientist. None the less, as his work developed it moved progressively away from hard science and more and more into a clinical and impressionistic realm. Late in his life he was the chairman of the first international conference on chemical concepts of psychosis, and repeated a hypothesis that he had made way back in 1903, namely that he was convinced then long before anybody else was, that psychosis had a chemical basis to it, that it was somehow rooted in the innate functioning of the brain.

Cupitt: Jung took it that all the data of the life of the mind were something like empirical data. He thought there actually was a thing called psyche, something like a ghost, a non-physical, non-spatial entity that accompanied the body. Events went on inside it, it had a kind of inner space that the scientists could explore, so in effect virtually anything that people said to Jung about their dreams or their imaginings was treated by him as evidence for what was going on in the psyche, and to that extent he thought he was an empirical scientist.

London analyst Andrew Samuels is one of the leading thinkers in the Jungian world today, prolific in publishing assessments of Jung's work and in challenging the more romantic views of Jung. He gave the following list of Jung's principal contributions:

Firstly Jung challenges the boundaries between different areas of knowledge that we have set up, or different areas of interest. I'm thinking specifically of psychology, religion and culture, which we tend to keep apart. Jung showed us, for example, that religion is an intensely psychological business. He also showed us that any psychological theory that doesn't take account of what he called the religious instinct is deficient theory. The second contribution has to do with Jung's providing for us a model of Life's journey that's not mystical. I think what Jung provides is a way of growth, a way of enrichment for anybody that does not require their moving out of their ordinary human level.

When Joseph Henderson first met Jung, in 1929, he was a directionless young man just out of college. He spent a year teaching at his old school in New Jersey in order to finance the trip to Zurich:

I taught for a year and made some money and then went to Zurich to work with Jung, to see what I should do with my life. It was more wonderful than I had expected even. A wonderful man to work with, a tremendous experience to meet Jung. It's almost impossible to describe what that was like. A kind of union of a Swiss peasant and a scholar and something of a more spiritual nature, it describes a man that technically should not exist, but did.

Marie-Louise von Franz met Jung as a schoolgirl, because Jung wanted to meet some young people. The impact he had upon her then has lasted for her entire life, during which her intellectual energies have given her a reputation as the principal successor to Jung's intellectual crown. She has published work on a wide variety of subjects, ranging from alchemy to fairy-tales. Her view of Jung's legacy was this:

Jung's work survives him because he has pioneered so far ahead, he has charted out a whole new continent, and the following scientists still have trouble to follow up and to map out what he explored. That will take a long time still.

In the chapters that follow, we attempt to introduce the major aspects of Jung's work in the world, particularly where it touches upon the everyday problems and difficulties that people everywhere share. We discuss the basic proposition that what is psychological is also 'real', and how that reality emerges in many forms. In particular the psyche likes to speak in images, and the ones which call to us nightly are in our dreams. We portray Jung's creative work, both in his own words and as others encountered him as patients and pupils. We consider the impact his travels had upon him, and the universal human connections he discovered, which he called the 'collective unconscious'. We consider what Jung's psychology has to say about the way people relate to each other, about the dominance of traditionally masculine values in society, and about the way our surroundings reflect our psychological identity. We observe the multiple and complex ways in which every individual seeks meaning in life; and reflect on the process of ageing and facing death, through the eyes and dreams of the many elderly analysts who gave interviews for the film series and this book.

Our participants' thoughts reflect the deep conviction which Jung's work lends to many people and their attitude to life. For Dr Marie-Louise von Franz, now elderly and ill, the secret was 'Jung's universality, his flexibility, his broadmindedness'. To Dr Jeffrey Satinover, the young and energetic Chairman of the C. G. Jung Foundation in New York, 'Jung's contribution was to restore a deep-rooted value system, based on the really unchanging elements of human nature'.

2

The Reality of the Psyche

Outward circumstances are no substitute for inner
experience. Therefore my life has been singularly poor in
outward happenings. I cannot tell much about them, for it
would strike me as hollow and insubstantial. I can
understand myself only in the light of inner happenings.
[Jung: *Memories, Dreams, Reflections*, p. 5]

We all dream. Humanity shares dreaming as it shares breathing. We
watch our children dream as they sleep; we even see the rapid eye
movement that is evidence of dreaming in the soupy ultrasound images
of the foetus in the womb. In all the great religions and cultures there
are significant dreams – Agamemnon's dream, or Jacob's dream of the
ladder to heaven – which are remembered because they contained
important messages. The aboriginal culture of Australia refers to its
earliest history as 'dreamtime'.

Carl Gustav Jung, more than any man or woman before him,
attempted to understand the meaning of dreams, for the simplest of
reasons: in his own life they seemed important. The more he investigated, the more he seemed confirmed in his assumption that dreams
were not just trivial nonsense in contrast to the meaningful events of
waking life.

Whatever else might be true of dreams, one thing was certain: the
dream was a real experience. No more, and no less, than the experience
of seeing a play or a film, the dreamer has experienced something. The
filmgoer is not physically transported into space when watching *Star
Wars* any more than the dreamer is soaked by dreaming about falling
overboard. But in many ways the dream experience is the more real,

because it cannot be reduced to matters of film technique, script, lighting and performance.

The reality of the dream experience is what gives rise to one of the central concepts in Jung's psychology: *the reality of the psyche*. Everyone who took their dreams to Jung had personal contact with exactly how real it was in his thinking. As an analyst, Jung's method was to treat dreams as facts which the doctor or scientist could observe and discuss. For example, Dr Gerhard Adler, who entered analysis with Jung in the late 1920s:

> My first interview with Jung was very significant. I had a dream the night before in which I travelled to India. I saw this great triangle of India, and I landed somewhere on the coast. I told this dream to Jung and instead of analysing, he took a large atlas out and sat down beside me, and he said: 'Now show me, where did you travel, where did you travel? Show me.' This was extremely important to me – it showed me immediately how seriously he took the reality of the psyche.

Dreams are the language in which all aspects of a person's individual psychology express themselves, in an uncensored form. Dreams are just the threshold into the unconscious from the conscious, or from the 'ego'. 'Ego' in Latin means 'I', and is really what we think of when we think of our identity in the first person – the aspect of ourself which thinks, judges, speaks and acts. To accept the reality of the psyche is to realize that there is something more, something deeper, something which doesn't express itself in thought-out language and ideas, but which somehow affects the ego part, and which is responsible or all our strongest emotions, from falling in love to racial hostility.

When an actress or a sportsman achieves sudden fame, the complaint is often heard that the publicity they receive about their personal life reads as if it concerns someone else, a quite unrecognizable person. The biographical portrait in a popular newspaper is as incomplete as seeing the conscious personality as the exclusive reality. As one of Jung's pupils, Dr Liliane Frey-Rohn, expresses it:

> ... the reality of the psyche means that what we feel, what we think, has a deeper basis, that it's not just what you read here and there in the newspapers. I mean that really goes very deep. The questions are directed towards who you are as a human being, what is really your deepest interest, how do you envisage life, what kind of person are you really?

Dr Michael Fordham, who jointly edited the English edition of Jung's *Collected Works* with Dr Adler, considers the essence of Jung's approach to be based in:

> ... even rather simple ideas. I mean the idea that we are not what we think we are only, or what we feel we are. We've got an unconscious which is a dynamic and active feature of your everyday life. And we owe that to Jung, I think.

Another analyst, the American Dr Edward Edinger, says:

> The human psyche is more than the ego. The human psyche has a non-personal dimension to it, a historical dimension and even a cosmic dimension. That's not a matter of doctrine or teaching, it's a matter of empirical discovery and once it's discovered, then the individual knows it for a fact and can live in relation to that non-personal dimension. It's still totally the property of Jungian psychology. No other school of psychology has any notion of what it's about.

The very word 'psyche' is somewhat overshadowed and coloured by 'psychic', conjuring up images of gypsy ladies in fairground stalls. We can roughly take it to mean the human source of what makes people say something is 'psychological'. But there lies another difficulty: 'psychological' is all too often used or misused to mean 'imaginary'.

Jung's work, and his attitude to the patients whom he treated as a doctor, exploded the myth that life does not have a psychological background. If there were none, then all our human problems, from the trivial to those which threaten the survival of the human race itself, would be capable of resolution by logical discourse. We do know that this is not true: we do know that our lives are not entirely 'practical', and our problems cannot be solved or understood by recourse to the doctor, the bank-manager, the school-teacher and employment counsellor alone. Something else – whether we call it 'psyche' or 'unconscious' or indeed 'religion' and 'spirit' – is there.

The essentially twentieth century medium of film, digested via television or, in earlier decades, in cinemas, arrived just in time to enable modern audiences to see examples of surviving 'primitive' cultures which progress has not yet destroyed. We marvel at healing methods which have no apparent scientific and materialistic basis, yet work; and we are fascinated by rites and rituals which have a power and emotion which we find difficult to explain. The rituals don't produce anything concrete, yet even as outsiders we have a sense of what Jung always called 'numinous' – 'indicating presence of divinity; spiritual; awe-inspiring', according to *The Oxford Dictionary*.

The disappearing world of original cultures remains a fragile connection to the historic truth that no age, no matter how developed in technical and practical life, can live as it were by bread alone. It is no coincidence that Jung was interested not only in dreams (of which he analysed about 67,000, according to one estimate), but also tribal cultures and societies which offered him the opportunity to learn about the European psyche, by comparison. He heard his patients telling him that their lives lacked meaning; and he saw tribal societies where the tribe's identity was the meaning for its members – and he tried to see where 'civilization' had lost its roots. Above all, it was obvious to him that in societies which had not yet become purely materialistic, an understanding of the reality of the psyche was a living presence.

In the developed world, there is a general reluctance to take the psyche seriously. Generally, people would rather not know about an aspect within themselves which is not really under their control. But this attitude is subject to change, and to variation. To our children, we will say 'Use your imagination!' as often as 'Think hard!' Yet in adult life, imagination has a low status: 'You're angry with me!' 'No, you're imagining it!' – and 'Do you seriously imagine? ...' don't leave much scope for imagination to be an active ingredient in life. As Carl Jung said to Richard Evans in 1957:

> ... it is demonstrated to us in our days what the power of psyche is, how important it is to know something about it. But we know nothing about it. Nobody would give credit to the idea that the psychical processes of the ordinary man have any importance whatever. One thinks 'Oh, he has just what he has in his head. He is all from his surroundings. He is taught such and such a thing, believes such and such a thing, and particularly if he is well housed and well-fed then he has no ideas at all'.

The English analyst Andrew Samuels pursues the same theme in his analytical practice today. The essence of Jungian psychology is to allow the psyche to express itself positively, very often in images, whether in dreams or paintings or in words alone. According to Samuels:

In analytical psychology, fantasy is valued. Even valued as a kind of thinking. Jung talked about fantasy thinking. And we know that even the most fantastical products of the unconscious, such as dreams or visions, often display a kind of rationality or thoughtfulness. There's a rationality of the irrational. . . . Pay attention to your fantasies, they make sense. They're not pathological, they're not misleading, they're not put into you by outside agencies like God or something like that. They are not only making sense, but they are sense-making.

Jung gave his interview to Dr Evans in the Federal Technical High School, where he had been Professor. He explained the simplicity of his view of fantasy as he gazed out of the window at the roofs of the city of Zurich sloping down the hill below.

When you observe the world you see people, you see houses, you see sky, you see tangible objects; but when you observe yourself within, you see moving images – a world of images, generally known as fantasies. Yet these fantasies are facts. You see it is a fact that the man has such and such a fantasy, and it is such a tangible fact, for instance, that when a man has a certain fantasy, another man may lose his life, or a bridge is built – these houses were all fantasies. Everything you do here – all of the houses, everything, was fantasy to begin with, and fantasy has a proper reality. That is not to be forgotten; fantasy is not nothing.

This is a way of thinking, and not a provable hypothesis, of course. But as we consider various aspects of human life, and not only our dreams, the truth of the fantasy or psyche-origin of much action and behaviour seems natural. In relationships, in groups, among colleagues or school-friends, in playgrounds and on battlefields, actions and emotions occur which are not based in logic and thought alone. But to acknowledge the existence and activity, even the influence of the unconscious, is one thing – attempting to define it is quite another. Jung himself was well aware of how difficult it is to be specific when speaking of the unconscious:

As soon as research comes to the question of the unconscious, things necessarily become blurred, because the unconscious is something which is *really* unconscious, and so you have no object, you see nothing! You can only make inferences, you know, and so we have to create a model of this possible structure of the unconscious because we can't see it.

The intuitive method of inferences and models baffled Marie-Louise von Franz when she first met Jung. The most distinguished of all Jung's surviving colleagues, her work has covered almost as wide a span as Jung's own – on alchemy, fairy-tales, dream symbols, mythology and science. Now in her seventies, and seriously ill, Dr Von Franz is striving to complete her final book on an Arabic Sufi alchemist. Her very first encounter with Jung came when she was an eighteen-year-old schoolgirl, educated to disregard what was not visible, material and evident to the mind. Then she was invited by a school-friend to visit Jung at Bollingen:

> I met him just before I finished High School, so I thought he was a Methuselah, an old bear or something. But I was very deeply impressed. He talked about case material, about a crazy woman and politics and all sorts of things. What stuck in my memory is that he talked about a crazy girl and said she was on the moon, and talked about it as if it was very real. And being rational I was indignant and said 'She hasn't been on the moon' and Jung said 'Yes she has' – and I thought 'That cannot be'. I said 'That satellite of the earth there which is uninhabited – she hasn't been there' and he just looked at me and said 'Yes, she has been on the moon!' And I thought 'That old man is crazy or I am stupid' – and then it suddenly dawned on me that he meant that what happens psychically is absolutely real to the one to whom it happens. So I suddenly realized the reality of the psyche.

The case had impressed Jung himself too. It has given him a sense that in looking at the symptoms or the diagnosis of a case of mental illness, the doctor was likely to miss an expressive side of the psyche. As he recalled the case of the moon-girl in later years:

> She was eighteen years old, and came from a cultivated family. At the age of fifteen she had been seduced by her brother and abused by a schoolmate. From her sixteenth year on, she retreated into isolation. ... She grew steadily odder, and at seventeen was taken to the mental hospital, where she spent a year and a half. She heard voices, refused food, and ... no longer spoke.
>
> In the course of many weeks I succeeded, very gradually, in persuading her to speak. After overcoming many resistances, she told me that she had lived on the moon. [*Memories, Dreams, Reflections*, pp. 128–129]

The girl told Jung of an elaborate fantasy involving a demon male vampire which kidnapped and killed the women and children who lived on the moon. She decided to kill the vampire, but at the moment when she should wield the knife, she was blinded by the vampire's beauty and was carried off herself. Jung felt that her flights of imagination were the result of the incest:

> She felt humiliated in the eyes of the world, but elevated in the realm of fantasy. ... The consequence was complete alienation from the world, a state of psychosis. She became 'extramundane' as it were, and lost contact with humanity. She plunged into cosmic distances, into outer space, where she met with the winged demon. ... By telling me her story she had in a sense betrayed the demon and attached herself to an earthly human being. Hence she was able to return to life, and even to marry. [*Memories, Dreams, Reflections*, p. 130]

Jung's therapeutic method was based on accepting the reality of psychic experience. To the psychotic patient, the moon-visit was real. Before Jung, psychiatrists would have paid little attention to what such a patient had to say; few would have attempted Jung's effort to get her to speak. But the fantasy she uttered made sense of her situation; after what she had suffered in 'real life', little wonder that she should flee into outer space! This was the reality to the patient, and Jung, attuned to that reality, and taking it seriously, was able to assist her – despite several subsequent outbreaks of instability – to reintegrate herself into the world of 'normal reality' from which she had fled.

> Thereafter I regarded the sufferings of the mentally ill in a different light. For I had gained insight into the richness and importance of their inner experience. [*Memories, Dreams, Reflections*, p. 130]

One of Jung's followers, herself an analyst, describes Jungian psychology as a psychology of commonsense. In examining certain cases, it makes sense to turn a hypothesis on its head: with the moon-girl, what else could possibly explain her fantasy but that she had a good reason to flee from life? In older cultures, it was taken as being natural and obviously true that dreams were important, and often curative. The Greeks, for example, believing that illness was a divine intervention, believed equally that the cure could come only from another divine action. Knowing perfectly well that the gods could not be summoned to the bedside like the family doctor, the approved method was to participate in some form of religious cult ceremony which enabled divine action to take place.

Professor C. A. Meier, a Jungian analyst now well into his eighties, worked alongside Jung for some thirty years and succeeded him in a number of professional posts – at the Burgholzli, at the E.T.H. (Eidgenossische Technische Hochschule in Zurich), and in international psychological bodies. He was the first Director of the Jung Institute in Zurich, and founding Chairman of the Zurichberg clinic established to provide a comprehensive analytical psychology and psychiatry service. He and his wife have lived for many years in a large apartment in Zurich, where the polished wooden floorboards creak reassuringly, and Oriental rugs ensure that no one walks too fast, for fear of skating across the hall. In his study, Professor Meier is dwarfed by the bookcases which rise from floor to ceiling, photographs of Jung, artefacts and objects from classical cultures, and a connoisseur's collection of pipes, cigars, cheroots, cigarillos, ashtrays and matches.

Permanently wreathed in cigar- or pipe-smoke, Professor Meier has the same sharpness of manner which Jung himself supposedly had, and stories of his battles abound. If he doesn't agree with you, or he thinks a question stupid, the answer will be brief and end with 'Damn it all!' or 'For God's sake!' Yet, again like Jung, his great good humour, loud laughter, and an evident relish for the engaging business of trying to understand the human psyche have won him many friends and admirers. His book, *Ancient Incubation and Modern Psychotherapy*, explains how Professor Meier observed what he thought were ancient symbols and motifs in the dreams and other material produced by psychotic patients at the Burgholzli.

> The content of this material showed quite plainly that, even in psychosis which medical science usually approached in a defeatist spirit, there was a factor at work that we call today, rather inadequately, the 'self-healing tendency of the psyche'. [*Ancient Incubation and Modern Psychotherapy*, p. ix]
>
> This was what instigated me to study incubation, which is the ancient ritual of going to the temple of the divine healer Asclepius to sleep there, and to receive the healing dream.

The Greeks saw the dream not only as man's access to the soul, and to healing, but as something that really happened, in contrast to modern's man's view of the dream as an imaginary experience. The cult of Asclepius was the most notable provider of the 'healing-dream' experience. Those in need of cure would make a pilgrimage to the Asclepian Temple among the pines at Epidavros (alongside the amphitheatre) as well as other places; the patient would make an offering, and go to sleep in a special dormitory where the God would ensure a healing dream would occur.

The process implies an essential connection in medicine (which retains Asclepius's staff with serpents entwined as its eternal symbol) with the irrational, or inexplicable power of the psyche or the unconscious to assist in the cure. Professor Meier emphasizes the connection with analytical psychology:

> I would say this is the closest connection to what we try to do in psychotherapy nowadays. We try to make people accessible to the messages, to create the atmosphere within which the unconscious can speak.

The age of materialistic proof, and pharmaceutical medicine, has overshadowed these ancient truths which humankind once knew about itself. Of course the reality of the psyche is a difficult reality; it is one which can be inferred, but not proved by the concrete standards we mostly now apply. What Jung did was to point out the wealth of circumstantial evidence for taking seriously what revealed itself as the psyche and its unconscious dimension.

What Jung was doing, in many ways, was to give new meaning to archaic ways of thinking. Observing the religious aspect of his patients' inner lives, he preferred not to speak of 'God' as an entity, but of the 'God-image': while every believer definitely has an image of God, nevertheless all the God-images don't add up to a single practical fact about the nature of 'God'. To Jung the 'reality of religion' went alongside his 'reality of the psyche'. His thinking has had a certain influence in modern theology, according to Don Cupitt, a Christian theologian and the Chaplain of Emmanuel College, Cambridge:

> Jung was a religious naturalist, that's part of his originality. That's to say he takes it for granted that religion is produced from inside us, it's a human expression. He doesn't accept any metaphysical or supernatural account of where religion comes from, and on that I agree with him. I sometimes provoke my fellow believers by saying that if the idea of God hadn't been produced from inside us, it wouldn't be of any interest to us. What is more, the gods that people worship quite obviously tell us a lot about the people who worship

them, which is surely evidence that our gods come from inside ourselves. That's where their interest lies.

For Jung the inner meaning was the real meaning, especially under modern conditions. As Jung would put it, in the Middle Ages it was all 'out there'. You looked up at the night sky, and you saw heaven and those stars were living beings and so on. But since Galileo, it's all got internalized within the self, so the things that used to be up in the sky are now in our hearts.

It is worth pausing briefly to consider who were the many patients whose inner lives represented Carl Jung's raw research material; and what they encountered when they met him. At the Burgholzli hospital, they were in-patients of a mental hospital, with the illnesses and difficulties that remain the stock-in-trade of such institutions today: schizophrenia (then called dementia praecox), different forms of psychosis, depression, perhaps epilepsy and so on. In his private practice, Jung's patients were largely middle-class or better. Increasingly, as his reputation grew, patients came to Jung from further afield, and many from America.

Among a number of wealthy American women patients, Jung saw two heiresses from the Rockefeller and Mellon families. He also had Hermann Hesse briefly as a patient; James Joyce's daughter; the painter Jackson Pollock and another alcoholic, the mysterious 'Rowland H.' who founded Alcoholics Anonymous. According to one legend (and Jung attracts them) the American playwright Thornton Wilder came to Zurich in the hope of seeing Jung. When Jung could not see him, as he was too busy, Wilder settled into the antiquated Hotel Sonne, a few hundred yards along the lakeshore from Jung's house in Kusnacht, and wrote *Our Town* while he waited. Jung, however, respected the fact that it was his patients who provided him with the material for his work; and reserved a preference for those who had scraped together the money to see him because they cared or needed to, rather than the wealthy and influential.

My patients brought me so close to the reality of human life that I could not help learning essential things from them. Encounters with people of so many different kinds and on so many different psychological levels have been for me incomparably more important than fragmentary conversations with celebrities. The finest and most significant conversations of my life were anonymous.
[*Memories, Dreams, Reflections*, p. 145]

Jane Wheelwright, an American analyst, first met Jung in 1932. She accompanied her wealthy but mad Aunt Laura – by ship from San Francisco, through the Panama Canal, to Europe – on a grand tour of the 'crowned heads of European psychology' as her witty husband, ex-ham actor turned psychiatrist and analyst Joe Wheelwright, puts it. Jane recalled Jung's reaction to the arrival in Kusnacht of 'a simple person'.

Jung always liked the level of the multitude – the simple person. He hated the educated. He hated specialists and all those fancy people. I remember once when a very simple guy came to Zurich. He saved up his money, he had a very simple job. He came to Zurich to meet Jung. It was his lifelong ambition. He was a little weedy guy and he was nothing to look at and nothing to talk with and Jung was so happy about him. I've never seen him so enthusiastic. He just thought it was wonderful. He cancelled everybody, he cancelled all his fancy or not-so-fancy patients and gave this guy time. And nobody coming into Zurich could get any time with Jung normally. But this guy did. Because Jung was so pleased. He was just delighted – he was bouncing around the place and talking about it.

Learning from the patient is the natural consequence of analytical psychology not being a theory to be imposed upon, or 'a cure' for, the patient which is in the doctor's power alone. The doctor can learn, rather than merely prescribe, because the unconscious of the patient's unconscious psyche *does* produce images and dreams. It is dynamic and spontaneous, in Jung's view – and other analysts confirm the reality of the psyche is such that they too can share in an experience of the patient.

Dr Harry Wilmer is a Texan psychiatrist who served in the US Navy before running a drug-dependency ward in San Francisco. It was in the late 1960s and early 1970s, at the time when Haight-Ashbury, the San Francisco city district, was synonymous with sex, drugs and rock and roll. This was the 'Tune In, Turn On, Freak Out' ward. Joe Wheelwright, who was a consultant to the ward, showed the famous *Face to Face* interview between John Freeman and Jung, and Dr Wilmer began to get a sense of the reality of the psyche which was absent from the medical psychiatric model of his training.

Something about Jung and the immediacy with which he appears in that film, something about personality rather than technique, something about the compensatory aspects of the psyche seemed to make a profound impression on me. And it was as if I could now see what these drug trips were like, as if I could see that there was a healing aspect to the unconscious.

In later years, Dr Wilmer began to work with Vietnam veterans who were psychological casualties of the war, in US Veterans' Administration Hospitals and Centres.

I was running a ward for schizophrenics, and we had dream seminars. ... A veteran told of a Vietnam dream, and I realized that I had been listening to dreams of Vietnam and not really hearing them. Suddenly in this group it was alive. You know, Jung talking about the reality of the psyche: it was as if I had the privilege – if you want to call it a privilege – of being in the Vietnam War, of experiencing it.

The paradox, that the dream can be experienced like reality, is one that Dr Wilmer is well aware of. Yet he argues that the dream is if anything more accurate as an account of the experience than the written or oral histories of the Vietnam War – or of any war, perhaps.

It's the world of images, in contrast to the world of words. The oral histories are necessary, they are important memories, they're important records, but the dreams to me represent the only uncontaminated history we have of the war. ... To hear it is to experience it as the living experience of Vietnam, uncontaminated by conscious thinking. It gets mixed up when people talk about it, with conscious thought. But the dream itself is pure memory.

The reality of the psyche is so central a topic in Jung's work and his thinking, that he wrote an entire paper on the concept of reality – 'The Real and Surreal' (1933). In it, he gave an ironic reply to the suggestion that somehow the psyche and its products were not, and could not be called, 'real'.

Reality contains everything I can know, for everything that acts upon me is real and actual. If it does not act upon me, then I notice nothing and can therefore know nothing about it. Hence I can make statements only about real things. ... Unless, of course, it should occur to someone to limit the concept of reality in such a way that the attribute 'real' applied only to a particular segment of the world's reality. This restriction to the so-called material or concrete reality of objects perceived by the senses is a product of a particular way of thinking – the thinking that underlies 'sound commonsense'. [*The Real and Surreal* (1933)]

Applying this standard of reality to matters of psychology and psychiatry was a radical departure. Nowhere did Jung find the limited 'sound commonsense' view of reality, which excluded fantasy and psychic life, more damaging or tragic, than at the Burgholzli Hospital for the Insane where he spent his early professional years as a young psychiatrist. Here he found professionals busily occupied with the process of describing symptoms and ascertaining diagnoses, dismissing on a wholesale basis the psychological reality of the insane. What was true and all-encompassing for the schizophrenic was dismissed as imaginary, delusional, hallucinatory, incurable, dementia or just plain madness. Jung's contemporaries were by and large uninterested in the question which preoccupied him:

What actually takes place inside the psyche of the mentally ill? [*Memories, Dreams, Reflections*, p. 114]

Jung's scientific method was now deployed to investigate the unconscious which he had experienced directly for himself and indirectly through his patients. The accusation is often made against Jung that he was incurably mystical or romantic about the psyche – but his approach was scientific in a field not considered amenable to such methods.

Through my work with the patients I realized that paranoid ideas and hallucinations contains a germ of meaning. A personality, a life history, a pattern of hopes and desires lie behind the psychosis. The fault is ours if we do not understand them. … At bottom we discover nothing new and unknown in the mentally ill; rather, we encounter the substratum of our own natures. [*Memories, Dreams, Reflections*, p. 127]

Jung began to find evidence for his hypothesis that the psyche spoke in another way than through conscious thought. So successful was he that the very familiar modern concept of the lie detector, or polygraph, is based quite straightforwardly on his early research. At the age of thirty Jung did experimental work on the word-association experiment, the most familiar (and widely-parodied) of all psychological testing devices. The test (see Fig. 1) gave rise to the first psychological term to be associated with Jung's name – the complex.

The test requires the patient to say a word in immediate response to the doctor's stimulus word; the speed of response, and the patient's pulse and respiration were measured at the same time. Jung's innovation was to consider why some test-words caused patients to hesitate or to become anxious. Fifty years after his first experiments, he explained to Richard Evans what was the real interest of the results.

> I made these association tests and I found out that the important thing in them had been missed, because it is not interesting to see that there is a reaction – a certain reaction – to a stimulus word. That is more or less uninteresting. The interesting thing is why people could *not* react to certain stimulus words, or in an entirely inadequate way. And then I began to study these places in the experiment where the attention or the capability apparently of the test person began to waver or to disappear, and I soon found out that it is a matter of intimate personal affairs people were thinking of, or which were in them even if they momentarily did not think of them, when they were unconscious in other words; that nevertheless an inhibition came from the unconscious and hindered the expression in speech. [Houston No. 1]

The word-association test consists of a list of 100 words which were designed to elicit emotional responses. The subject was asked: 'Respond as quickly as possible to each word with the first word that occurs to you'.

Jung discovered that delays in response time were attributable to feelings that were raised by a particular word. These 'feeling tones' of which the patient is unconscious disrupt his ability to answer as quickly as possible. In later studies, Jung employed a machine which measured galvanic skin response (the electrical conductivity of the skin surface, influenced by the slightest amount of sweating) and also measured pulse, respiratory rate and volume of blood in the finger. This was the first polygraph or lie detector machine. According to Professor Meier:

> That's exactly the beginning of the whole development of Jungian psychology, when he did this word-association test and discovered that there were strange interferences from somewhere else or somebody else, in the way in which we try to react, to answer. And then it became clear that something else is at work as well,

Nr.

I.   (1908)

Name: _____   Krankheit: _____

Beruf: _____   Datum: _____

1. Kopf

2. grün

3. Wasser

4. singen

5. Tod

6. lang

7. Schiff

8. zahlen

9. Fenster

10. freundlich

11. Tisch

12. fragen

13. Dorf

14. kalt

15. Stengel

16. tanzen

17. See

18. krank

19. Stolz

20. kochen

21. Tinte

22. bös

23. Nadel

24. schwimmen

25. Reise

26. blau

27. Lampe

28. sündigen

29. Brot

30. reich

31. Baum

Fig. 1 Jung's word-association test.

and interferes. .... So then he started to understand that here is something which tries to express itself without being given a chance, and therefore disturbing the reaction. Therefore he or they began to call this, in their discussions at the Burgholzli, they began to call it a complex. In other words, something that exists without our knowing it, and then at certain occasions it has a chance to come through. It has its own sort of separate existence within our system.

In the plain language which Jung always liked to use:

I took the existence of the unconscious for a real fact – for a real autonomous factor, capable of independent action. ...
Consciousness is one factor, and there is another factor, equally important, that is the unconscious, that can interfere with consciousness any time it pleases. And of course, I say to myself now – this is very uncomfortable, because I think I am the only master in my house, but I must admit that there is another – somebody in that house that can play tricks, and I have to deal with the unfortunate victims of that interference every day in my patients. [Houston No. 4]

Not only in his private practice, but also with the mental patients at the Burgholzli Hospital, Jung was able to see with the word-association experiment that a second 'voice', that of the unconscious, was able to express itself – and to make some sense.

Much of what we had hitherto regarded as senseless was not as crazy as it seemed. More than once I have seen that even with such patients there remains in the background a personality which must be called normal. It stands looking on, so to speak. [*Memories, Dreams, Reflections*, p. 126]

In no way has Jung's early research gone out of date – the word-association experiment was a dramatic discovery which continues to be used and improved technically even today, in the form of the polygraph, or lie detector test.

Jeffrey Satinover is an analyst and psychiatrist in Stamford, Connecticut, who employs the latest computerized generation of neurological testing devices. One of these tests, known as 'brain-mapping', is based upon the principles underlying Jung's original word-association experiments. Unlike many analysts whose deep personal need, or an overwhelming dream, represented a conversion on the road to

Kusnacht, Dr Satinover came to Jungian psychology for more prosaic, though personal reasons. In high school and college he dated two young women, both of whose fathers were Jungian analysts. Later on, in what he calls a 'first half of life crisis', he sought out a Jungian therapist, and ultimately decided to become a Jungian analyst too.

> I was referred to Freddy Meier, I went to Zurich, enrolled in the
> programme, got into analysis with Meier, that was it. Now there's
> another side to it too, which is that I've always loved the mountains,
> and even since I was a kid, had fantasies of going to Switzerland.
> So this was a great way to kill two birds with one stone.

Dr Satinover conforms more to the fast-track, high-achievement model of American medicine than the dream-based, myth-oriented stereotype of analytical psychology. He expounds with enthusiasm his efforts to integrate a Jungian analytical approach into mainstream American medicine. With others, he has established a private clinic specializing in two fields which Jungian traditionalists have regarded as the least amenable to the archetypal and analytical approach: drug addiction and alcohol abuse, and Alzheimer's disease and premature senility.

Jeffrey Satinover is the current President of the C. G. Jung Foundation in New York, and in the clinical work he does, and in his lecturing post at the ivy league Yale University, he gives credit to Jung's pion-eering work. Today, with computer technology, Dr Satinover can measure the functioning of the brain far more precisely than Jung was able to do eighty years ago. But in one of the treatment rooms he demonstrated the connection to Jung's experiment.

In the modern technique of 'brain-mapping', the patient sits before a television monitor, which shows a variety of patterns, which change from time to time. With every change in the picture, the brain's reaction – its electrical activity, monitored by a skullcap of electrodes on the patient's head – is timed in microseconds. When this information is turned into a picture, the normal brain will look a bit like a bull's-eye pattern of concentric circles. But a brain which is functioning in a distorted or imbalanced way will produce a picture where the colours and pattern are themselves distorted or lopsided. As Jeffrey Satinover explains:

> Basically what Jung did with the word-association experiment was
> use a stimulus and then measure physiological responses as they
> correlated to psychological responses. So at the same time that he

was taking careful note of the patients' associations – the thinking that was taking place cognitively – he was also observing pulse, respiratory rate, volume of blood in the finger and skin conductivity, all of which are essentially measures of anxiety. He didn't conceptualize it that way at the time, but basically what he was doing was identifying the physiological components of an anxious reaction. And he noted that when the cognitive content of a patient's response was emotionally laden, that there were disturbances found physiologically – the patient had an anxious response to it.

So he was looking at precisely the same kind of activities that we're mapping here. What technology has allowed us to do is to set aside the cruder peripheral measures of disturbed response and look directly at the functioning of the brain which Jung could only infer was disturbed as a consequence of the peripheral disturbances. I'm sure that if he were alive and had access to this kind of technology and was still seeing a patient population in the Burgholzli, he'd probably be scurrying around brain-mapping everybody he possibly could.

Another parallel development from Jung's experiment is the poly-graph or lie detector test. The word-association test conclusively ident-ified the existence of an unconscious voice, separate from the conscious mental processes of the individual, but able to identify itself, or to interfere, when a difficult emotional situation arises. Since questions of truth and lying fall into this category, it is this alternative version or voice that the polygraph can detect, through physical evidence. Recalling Jung's phrase about being 'master in my own house', the American analyst Dr Edward Edinger describes the lie detector test in psychological terms:

It's a very interesting phenomenon, the lie detector test. What it does is to measure certain physiological responses to a psychological situation. What it reveals is that the physiology of the individual is a separate entity from the ego. So it's as though a second personality is standing behind me when I'm taking a lie detector test, and you ask me a question that I don't want to acknowledge, and I'll say 'no' and the man standing behind me will say: 'Oh yes, that's what the physiological response does'. So it tells us just in irrefutable terms that there is a second entity, second psychic centre, in the human psyche and it's interested in truth.

The relevance of Jung's work does not only lie in procedures of psychological testing. His view was that the whole of life is psychological, more or less. Psychological truth, therefore, does not only reveal itself through tests, but also in dreams, and arguments, and high emotion. It also emerges in public rituals and ceremonies – and the one that was perhaps most familiar and dynamic as a personal experience for Carl Jung was the annual Swiss Fasnacht carnival. All over the country, but especially in the city of Basel, in the north-western corner of Switzerland and close to both France and Germany, normal Swiss order surrenders to the fifes and drums, the piccolos, the confusion and colour of a vivid Lenten carnival – a carnival of truth. Many of Jung's friends and pupils went to Basel to see the Fasnacht, some at his suggestion, and others with him. One of these was the analyst Gerhard Adler:

> It tells us the truth, that the real depths of human psychology – this is usually hidden. If you take the proverbially reticent Swiss. Suddenly it breaks out. Suddenly it is something there that one wouldn't expect. But it is of course the truth.

Fasnacht is a licence for misbehaviour instead of the usual staid and respectable Swiss city life. For three days and nights the carnival invades the streets, stops the traffic, and brings a spirit of medieval rabble into the ancient but elegant city. The carnival allegedly has pagan roots, and one analyst recalls visiting Fasnacht and a simultaneous sun-worship ceremony nearby. It takes place, not on the three days before Lent, but has slipped to five days later. While the participants of the Mardi Gras, the Venice Carnevale, and Carnaval in Rio are all recovering in the first days of Lent, the Fasnachters are just getting started.

While the façade of Basel is of an expensive and sophisticated European city, its backstreets are full of mask-making ateliers and costumiers, who work all year round on their designs. Every Fasnacht mask is new, every year – and at a minimum price of 200 Swiss Francs (£75 or $130) it is a substantial mini-economy. The artistic and bohemian life of the city – which seems invisible – in fact thrives all year round, and has three days of supremacy each year. Jung saw Fasnacht as a medical student in Basel, and later took some of his friends and pupils to witness the eruption of the Swiss unconscious at first hand – perhaps seeing the true identity of the Swiss. Gerhard Adler saw it for himself:

> Well, true identity in the unconscious sense – they had a side to themselves, or a layer to themselves which usually didn't come out, and it was in this orgiastic experience of the wild Fasnacht that they could let themselves go. Of course it isn't orgiastic in any extreme sense. It is only orgiastic in the sense that it shows the true nature of the wildness. The Swiss are really very wild people, but very reticent people.

Fasnacht begins at four o'clock on a Monday morning. In the cold February night, thousands of people, all organized into 'cliques', wait for the *Morgenstreich* to arrive. This is the 'Drumbeat of morning': all the street-lights are turned out, and as the Cathedral bells toll the hour, the cliques light the elaborate lanterns each one has designed, and every individual lights his own lamp – often carried on top of the head – while at the same time the drums begin to beat and the piccolos to whistle. Every clique is playing a different tune, at a different rhythm; the theory that there is a route for the marchers to follow immediately breaks down. The Marktplatz, the main square of the city, and all its neighbouring streets are immediately filled with a total confusion of noise and flickering lights. Tens of thousands of spectators are in the streets too; watching something reminiscent of a tribal war ritual, in which the weapons and expressions of hostility are in the form of musical noise and outlandish costume.

As dawn breaks, and the light comes up, the masks, costumes, and lanterns begin to be revealed. It requires no great imagination to begin psychological speculation. There are men in women's clothing, and women in men's. There are battered aristocrats and courtiers from earlier ages, witches and fairies, a whole impromptu congress of fairy-tale characters and real or mythical animals. There are pigs, rats, Phoenixes, and bumble-bees – and they all play their piccolos still.

Jane Wheelwright, who also saw Fasnacht when she was working with Jung in Switzerland, sees the continuation of such rituals as keeping people in touch with an earlier, less sophisticated form of life.

> There's a lot of ritual in Europe. Fasnacht apparently is still connected very much to the archetypes, and it's like a holiday from being civilized, and when you think of the primitive tribes, they had that too. To behave yourself all the time is too tiresome,

it gets you down, finally. So if you can cut loose ... and apparently, in the old traditional way, you could cut loose and you knew when to stop.

One of the great carnivals which has been lost from European life was London's Bartholomew Fair. The alternative title for Ben Jonson's vivid comedy set at the Fair was 'The World Turned Upside Down' – a dimension of Fasnacht which still seems important. Gerhard Adler draws a parallel with another example of reversal – the religious ceremony of Maundy.

Maundy is an old ceremony in which the Pope and the Bishop wash the feet of the common people. It is also a reversal of things, but here is an aspect that the uppermost become the lowest, and the lowest becomes the uppermost. There is something coming from underneath and something from above that goes down.

In the main Fasnacht parade, which takes place on the Monday afternoon and again on Wednesday, the cliques parade in the new masks which they have designed, this time identical for each member. Cliques can be professional groups, or an assortment of friends; in recent years there have emerged a number of all-women groups in response to a general exclusion of women before. In this as in other ways, Fasnacht is a microcosm of Swiss society; and the themes that the masks illustrate, and which is indicated most clearly by the main lantern which the clique parades through the streets, are also topical. The aftermath of the massive pollution of the Rhine by a chemical plant near Basel was to be seen in the 1988 Fasnacht in a wide variety of satirical lanterns on ecological and environmental themes, combined with negative or even slanderous visual attacks on local politicians. This is a major facet of the Fasnacht mask, both in social terms and at an individual level.

At Fasnacht, everyone is masked, and anybody in a Fasnacht mask may insult his friends or colleagues by telling them the naked truth which for the rest of the year he would suppress. It is the opposite of the mask which we normally wear in order to take our place in the world. The Latin word for an actor's mask was *persona* – Jung himself coined the use in psychological terms for the manners and style we assume as our outer image – which may be very different from our inner psychological reality, as Gerhard Adler explains:

We wear masks all the time and we have to get behind the mask, we have to realize that we have the mask. Persona was also on the other hand something necessary, because we can't jump with our true being at everybody. We have to be careful.

Jung established the idea of persona by observing that his patients had a certain way of presenting themselves, which was not, as he investigated the reality of their individual psyche, the real personality. In Fasnacht, one observes people assuming a persona or mask which permits them to express and demonstrate the things that they might feel quite prohibited from expressing during the other 362 days of the year.

Wherever one turns during the Fasnacht parades, whether in the sidestreets or the open squares, one sees extraordinary and startling figures: three snowmen on horseback, a regiment of high-stepping military rats, a battalion of Hausfrau Brunnhildes, wearing colanders as hats; a whole troop of boy pilots march by, bearing a remarkable resemblance to Mathias Rust, who flew into Red Square; the waiters' clique wear masks that have a hand carrying a tray where the head should be, while the industrial scientists are dressed as 'Wockis', the grotesque parody of simple country peasants in the nearby Alsace countryside. There are fire-birds, people whose heads have become coffee tables laden with decorative vases, masks in the shape of giant flies' heads, and cheery rotund men's mouths munching insects, too. And among many others, there is a team of monks or nuns whose heads are naked buttocks – pulling a vast chariot where a smiling Satan beats his drum.

The painter Pablo Picasso once wrote about masks in a letter to Françoise Gilot:

Men had made those masks for a sacred purpose; as a kind of mediation between themselves and the unknown hostile forces surrounding them, in order to overcome their fear and horror by giving it a form, an image. Painting isn't an aesthetic operation; it's a form of magic designed as mediation between a strange hostile world and us; a way of seizing power by giving form to our terror as well as our desires.

It is interesting to note that despite the coincidence of views on masks and their psychological meaning, Jung once attended an exhibition of Picasso's work and felt able to question the painter's sanity.

Jung's grandson Dr Dieter Baumann, who himself is an analyst, is an enthusiastic participant in the Fasnacht – both as a ritual to be enjoyed and experienced enthusiastically, and as a psychological revelation:

> I happened to be in the army, in the barracks on the other side of the Rhine, and I was awakened by the *Morgenstreich*. I went to the window and in the distance I saw the *Mittelerrhein* bridge and on the bridge these circulating lights – and my impression was very very special – eerie, like elves coming out of the ground. At a given point, I think it has also to do with my age, I bought myself a piccolo and I started to practise, and then I went – because I liked it, and because I have one quarter of Basel blood by Jung, by this ancestor. I liked the music and the whole love and skill and pains people take to create Fasnacht. It is the spirit of the dead who become alive again. It's the ancestral spirit. One cannot really explain it, but an aspect is certainly that the unconscious comes out ... on the one hand it is a reconnection with the heathen past and with the natural past. Basel is a city and a very densely constructed city with all these chemical plants and so on; and I have the impression nature here reminds us psychically that actually we are peasants and should take care of the earth. I think the Fasnacht is unconscious religion.

At the end of Fasnacht, and at intervals within the three days of festivities, the masks are taken off in order to enable a return to the respectable, normal life of the sophisticated European city. The pagan and the unconscious impulses of Swiss life are concealed once again under the everyday mask of business as usual. As Jung himself observed about the concept of persona in everyday life:

> Such a performance of the persona is quite all right, as long as you know that you are not identical with the way in which you appear; but it you are unconscious of that fact, then you get into sometimes very disagreeable conflicts.

The wild eruption of imagination, vulgarity, irreverence, wild costumes and fantastic masks, a cacophony of clashing music, played deliberately badly – all of Fasnacht represents a vivid reminder to the Swiss of an unconscious facet of the national personality which demands expression. It is worth considering the effect upon other nations – England perhaps above all – or smaller communities, where no such safety valve exists.

Whether one finds the evidence for the reality of the psyche in dreams, in madness, or in social ritual, Jung's ideas about the unconscious psyche have infiltrated modern attitudes to a remarkable extent. The reality of the psyche is essential to the Jungian way of seeing life – through the undeniable existence of an inner life.

If Jung was a twentieth century man, or even the author of the psychology of the twenty-first century, there can be no doubt that his work goes against the grain of our intellectual tradition. Life is very widely dominated still by the belief that rational solutions exist for all problems, and that problems which don't respond to reason cannot be real; or that their inability to be resolved is attributable to human weakness or failure. Jung once noted:

> The true problems of life are never really solved, and if ever we think they are, that is probably a sign of deeper difficulty. ('The Stages of Life', *Collected Works*, Vol. 8, par. 771)

In the chapters that follow, we will consider individual aspects of Jung's thinking which touch on 'real life' in a variety of ways. But none of it means anything unless we first have understood that for Jung, the most real dimension of life was the one that many of us find it impossible to recognize at all – the reality of the psyche.

> All my writings ... represent a compensation for our times, and I have been impelled to say what no one wants to hear.... I knew that what I said would be unwelcome, for it is difficult for people of our times to accept the counter-weight to the conscious world. [*Memories, Dreams, Reflections*, p. 222]

3

The Wisdom of the Dream

Among the many puzzles of medical psychology there is
one problem child, the dream.
['On the Nature of Dreams', *Collected Works*, vol. 8, par. 531)

Aniela Jaffe is eighty-six years old now but her apartment in Zurich is
filled with the flowers of a young woman continually visited by suitors,
bearing witness to her grace, charm and intelligence. Still a beautiful
woman, though almost blind and as fragile as paper, her hospitality
is definitely that of old-world Europe: Lapsang Souchong tea and
chocolate biscuits never tasted so good as at Hochstrasse at four
o'clock on a Sunday afternoon. Our interview was filmed, appropriately
perhaps, on Valentine's Day 1988.

Aniela is a woman who has a strong sense of who she is in this
world and what that means to her; that includes a perspective on her
advanced age. It is not a compliment to Mrs Jaffe to be told she is
looking young; she is happy to look and feel as old as she is, and to
embrace the positive and negative aspects of the end of life.

Mrs Jaffe first met C. G. Jung in 1938, when she was in Zurich
having been thrown out of Germany – she is Jewish. At the time, she
says that she was living a very extroverted type of life, until an accident
changed all that, and her dreams began to comment.

It was a sort of nervousness, very extroverted behaviour. But that
was not my true type. So I was punished. I broke my leg – or IT
broke my leg, because I was not allowed to live as an extrovert. I
came to the clinic for many weeks, and there I had many very

interesting dreams.... I'll tell you one of the dreams I had at the clinic. I walked down the Bahnhofstrasse here in Zurich, and I looked at the station clock. And all at once the clock stopped and after a short moment it started again but anti-clockwise, you see. In the other direction. So that was very clear, from the outside to the inside. And it's what I told Jung in my first lesson.

For those who have followed Jung's ideas, the dream is an invaluable commentator and illuminator of life. To Aniela Jaffe, a dream would naturally provide insight in this way. With this dream, and with an introduction from a friend, began Aniela's long association with Jung. After she analysed with him she went on to be the secretary of the Jung Institute in Zurich, then Jung's personal secretary for the last seven years of his life. Jung's autobiography, *Memories, Dreams, Reflections*, was 'recorded and edited' by her, with the result that Mrs Jaffe is, apart from Jung's own son and daughters, perhaps the very best source of insight into Jung's work and how he himself saw it in retrospect at the end of his life.

She herself became an analyst and has published numerous articles and books. After all these years and accomplishments, and over twenty-five years after Jung's death, she says without a hint of embarrassment 'I have still a transference on Jung'.

A transference is a projection of an inner image on a person, so the old wise man, old father figure, I saw that in Jung. He awoke this figure in me and provided a hook to hang up the inner figure. It was probably what I was looking for – a wise man who showed me the world. What made Jung famous was that he was not just a wise man, but he was much more. He was a human being, *ein Mensch* – and that's much more. But you see what made him great was his being seized by inner images.

Jung discovered that by taking first his own and then his patients' dreams and fantasies seriously, he could find the key to understanding, 'the secret background to life', which contained hidden solutions to life's problems. It was as though he had found the hidden field in which the vital missing pieces to the puzzles of peoples problems lay. Jung discovered that the psyche contained its own healer which could be activated by the process of exploring dreams and fantasies. For Aniela Jaffe and many others, he, as the analyst, strove to be the 'hook' or outer personification for that which he showed them actually came from within the depths of their own psychology.

Jung always maintained that he was a medical doctor first and foremost. What turned into a life-long exploration of the psychic history of mankind began with the practical problems of a working psychiatrist. His sometimes controversial reputation was built largely upon his insistence upon investigating what his psychiatric patients and common people found real or of interest rather than that which intellectuals deemed appropriate for investigation.

From his earliest childhood, Jung remembered and considered his own dreams and fantasies. He thought it was worth knowing what dreams were; what purpose or information they might contain; how we might find them useful or informative about the meaning of events in our 'real life'. As a young man, considering which direction his university studies should take, Jung hesitated between pursuing archaeology and anthropology on the one hand, or the sciences on the other, when he went to university in Basel. But even in his late teens, such was his conviction in the wisdom of his dreams, that he allowed two powerful and impressive dreams to guide him.

In the first dream I was in a dark wood that stretched along the Rhine. I came to a little hill, a burial mound, and began to dig. After a while I turned up, to my astonishment, some bones of prehistoric animals. This interested me enormously, and at that moment I knew: I must get to know nature, the world in which we lived, and the things around us.

Then came a second dream. Again I was in a wood; it was threaded with watercourses, and in the darkest place I saw a circular pool, surrounded by dense undergrowth. Half immersed in the water lay the strangest and most wonderful creature: a round animal, shimmering in opalescent hues, and consisting of innumerable little cells, or of organs shaped like tentacles ... It aroused in me an intense desire for knowledge, so that I awoke with a beating heart. These two dreams decided me overwhelmingly in favour of science, and removed all my doubts. [*Memories, Dreams, Reflections* p. 85]

For Jung, the message of such dreams was simply experienced as fact, and within the context of analytical psychology, the meaningfulness of dreams is more or less taken for granted; outside it, such a proposition is very far from being widely accepted, though what acceptance there is may be due to Jung's work more than any other person's.

However, it is very often the case that Jung is only considered in relation to his older colleague, the Viennese psychiatrist Sigmund Freud. At the popular level, Jung's thought is more accessible and better understood than the more technical Freud – but within the profession of psychology, Jung's reputation is as the less rigorous intellectual, and more the romantic mystical healer. Both men were responsible for the birth and development of modern psychology; the proportion of credit is impossible to define. For many years there has been outright hostility between the two schools of followers, but particularly the Freudian tradition attacks Jung on matters which have nothing to do with the quality of his psychology. In this context, in the attempt to bring the merits of Jung's work to a wider audience, there is no pretence of neutrality or 'balance'. However it is illuminating of Jung's own work – and perhaps, incidentally, of Freud's – to hear what Jungians believe were the essential differences between the intellectual and philosophical outlook of the two men.

As Jung himself observed, Freud had no philosophical education at all, whereas Jung had studied the history of philosophy with the same attention as his scientific courses. Freud, the older man by some thirty years, was educated in the nineteenth century, in the intellectual climate of what is called 'scientism' – that everything could be known, that material explanations could be found for every possible phenomenon – even psychological ones. It was the third or fourth generation of the Age of Reason, by then running in high gear. Jung, born in 1875, and scarcely out of medical school at the turn of the century, was educated in a changing intellectual climate as the twentieth century approached. His father and other relations were ministers of the Swiss Protestant Church, so religion was a part of his background in addition to childhood and adolescent experiences of his own, apparently dynamic, unconscious. At Basel University he studied Kant, whose Critique of Pure Reason sowed doubts about rationalism, and Nietzsche, whose mythological style of philosophy had made a great impression on the Basel faculty in recent years.

The English theologian Don Cupitt makes the following comparison between the two men:

Freud is the more respectable thinker, at the moment, because he was a better writer and I suppose he was more of an orthodox pessimistic Victorian scientist. Whereas Jung is something like a gnostic, he's a heretical underground thinker. Some of his ideas are very original, but he was not so persuasive a writer as Freud.

To James Hillman, the American 'post-Jungian' analyst and critic, the essential difference between the two men is that they belong to different intellectual traditions:

Being critical is much more Freudian than Jungian. The faith aspect is more Jungian than Freudian. You see Freud revised his work all the time, and then said 'What I didn't do then, now I would do it this way.' He made revisions because he had a kind of systematic theory. Jung didn't revise anything. He built on it, he didn't have a critical mind in that sense. Freud comes from a different tree than Jung. Jung comes from a Romantic tree, from a Neoplatonic tree, from a Gothic tree. Freud comes out of an Aristotelian kind of thinking, with a rational, empirical angle – that's the kind of tree he grew on.

Aniela Jaffe, Jung's secretary in his last years and the compiler of his autobiography, believes that the patient will gravitate towards one or the other school of thought according to his or her inner mode of functioning:

They go to a Freudian, they go to a Jungian. That is of course their fate, whom they choose. And I should say from the character, if they are more rationalistic, they go to a Freudian, if they are more religious and irrational they go to a Jungian. What is important for Jung is not knowing and understanding, but experience.

In the words of one Jungian analyst, Freud was essentially nineteenth century in his outlook, while Jung was a twentieth-century thinker who had moved away from the 'I must know' themes of scientific research and realized the importance of mystery, religious experience and wholeness for man. Jung wrote in 'Retrospect', the last chapter of his autobiography:

It is important to have a secret, a premonition of things unknown. It fills life with something impersonal, a *numinosum*. A man who has never experienced that has missed something important. He must sense that he lives in a world which in some respects is mysterious, that things happen and can be experienced which remain inexplicable, that not everything which happens can be anticipated. The unexpected and the incredible belong in this world. Only then is life whole. For me, the world has from the beginning been infinite and ungraspable. (*Memories, Dreams, Reflections,* p. 356)

Jungian analysts today have a variety of impressions – all tinged with their subjective preference for Jung, naturally – of how and why Freud and Jung differed so deeply. As they became pre-eminent in their field, and their ages were such that they could have been father and son, a clear power struggle developed between them and their groups of followers, with the usual consequences, as Andrew Samuels points out.

What happens in a power struggle is that it becomes life and death. The two men were absolutely invested in their own ideas, and that's good because without the kind of passionate conviction in one's ideas, they lack something. But what you start to get is the rubbishing of each other's main concerns. So Freud eventually castigates Jung as a kind of nutcase mystic, and Jung castigates Freud as a materialistic bore. But what it's really about is leadership.

Another difference was undoubtedly the general purpose of the psychoanalysis (Freudian) or analysis (Jungian). In the opinion of Dr Joe Wheelwright:

Jung was primarily interested in where you were going to, and Freud was primarily interested in where you came from. Who's to say which is more important?

Unlike Freud, who believed that the function of the unconscious mind was to contain those things which the conscious mind found unbearable and therefore repressed, Jung believed that the split between conscious and unconscious was the result of the psychological evolution of the human mind. The ego – what we describe when we use the word 'I' – was the part of the mind that had grown away from the rest of the psyche when man developed consciousness, the quality of thinking which differentiates him from the rest of animal life and nature. Although the unconscious for Jung did contain material which the ego had repressed, it also contained the collective psychic history of mankind and the image of man in nature before the development of the self-aware, thinking mind, capable of reasoning and judgement.

Jung himself explained the difference between his view of the unconscious and Freud's in 1957, to Evans:

A content sinks below the level of consciousness and thus becomes unconscious. That is Freud's view too, only he says it sinks down because it is helped, it is repressed from above. That was my first point of difference with Freud. I said there were cases in my observation where there was no repression from above, but the thing itself is true. Those contents that become unconscious had withdrawn all by themselves, they were not repressed. On the contrary, they have a certain autonomy. I discovered the concept of autonomy because these contents that disappear have the power to move independently of my will. [Houston No. 1]

Of all those people who knew and followed Jung's work, it was possible only to find one who had also had a personal encounter with Freud. Professor Freddy Meier studied for a time in Vienna, and was invited to a weekly seminar which Freud gave to his students.

That was a very odd experience. This group of his pupils, who discussed their cases on Wednesday, gave me a strange impression. They were all in fear and trembling before Freud.

Meier then asked for a private meeting with Freud, which was filled with pleasant talk about the Jung family. Freud offered to take Meier for analysis, if he so wished. Then, as he left, Meier felt paralysed, and could not move from the porch of Freud's house.

We had to deal with a pathological condition – I was paralysed, when I stood there outside of the house, and I couldn't move and I had to ponder, what this terrible gentle man as he was had possibly done to me. And after a while, a minute or so, it dawned on me that this man is trying to kill you. But spiritual murder of course. And so I was liberated and could walk off, and that was the end of my acquaintance with dear old Freud. The limitations he put on the functions of the human psyche simply didn't agree with me. He was too narrow.

The first and most important theme in the Jungian approach to dreams is that the dream itself is a natural human activity. Jung's view that the unconscious is active and independent automatically suggests that the expression of the unconscious, in the form of a dream, is something worth considering in its own right. On this fundamental point, as on the general view of the unconscious and its contents, Jung wrote:

I was never able to agree with Freud that the dream is a 'façade' behind which its meaning lies hidden – a meaning already known but maliciously, so to speak, withheld from consciousness. To me dreams are a part of nature, which harbours no intention to deceive, but expresses something as best it can.... To him the unconscious was a product of consciousness, and simply things consciousness had discarded were heaped up and left. To me the unconscious then was already a matrix, a basis of consciousness of a creative nature, capable of autonomous acts, autonomous intrusions into consciousness. [*Memories, Dreams, Reflections,* p. 161]

Inevitably Jung believed these intrusions to be purposeful, as his personal experience was that dreams offered a perspective on matters in his conscious life. At about the age of fifty Jung began to study alchemy, a breathtakingly obscure subject which mingles a kind of early history of natural science with highly inventive mystical and mythological interpretations of physical experiments. Despite the profound difficulty of the subject, Jung dived in, and persevered: not least because of a series of dreams which indicated to him that there was something new he had to try to understand:

I had a series of dreams which repeatedly dealt with the same theme. Beside my house stood another, that is to say, another wing or annex, which was strange to me. Each time I would wonder in my dream why I did not know this house, although it had apparently always been there. Finally came a dream in which I reached the other wing. I discovered there a wonderful library, dating largely from the sixteenth and seventeenth centuries. Large, fat folio volumes, bound in pigskin, stood along the walls. Among them were a number of books embellished with copper engravings of a strange character ... only much later did I recognize them as alchemical symbols. [*Memories, Dreams, Reflections,* p. 202]

The nature of the material in dreams prompted Jung repeatedly to ask the same question. Were the images or complexes in the unconscious purely the result of repressed, uncomfortable feelings from conscious life, or did they have an independent existence, as if inherited from human evolution, rather than the chronological lifetime of the individual? The evidence Jung found most persuasive was that in dreams, and schizophrenic fantasies, detailed material emerged which, he was quite satisfied, the individual in question could never have come across in conscious life.

After my association experiments – when I realized that there is obviously an unconscious; the question holds, now what is this unconscious? Does it consist merely of rests – of remnants of conscious activities, or are there things that are practically forever unconscious? In other words, is the unconscious a factor in itself – and I soon came to the conclusion that the unconscious must be a factor in itself, because I observed time and again that people's dreams, or schizophrenic patients' delusions and fantasies, contained certain motifs which they couldn't possibly have acquired in our surroundings. [Houston No. 4]

The most famous example of duplication concerns the idea that the sun has a phallus. Jung was called to the window by a schizophrenic patient, who told him to squint at the sun. If he did, he would see a tube hanging from the sun, its phallus, which was the source of the wind. Jung was bemused, but not particularly struck – until several years later, when he came across a translation of a newly-discovered Greek text with exactly the same mythological reference contained in it.

Nevertheless, the appearance of similar material from some deeper source did not amount to a theory of how it happened. An explanation which began to make sense to Jung first emerged from another of his own dreams, and an irrevocable split also opened between Jung and Freud with this, Jung's most original and controversial discovery, of what he called 'the collective unconscious'.

I was in a house I did not know. It was 'my house'. I found myself in the upper storey, where there was a kind of salon furnished with fine old pieces in rococo style. On the walls hung a number of precious old paintings. I wondered that this should be my house, and thought 'Not bad'. But then it occurred to me that I did not know what the lower floor looked like. Descending the stairs, I reached the ground floor. There everything was much older, and I realized that this part of the house must date from the fifteenth or sixteenth century. The furnishings were medieval; the floors were of red brick. Everywhere it was rather dark. I went from one room to another, thinking 'Now I really must explore the whole house'. I came upon a heavy door, and opened it. Beyond it I discovered a stone stairway that led down into the cellar. Descending again, I found myself in a beautifully vaulted room which looked exceedingly ancient. Examining the walls, I discovered layers of brick among the ordinary stone blocks, and chips of brick in the mortar. As soon as I saw this I knew that the walls dated from Roman times. My interest by now was intense. I looked more closely at the floor. It was of stone slabs, and in one of these I discovered a ring. When I pulled it, the stone slab lifted, and again I saw a stairway of narrow stone steps leading down into the depths. These, too, I descended, and entered a low cave cut into the rock. Thick dust lay on the floor, and in the dust were scattered bones and broken pottery, like remains of a primitive culture. I discovered two human skulls, obviously very old and half disintegrated. Then I awoke. [*Memories, Dreams, Reflections*, pp. 158–159]

The dream occured while Jung and Freud were together in the USA in 1909. Jung's interpretation of his dream was quite different from that of Freud, who implied that the skulls might indicate a death wish against someone by Jung. 'My wife and my sister-in-law', said Jung. 'Myself,' thought Freud. But Jung's own opinion was quite different.

It was plain to me that the house represented a kind of image of the psyche – that is to say, of my then state of consciousness, with hitherto unconscious additions. Consciousness was represented by the salon. It had an inhabited atmosphere, despite its antiquated style. The ground floor stood for the first level of the unconscious. The deeper I went, the more alien and the darker the scene became. In the cave I discovered remains of a primitive culture, that is, the world of the primitive man within myself – a world which can scarcely be reached or illuminated by consciousness. The dream pointed out that there were further reaches to the state of consciousness I have just described. It obviously pointed to the foundations of cultural history – a history of successive layers of consciousness. My dream thus constituted a kind of structural diagram of the human psyche; it postulated something of an altogether impersonal nature underlying that psyche. [*Memories, Dreams, Reflections*, pp. 160–161]

Jung's therapeutic attitude to dreams – his own and other people's – was that the unconscious attempts to communicate something of value in the dream, often something to balance the conscious attitude. Patients who enter analysis do so because they are suffering – often caused by the disconnection of the conscious and unconscious mind.

Robert Johnson is a tall, limping figure whose Oregon roots, deep in lumberjack country and culture, gave way to a near-monastic life in which the impact of a single dream has dominated for almost forty years. He is a quietly-spoken man, almost immobile in his chair, whether at his beachside house north of San Diego, California, or in one of his favoured retreats – in the baking-hot desert of Borrego Springs, three hours' drive east from the Pacific coast, or in the Indian ashram at Pondicherry of the Hindu teacher, Sri Aurobindo (a near-contemporary of Jung), where Johnson spends three months of every year. In recent years he has been in great demand as a speaker, combining Jungian insight with Hindu wisdom, and offering his audiences a psychological understanding of Indian, European and Greek mythology.

In 1948 Johnson found himself in Zurich, an 'unhappy youth', and entered into analysis with one of Jung's formidable woman followers.

> I began analysis with Yolande Jacobi, who is probably the most unfortunate choice I could have made – I being the introverted feeling-type that I am, and she being an extroverted Hungarian, who conducted her analytical hours pacing the floor, which always annoyed me. She told me that the apartment owner, next floor down, took her to court in Switzerland because she paced. The Swiss judge heard her plea that 'I am a Hungarian and I pace, that is part of my nature, it is my right to pace', and he said, 'All right, you may pace between 8.0 a.m. and 10.0 p.m., but not in the night'.
>
> I had a very large dream, one of these great, epoch-making dreams which are so important in one's life, really a summation of who I am, and what I am for, and what I am on the face of the earth to do. I think the dream frightened Dr Jacobi, because her comment was: 'You're a young man, that's an old man's dream, and you shouldn't dream dreams like that' and she refused to discuss it.

Robert Johnson walked out on his analyst, and armed with his big dream promptly began analysis with Emma Jung, Carl's wife, who was then teaching in the Institute. The dream was impressive enough for her to speak of it to her husband.

> Mrs Jung apparently took the dream to Dr Jung that night, because he phoned the school the next day, got me on the phone, and said 'You get out here, I want to talk at you' – *at me* – and it was precisely that. Dr Jung occupied about three hours in our first meeting, telling me who I was, what I should do, what I should not do, what kind of a life I should lead, and made it quite clear

that he didn't want me to interrupt him. He had some information
to tell me. And what he told me has been remarkably accurate
and true, but has taken me this much of my lifetime to come to an
understanding of some of those things.

In essence he told me: 'It is your place on the face of the earth
to live the inner life, and to do the work in the refinement or the
evolution of the collective unconscious. And even if you never do
anything else but that, your life will have been well spent.' He said:
'Don't marry, you live alone, spend most of your time alone, and
don't ever join anything.'

To anyone hearing this story, Jung's response could seem an arro-
gant imposition of a tenuous point of view about the value of a dream
on an impressionable young man. But Johnson has no qualms about
the essential truth of what Jung found in his dream.

I don't feel it was Dr Jung who was speaking. He was spokesman
for my dream, and that was the authority he needed. I still work
at that dream, it's that important to me. That dream was like the
book review of my life, which was to come. Dreams have an
extraordinary capacity for outlining who one is and often give good
information on how one should or can lead his life. Dr Jung's
interpretation was remarkably accurate, I don't think there's any
detail in which he was in error. One of the things Dr Jung said
was: 'I don't care how old you are, you have to live that dream
now'.

Robert Johnson was insecure as a young man, and remains shy and
self-effacing now, in his sixties. The places where he seeks refuge are
a contrast: in the desert, almost a wilderness where he can be alone
or share his space with one or two close friends; and in the ashram, a
community where human feeling fills the atmosphere. His explanation
of the attraction of the desert was this:

Great things of the interior world seem always to have happened
in the desert in Western culture. I come here principally to store
energy, which is almost a lost art in the modern world. Wonderful
things happen if one stores energy. The creative process is
stimulated; one's best faculties go to work. This is a wonderful place
to store energy. To go to a place which is quiet, in which one lives
something like a natural rhythm of life – that's a very salutary
experience for one. For my patients I often prescribe for them: just
go and be quiet for a few days.

The prescription of Johnson's 'big dream', interpreted by 'spokes-man' Jung, was to live alone, never join anything.

I promptly went out and tried to join something, because I was such a lonely youth, and wanted to belong somewhere. The church, or the university, or the Jung societies, or anything that I could fit myself into, to alleviate the solitariness. They all blew up in my face, nicely. For instance, I put myself into a Benedictine monastery at age forty, stayed two years, and had to battle my way out of it, at great pain and great difficulty, and considerable danger to myself. One doesn't tear one's life apart at forty and again at forty-two easily.

For many years, Robert Johnson has permitted himself to live in the way that the dream indicated: not alleviating the solitariness, but accepting that it was his way. Like Aniela Jaffe, who suffered when she behaved in a falsely extroverted style, Johnson found that joining things and trying to belong was to ignore the commitment the con-conscious demanded of him.

In using the phrase 'big dream', Johnson is referring to the attitude towards dreams which Jung observed during his expedition to Africa in 1925. Together with the English psychiatrist (for some years Jung's assistant in Zurich), H. Godwin Baynes, and an American friend, George Beckwith, Jung had undertaken what the British colonial authorities in East Africa named the 'Bugishu Psychological Expedition'. According to Aniela Jaffe:

When he was in Kenya, he was fifty or fifty-one, and there he was called 'Mzee' – that means 'old man'. That astonished him. But he said 'My hair was already grey and white', therefore he was an old man.

While Jung was the 'Mzee', Baynes was known as 'Red Neck' – because all Englishmen had red necks – and the well-dressed American 'Bwana maredadi', 'the dapper gentleman'. Jung's interest had been sparked by a visit to the Wembley Exhibition in London early in 1925, which included a survey of the African tribes under British rule.

They sailed through the Suez Canal to Nairobi; among their fellow passengers was Ruth Bailey, a young English woman who thirty years later came to Zurich to become Jung's housekeeper after the death of Emma in 1955. Jung and Baynes had a cumbersome 16 millimetre black-and-white film camera with them to record the expedition, and which provides some very rare footage of the African interior in the 1920s, though sadly relatively little of Jung himself. Their goal was to live and study with the Elgonyi tribe, a sub-group of the Masai who lived on the foothills of Mount Elgon, on the borders of Kenya and Uganda.

The tribesmen were as fascinated by the white European doctor as he was by them and their alien culture and habits. Jung had learned some pidgin Swahili, and as always he asked everyone he met about their dreams, and the importance they gave to dreams. The analyst Joe Wheelwright, who trained with Jung in the 1930s, heard from him first-hand about his travels and 'big' and 'little' dreams.

> His visit to Africa certainly helped to inform him on the subject of dreams and to differentiate between what he called big dreams and little dreams, and this had to do with whether the dream was from the collective unconscious, from the deepest layers, or whether it was from the personal unconscious. Because a big dream came from the collective unconscious and was really universal in its import.

Jung himself wrote in his study 'On the Nature of Dreams (*Collected Works*, vol. 8, par. 554):

> Not all dreams are of equal importance. Even primitives distinguish between little and big dreams. I have examined many such dreams and often found in them a peculiarity which distinguishes them from other dreams: they contain symbolical images which we also come across in the mental history of mankind. Thus we speak on the one hand of a personal and on the other of a collective unconscious which lies at a deeper level. The big dreams come from this deeper level.

Jung's expedition party spent six weeks living among the Elgonyi. In palavers with the men of the tribe, Jung asked them about their religious practices, and their dreams. He found them reluctant to speak, and deduced that they might fear that harm could come to them from anyone who has knowledge of their dreams. The attitude of the Somali and Swahili expedition porters was quite different, however:

> They had an Arab dream book which they daily consulted during the trek. If they were in doubt about an interpretation, they would actually come to me for advice. They termed me a 'man of the Book' because of my knowledge of the Koran. To their minds, I was a

disguised Mohammedan. [*Memories, Dreams, Reflections*, p. 265]

In the flickering monochrome images of the Jung-Baynes home movies, the expedition is seen to trek through the bush and into the highlands, with vignettes of tribal life interspersed through the film. At one point, in a cave apparently occupied by a family and its goats, Dr Jung is seen to be prodding and tickling a wide-eyed African boy of three or four years old; at another, he applauds as two boys re-enact the incident in which the expedition cook was almost attacked by a hyena in his tent. Seemingly as comfortable in his colonial role of expedition leader (seen distributing wages to the bearers at a folding card-table) as he would be in his Zurich study, Jung regarded the African visit as enjoyable and informative.

> Our camp life proved to be one of the loveliest interludes in my life. I enjoyed the 'divine peace' of a still primeval country. Never had I before seen so clearly 'man and the other animals' (Herodotus). Thousands of miles lay between me and Europe, mother of all demons. [*Memories, Dreams, Reflections*, p. 264]

Among the African tribesmen, Jung wanted to understand the status of dreams, and the meaning or value they attached to them. In particular, the Swiss doctor of medicine conferred with the Elgonyi *laibon* or medicine-man.

> When I asked him about his dreams, he answered with tears in his eyes 'In old days the *laibons* had dreams, and knew whether there is war or sickness or whether rain comes and where the herds should be driven'. His grandfather, too, had still dreamed. But since the whites were in Africa, he said, no one had dreams any more. Dreams were no longer needed because the English knew everything!

The important thing, wherever the real power lay, was that dreams were important. In the ancient Anasazi culture – the Indian tribes who are the original native Americans – dreams have significance. Dr Joe Wheelwright has spent a lot of time in the American south-west, and on one occasion observed a Navajo medicine-man's 'chant' – a ceremony either to cure an illness, or to mark an important day or rite of passage for an individual, a family, or the tribe.

I went to a chant and I talked to the head medicine-man afterwards, named He Who Lives By The Yellow Bitter Water, and I had to have an interpreter, because I can't speak Navajo and we got somehow onto dreams, and he said 'Do you believe in dreams?' I said 'Of course I do, I work with them constantly.' 'Why,' he said, 'There may be some hope for the Anglos.' The Anglos are the white people, the non-Indians. I thought of Jung at this point, because they were very sympathetic to him, they felt that he was on the right track.

Africans, Indians, and Jungians all take it for granted that the dream is a natural occurrence; and that the dream is nature's way of communicating with the conscious mind. Dreams are the vehicle by which all aspects of the psyche make themselves known in an uncensored form. Since they are a natural phenomenon they provide information which is not according to conscious human expectations, either in the method of communication or the style and content. As Jung wrote:

Of all psychic phenomena the dream presents perhaps the largest number of irrational factors ... such as lack of logic, questionable morality, uncouth form and apparent absurdity or nonsense. People are therefore only too glad to dismiss it as stupid, meaningless and worthless. ['On the Nature of Dreams', *Collected Works*, vol. 8, par. 532]

Dr Sonya Marjasch is a Jungian analyst in Zurich, and lives in a rambling farmhouse a few miles outside the city. She is a collector of folk art from India and Afghanistan, and is particularly interested in the emergence of modern images in traditional folk art forms: for example, the appearance of helicopters and tanks in contemporary handmade Afghan rugs. Dr Marjasch believes that:

Making symbols is the self-defence of the soul against petrification and against being invaded or overwhelmed. Folk art and dreams are the same in performing these functions.

Her sense of the modern European life is that sheer time-pressures, and materialistic attitudes, give us little time for our dreams.

What is really important is the relationship of the dreamer to the dream, and that this relation should be kept alive as long as possible, and that he should not too early abdicate – in order to save time – and trust another's interpretation, even if it may be very much to the point, instead of his own emotions and his own curiosity. This is something precious, this moment, to be alone with one's soul, and this should be enjoyed and also respected as long as possible. It can be that time is a problem, that there simply isn't time enough in the morning, because the clock time, chronological time, is very hostile to all this. There may be children rushing in and an office calling.

Not only is it difficult to find the time for dreams, to remember them in a half-waking state as the pressures of the day begin, but dreams themselves are often so strange that we can find them unwelcome. Partly, this was explained by Jung as demonstrating the independent vigour of the unconscious – that it is not subject to our conscious values.

Since the meaning of most dreams is not in accord with the tendencies of the conscious mind but shows peculiar deviations, we must assume that the unconscious, the matrix of dreams, has an independent function. This is what I call the autonomy of the unconscious. The dream not only fails to obey our will but very often stands in flagrant opposition to our conscious intentions.' ['On the Nature of Dreams', *Collected Works*, vol. 8, par. 545)]

Aniela Jaffe recalls the vividly ironic way in which one of Jung's own dreams responded to a conscious wish he expressed to himself.

When he was a young man, he had a great wish to experience the numinous. Then he had a dream, and a voice said 'If you open the curtain here, you will experience the numinous'. And he did, and what did he see? A pile of manure and a sow upon it. So that was a 'numinous experience'.

The heart of a Jungian analysis – and it is the heart, and not the mind, that seems to be engaged – is the consideration of dreams. Sometimes this amounts to 'interpretation', but above all the process allows the dream to be valued for what it is – as an expression of an essential compensation to the mental, conscious life which rules us all, almost all of the time. Jung wrote:

But if dreams produce such essential compensations, why are they not understandable? ... The answer must be that the dream is a natural occurrence, and that nature shows no inclination to offer her fruits gratis or according to human expectations. ['On the Nature of Dreams' *Collected Works*, vol. 8]

If the dream is natural, then there is perhaps a need to hesitate before seeking an interpretation. Sonya Marjasch sees the need to allow the dream, or nature, to express itself without urgently translating the 'message' into conscious terms.

I feel all this experience is getting lost by immediately wanting to carry away a meaning and in a way it's perhaps exaggerated, but still, getting rid of the dream. Because the dream by its nature is challenging the conscious attitude. It is something different or else it wouldn't be worth doing. A French author wrote that it is more shocking, for instance, in the morning to go and look in one's pocket and find that pencil that one could not find before, and then realize that one has dreamt about it – than to dream about pink elephants somewhere, because one knows exactly that that is a dream.

Nowhere in his writing does Jung refer to dreams of pink elephants; but every dream, by its very nature, is of interest to him.

The dream ... by virtue of its source in the unconscious, draws upon a wealth of subliminal perception, [and] it can sometimes produce things that are very well worth knowing. ['On the Nature of Dreams', *Collected Works*, vol. 8. par. 531]

As Jung told Richard Evans, he had a case of an intelligent young woman, a student of philosophy, who became dependent upon Jung and had a series of dreams in which he himself appeared as a father figure – though consciously she was able to say that she knew perfectly well he was not.

In her dreams she is a little infant, sitting on my knee, and I am holding her in my arms. I have become a very tender father to the little girl. . . . In the final dream, I was out in the midst of nature, standing in a field of wheat. I was a giant and held her in my arms like a baby, with the wind blowing over the field. When the wind is blowing over a wheat field, it waves, and with these waves, I swayed, putting her to sleep. She felt as if she was in the arms of a god, of the 'Godhead'. I thought, 'Now the harvest is ripe, and I must tell her,' so I said, 'You see, what you want and what you are projecting onto me, because you are not conscious of it, is that unconsciously you are feeling the influence of a deity which does not possess your consciousness; therefore, you are seeing it in me.' That clicked, because she had had a rather intense religious education, that enabled her to understand.

The dream has a capacity to tell us something useful, even in the most surprising or even grotesque language, or rather, images – for images are the language of dreams, not words. Dr Joseph Henderson, the American psychiatrist and analyst who with Joe and Jane Wheelwright was instrumental in establishing the Jung Institute in San Francisco, and has worked all his life on exploring what he and Jung decided to call the 'cultural unconscious', has considered the significance, among many other dream images, of the bear.

> The bear is often associated with the mother goddess in the ancient traditions, because the mother bear is so careful with her young and protects it, and teaches it and educates it for life. No other wild animal takes such good care of its young for such a long time. So the idea that the mother is an archetypal force is embodied in the bear. The bear seems to have been a symbol for the power of nature itself to survive. It lives in the wild, supports itself entirely on nature, it has no predators, it is completely independent, completely confident that it can survive. It also goes through a hibernation in the winter, so that it is associated with the idea of death and rebirth. It seems to die in the winter and come to life again in the spring.
>
> I did the research on the bear because of a dream a patient of mine had in which, in her grandmother's house, she saw a woman that turned out to be a bear with a woman's dress on, and this bear woman was dancing around the dining-room table, and frightened the patient very much, but at the same time stimulated her to a certain kind of determination, and it was that image which made me wonder what the bear meant. And so it turned out that this woman's personal problem was precisely the one that I found in the collective representation of the bear – the ability to survive, courage, confidence, and a maternal strength.

It is very often the case that the dream suggests in images what the conscious life lacks or needs as a way of getting back into balance. It was Jung's view that the psyche always seeks balance between the unconscious and conscious aspects, and that imbalance, simply put, causes suffering. The dream is a way of compensating for the one-sidedness of our conscious life.

> Compensation, as the term implies, means balancing and comparing different data or points of view so as to produce an adjustment or a rectification. ['On the Nature of Dreams', *Collected Works*, vol. 8, par. 545]

Mary Briner is an American who married a Swiss businessman and has lived in Switzerland for sixty years, for most of that time in an old house almost opposite the Jungs' house in Kusnacht, a mile or so across the lake. Mrs Briner was in the first group of analysts to graduate formally from the training programme of the Jung Institute in Zurich. Now in her eighties, she continues to see patients, and finds herself working with women, and with older women especially, more than ever before. On the question of the dream compensating for a conscious attitude, she tells this story from Jung's practice:

> Now take for instance a very simple example of a woman who thought she was highly virtuous and had all sorts of inflated opinions about herself; she dreamed that she was a prostitute. Now of course she wasn't a prostitute, but she'd cut out all knowledge of this feminine side of her nature and so the unconscious reminds her: 'Look, you too could be a prostitute if life were different'. Jung told me that one of the motivating forces of his research had been to try to reconcile the opposites in the psyche.

Just as the word-association test proves – in a negative way – that the unconscious is interested in truth, so the dream very often expresses a truth, and opens up the conscious mind to a consideration of an alternative point of view. As Aniela Jaffe points out, it is hard to ignore an impressive dream:

> If you have a dream which tells the truth, like the one I told you, it is an experience of your soul.

Or, as Joe Wheelwright realized when he first found himself in the process of analysis with Jung:

> I realized with reflection that people had always been the thing for me, and as I subsequently learned from women who listen to the inner voice – by some freak, because men aren't supposed to be feeling types – I realized that I really was listening to the inner voice.

The inner voice, as Dr von Franz points out, can disagree completely from what one 'thinks' in conscious life.

> There is a man whose life was a complete failure. He was always sick and his profession was a failure. He was a neurotic wreck, and when he was dying he had the feeling 'My life has been a failure'. In a dream he saw a battered tree with no leaves on it any more, and only two golden fruit, and a voice said 'The suffering which you have stood so well will help generations after you to survive'. So the unconscious reversed his opinion completely.

Dr Joe Wheelwright is something of a phenomenon in the Jungian world: not only, as he says, a feeling-type of man, but also an extrovert, which is also rare; a former actor and teacher, a former reporter who almost got the story of the Long March of Mao Tse-Tung but was scooped; a former speak-easy jazz musician in the prohibition years. It is by far the most varied resumé of any Jungian analyst.

Joe is now eighty-two, but he talks and cracks jokes with truly youthful enthusiasm. He is well over six feet tall, and dresses in an elaborate mixture of styles reflecting his varied career: the sober, well-tailored grey pinstripes of the well-educated, well-heeled Boston background; two wrist-watches, both on bejewelled Navajo straps, as well as the gold watch-chain of the typical British-trained consultant; the walking stick that serves in London and Zurich, as well as on the wilderness ranch in California where he and Jane spend half of each year. In 1932, he accompanied Jane and her mad Aunt Laura to see Jung – the consultant in San Francisco said he was 'the only man in the world who could cure schizophrenia' – and was so instantly convinced by Jung's approach to the psyche that he decided, almost within days, that he too wanted to be an analyst.

> I had tried by trial and error all those different things, music and teaching and all that stuff, and writing – and all the bells were ringing and all the lights were flashing and I realized that this was my calling. . . . So I said I would like to be an analyst, and Jung threw his hands up and said 'Oh God! It happens over and over again. . . . The patients say 'I want to do what you do'. I said 'Oh hell, I'm not that conceited, I don't suppose – I mean I do in a sense, but of course I couldn't do it as well as you, Herr Geheimrat, Sir'. And he said 'Well, it's too bad.' And I said 'No, but this is real – I'm different!' To which he replied – he loved American slang – he replied 'I'll bet!'

Joe Wheelwright then followed Jung's advice, and spent seven years training first as a doctor, and then as a psychiatrist, at St Bartholomew's Medical School in London, returning as often as possible to Zurich to work with Jung. Throughout his training, he had failed to get Jung's positive blessing for his ambition as an analyst. But having qualified in London, Joe went to Zurich in 1938–39 for an intensive period of analysis with Jung; and a dream had a powerful impact on both Joe and his mentor.

I'm a reluctant dreamer, a very poor dreamer. But I said to Jung one day, 'I had a dream last night that I was being initiated into the mysteries of Isis as a priest.' He was always interested in the context, of the day before when a dream came. He said 'What were you doing yesterday?'

And I said 'Doing? I don't know, what the hell can you do in Zurich?'

He said 'No, no, what have you been *doing?*'

'Oh,' I said, 'it is true that our friends the Briners took us to Einsiedeln' [the Benedictine monastery and cathedral].

'That explains it,' he said.

I said, 'Well, I'm glad it explains it to you, it doesn't do much for me.'

He said 'What did you see?'

'I saw a Black Madonna.'

'And what did you think?'

I said, 'Well, you know, I asked one of the priests about it and he said that it was Mary and Jesus and they'd been scorched in the fire.'

And he said, 'Did you believe that?' And I said 'no.' And he said 'Ah, now we're getting somewhere.'

What Joe Wheelwright had dreamed was in some ways 'the truth' about the Black Madonna. As Jung explained to him, the older, pagan cult of Isis and her son Horus had been incorporated into early Christianity at the time of Roman persecution – and all over Europe, supposedly scorched statues of the Virgin and Child in fact remain as reminders of this long-forgotten, but separate, religious phenomenon. Joe's dream had delved very deeply indeed.

Whereupon the trap-door opened and I fell down and began splashing around in the primordial slime – I mean the collective unconscious. And I became, from the point of view of the man in the street, as crazy as a bedbug. I was absolutely off my rocker. From the Jungian point of view, I was having an experience of the unconscious, and that meant that I would be able to work with people in depth. So Jung, almost at that point, stopped saying that I would make a very good psychotherapist – which in those days meant you could be a very good second-class citizen – and so he said 'You have the makings of a good analyst, after all, Wheelwright'. I almost kissed him. I forebore, and I don't think he would have liked it very much. In effect, he got hold of Excalibur and he cracked me over the head and said 'I dub thee an analyst,' you know, and then I took off in the cloud – a crazy man sitting in the cloud.

Dr Gerhard Adler, who met Jung at about the same time, and subsequently became the father of the English Jungian community, and spent twenty years editing Jung's *Collected Works and Letters* in English, had an opposite experience to Joe Wheelwright's when he first met Jung.

In 1931 I went out to Jung. I was very disappointed: nothing had happened. But all my friends told me that I had changed completely. I expected the old wise man to change me, but he was very quiet and he didn't push anything. Sometimes one went to him with a very important dream and he seemed to ignore it. He would talk and talk – but he was talking about that dream all the time. It was intuition – he had a great inter-relatedness.

Perhaps the most important of Adler's dreams evoked a very specific response from Jung:

I had a dream that Jung had died, and I was very upset and went about in the ante-room where he lay in state, and suddenly I felt: 'It's up to us, the old man has died, it's up to us now.' I told this dream to Jung. Jung simply said, 'Now *you* can analyse yourself.' And he sent me a patient the next day, clearly a schizophrenic patient. And I had a dream that night, and the dream was nothing but a notice-board on which was written: 'Madman'. And I went to Jung the next day and said to him: 'Dr Jung, you sent me a schizophrenic.' And he said, 'Yes, he bored me so much!'. And that of course was not the truth of the matter, it was in fact a test of me, if I was able to sense a man and realize what was wrong with him.

In two further examples, one can observe a dream which comments and sharpens the dreamer's perception of a real situation; and a general trend of dreams, collected by an analyst who is trying to identify a shift in the collective psyche of the Western world.

To John Beebe, the film buff analyst, the reference to a film actor highlighted a half-concealed truth about his own family background:

> Rather early on in my own analysis, I dreamed that my grandmother and some older people were reminiscing about an actor that they had known, oh back in 1909 or 1910 or something, and this was anachronistic but in the dream the actor was Spencer Tracy, and they were musing about him and saying 'You know he was a really good actor.' As I began to muse on what that might be about, that period (1910) was the last time on either side of my family that there had been a particularly strong and outstanding father figure. Somehow all after that there'd been various marriages that ended in divorce and this and that, and perfectly fine people, but no one who would fully embody the traditional father archetype. And where did my unconscious go, and where in the dream did my grandmother's psyche go? Not to some political figure – no, to a movie star, to Spencer Tracy. He carried the image of the good father.

James Hillman has been recording all the dreams he comes across as an analyst which refer to animals – and in particular to insects, or bugs. Now he has written a long paper on the theme of the human attitude towards the natural world which animal and insect dreams reveal.

> The paper is called 'Going Bugs' and it has to do with what bugs do in dreams, and the fear, and the way that humans react to the bugs. You might call it psychic ecology – it bears on pesticides and insecticides and the pollution of the world. You see we imagine the bugs are killing us, so we overkill the bugs. We are actually infecting and polluting and poisoning the world, but attributing to the bugs that they are poisonous, infectious, carrying disease and so on. So if we don't remove the bug problem in the psyche, and the fear of going bugs, and the bugs in the computers, and trying to get rid of bugs everywhere, we go on with the insecticide till we've actually poisoned ourselves out of existence.

> In what people dream about insects, one major motif is that the bugs have an intention, that they come at the dreamer and they

do something to the dreamer. They want something, they want to get into your blood, they want to get into your hair, they want to get you, and they have an intention, they're like little demons or little angels, to change your way of behaving.

It's absolutely crucial that there's a change within the personality regarding the animals. Not merely through the World Wildlife Fund and what Prince Philip is doing. All that's great, but if inside the person, he's still shooting wolves and beating bugs and afraid of snakes, he's still in the same place, he hasn't a psychic ecology.

For twelve years a man named Bill had the following dream several times a week. It was the repetition of an incident which happened to him while serving as an American soldier in the Vietnam War. The dream haunted him, and he suffered from severe depression. He wanted desperately to get rid of this painful, crippling memory. Only when he told his dream to Dr Harry Wilmer was there any possibility of erasing the nightmare.

We're on a search and destroy mission, and we're going through a friendly village. A baby was crying in a hooch – that's a little native house – and no one else was there. My buddy went into the hooch and he saw the crying baby. The captain at the outside shouted: 'Don't pick it up, don't pick it up!' But he didn't hear the words, and he reached for the baby and the baby exploded; it was booby-trapped. There was nothing left of the baby and just parts of my friend.

Dr Harry Wilmer is a soft-spoken, introverted man with a gentle manner. He lives in Salado, Texas in the heart of mid-western America. Salado is a small town, known mostly for its antique shops, blessed by a beautiful stream, which has water-cress growing wild on its banks. The creek has a swimming hole and a rope swing, adding to the traditional small-town atmosphere of the detached clapboard houses with screened-in porches. But there, in the peace of truly rural mid-America, one talks with Dr Wilmer of the nightmares, atrocities, and maimings of war.

Fourteen years after the end of the Vietnam War many veterans still find their lives in ruins, unable to cope with marriages, jobs and drug or alcohol addictions they acquired during or after the war. They are often among the growing population of homeless in America. The 350 dreams of the Vietnam War which Dr Wilmer has collected

frequently contain experiences of killing, massacre and grisly muti-
lation.

Like Bill, many of Harry Wilmer's patients had an overwhelming
sense of personal guilt for what happened to them in Vietnam, and
their dreams recycled the horrors:

> Because the subjects were unable to stem the tide of destruction of
> other people, in order to overcome the trauma it was essential that
> they be able to form a bond with another human being.

Almost all the dreams that we have heard until now have concerned
images or ideas that were not 'literally true'. But the dreams of the
veterans almost always repeated real events which had happened to
them, or events which were entirely plausible in the context of their
war experience. According to Dr Wilmer, because the dreams recorded
'what really happened' to these men, rather than containing the usual
symbolism psychoanalysts are used to interpreting, they were not
easy to interpret; and even the psychoanalytically oriented Veterans
Administration Hospital staff expressed little interest in the vets'
dreams.

> Reducing the experience to the traditional Freudian psychoanalytic
> model based upon childhood experiences is not doing justice to the
> material. This material was about the archetypal aspects of terror.

Harry Wilmer is well qualified to discriminate between the relative
merits of a traditional Freudian and the more archetypal Jungian
approach. He is one of the few analysts in the world who has trained
as both a Freudian and Jungian.

> The first thing is to listen, to honour this as an experience and to
> listen with the conviction that this is happening to him for some
> psychological reason, and that to get it out of his head, somehow
> or another it has to come out to some other human being who
> listens without making any great interpretations.

After a while, Harry found that a significant number of his patients
had what he called a 'healing nightmare', in which some aspect of the
traumatic dream changes so that the dream contains something that
couldn't have really happened; thus moving towards the manner in
which dreams more usually express themselves.

One former sergeant was responsible for leading seventeen men into
an ambush in a ravine and had to watch helplessly while they were

slaughtered. He escaped and returned the next day to find them all decapitated. He repeatedly dreamt of this horror. One day he told Dr Wilmer:

> I came into that ravine and looked down there, and instead of these decapitated people, there you were, and you were leaning against a tree, wounded, badly wounded. There was also a nurse from the ward (who incidentally was pregnant). She and I descended in there and rescued you, we carried you up. When I woke up that's the first time I've ever cried after one of these dreams.

Dr Wilmer has observed that transformation and healing begins when a new, unrealistic element arises in the dream: something which did not happen and could not have happened in the real situation – like his own presence on the Vietnamese battlefield.

> Something comes into the dream that didn't really happen. After all, if you dream twelve years of this, and wake up in a cold sweat and a horror, thinking you're still there, when something happens in the dream that didn't really happen, it begins to take you out of that primal experience. Then that dream became a dream you can analyse ... in which he in the dream is rescuing me. He is helping me out of his nightmare and that was the beginning of the end of his continual obsession with his horror.

Finally, there will be a further transition in the dream; it will recur with a new and fantastic element that is beyond the scope of reality, but demonstrates that the unconscious is once again beginning to produce its own images, in its own way.

> The next stage is what I call the healing nightmare, when it is transformed or when it becomes a stage of an ordinary hallucinatory nightmare. Didn't happen, couldn't have happened, far out – the kind of dreams that we all have from time to time.

The healing nightmare finally allows the psyche to adapt from the terrible memory of combat to the normal processes of the unconscious, but using no more than the resources of the unconscious itself, and the human connection of someone to listen. Dr Wilmer's experience is that too few people are willing to listen to the dreams or any other aspect of the Vietnam experience, wanting to forget the war and its soldiers entirely. But the healing nightmare is not a phenomenon limited only to the Vietnam War. It was from Dr Marie-Louise von

Franz that Harry Wilmer learned of Jung's own unpublished experience of listening to the trauma of war. He was treating a British
veteran of the First World War, who came to Zurich to see him because
of a recurrent nightmare. Harry reported the soldier's dream as follows:

> The night would come and he would become frightened and would
> go around the house closing all the windows and shutters, locking
> them. He did this on all three floors. When he came to the last floor
> and closed the window, just as he did, there was an explosion, a
> bomb, and he woke up terrified.
> A few months later the man dreamt that he went through the
> same procedure that he had performed countless previous times in
> his dream but this time something different happened. When he
> came to close the last window, instead of the bomb there was a lion
> roaring.

Dr von Franz told Harry Wilmer that Jung felt that this was a good
sign. The lion is an instinctual animal, of the earth; it was something
of a primitive nature that the man was now facing in himself.
The dreams continued. One night he had the same dream again;
except that when he came to the last window and went to close it,
just before he could do so, he saw a face, and it was his own.

> He was facing his own image. And that was when Jung said: 'Well,
> he's not going to dream it any more' – and he didn't.

Whether dreams replay the horrors of war, direct us to a lost pencil,
commentate upon our attitude to the natural world, or review the
whole sum of our individual life, there was no doubt in Jung's mind
that the dream had wisdom. Aniela Jaffe, looking back at the end of
her life, still remembers a dream which she had fifty years ago:

> After one of my first lessons with Jung, I dreamed that I stood at
> the street corner and an enormous open truck, full of books, passed
> by with great speed, and away. And Jung laughed and said in Latin
> 'rumpantur libros nec corda cestra rumpitur' which means 'Destroy
> the books so that your heart might not be destroyed'. It was to do
> with my being blind, now books are for me destroyed, I cannot
> read any longer. At the time, I was in my late thirties, it meant
> 'Don't be too intellectual, it's of no value because your heart suffers.
> Experience is of greater value than books'.

Jung's sense of the importance of his early 'house' dream was itself ultimately vindicated. For he discovered, years afterwards, that two houses connected to his family in Basel – which he had never entered – bore remarkable similarities to features of his dream. His mother's former home, when renovated, had traces of Roman ruins in its foundations; and his uncle's house, built in the moat of the old city, had a double cellar, one beneath the other. To Carl Jung and his followers, the dream is experience too, and its wisdom can be understood, and applied, with positive results.

4

A Creative Life

When C. G. Jung reluctantly began to collaborate with Aniela Jaffe in recording and editing his autobigraphy, he said that his life could only be expressed as a narrative of inner events. But his life could equally be described as a series of creative and imaginative actions and ideas. Jung was a trained scientist and psychotherapist, but he was also a poetic thinker, a painter, and a dreamer. He saw and healed thousands of patients, but he was also an enthusiastic sailor, cook, and stone-mason. The commitment to 'fantasy thinking' underlay the creative mix of Jung's life, and enabled him to combine a genuinely scientific approach to medicine with the carving of wooden dolls, wearing fancy dress, getting his friends and colleagues either drunk or angry, retreating into the isolation of Bollingen, and carving out the images he saw concealed in the stones of his beloved Tower.

Throughout his life, Jung allowed the open expression of the opposites that we all feel contending for supremacy within us. He gave this a concrete, personalized form in his memory of feeling as though he had two more or less distinct personalities in childhood – which he called Number One and Number Two.

Somewhere deep in the background I always knew that I was two persons. One was the son of my parents, who went to school and was less intelligent, attentive, hardworking, decent and clean than many other boys. The other was grown-up – old, in fact – sceptical, mistrustful, remote from the world of men, but close to nature, the earth, the sun, the moon, the weather, all living creatures and above all close to the night, to dreams and to whatever 'God' worked directly in him. [*Memories, Dreams, Reflections*, p. 44]

However real the psyche, it cannot be touched or held: Dieter Baumann recalls Jung saying once 'that he had to express himself in stone as well'. In a letter to his daughter Marianne, in the summer of 1956 after his wife Emma's death, Jung wrote:

> The stone I am working on (like the one I carved in the winter) gives me inner stability with its hardness and permanence, and its meaning governs my thoughts. [17 July 1956]

While Jung's practical creativity was devoted to carving stone among other activities, his imaginative creativity was devoted to the immense task he had set himself, of tackling the mystery of the nature of the human unconscious, and bringing some essence of its truth and value to light. As the analyst James Hillman points out, it is 'a work against nature'. People don't want to know about the psyche, generally – they prefer to think life is just the concrete, visible, tangible world.

> Certainly one of the essential facts about analysis is that it is a work, and Jung used the term *opus* from the alchemists – an *opus contra naturam*, which means a work against nature. Which doesn't mean against NATURE, it means against doing things easily. There's some kind of struggle in it. There's a work in it. And that costs.

Several members of the Jung family have followed in their grandfather's footsteps and become analysts or psychiatrists. Dieter Baumann is perhaps the closest to his grandfather's memory, and the most influenced by the personal relationship he had to Jung. He is an analyst, and works (in four languages) in Zurich and Milan. His manner is gentle, and his deep voice seems to provide evidence that he learned to speak English from his grandfather, so alike do they sound. And like 'C.G.', as he is often known among family members, Baumann embraces a philosophy and *modus vivendi* based upon the authority of the inner life. This was evident in making arrangements to interview him. Despite a basic willingness to help in communicating both a professional and personal sense of Jung, Dr Baumann was reluctant to be pinned down in front of the camera, surrounded by seven or eight crew and production team members, dazzled by artificial lights and hemmed in by the four walls of his study or any other room.

Until it felt absolutely right to Dr Baumann, he was not going to

70

succumb to the process. After last minute, late night discussions, he struck upon the right setting; on the banks of the Rhine, at the little town of Eglisau north of Zurich – just himself and three others to record the interview. There beside the cold water, the interview flowed naturally and without inhibition. But the first question to Dieter Baumann was inevitably 'Why here?'.

> Jung's life is very much connected with the Rhine and with water in general. He dedicated his life to going upstream, to going against nature. Namely, not going with the crowd down the river.

Jung was born in 1875 by the Rhine, a son of the parsonage. His father Paul was a Protestant minister, whom Jung perceived to have lost his faith. This was to affect Jung's life deeply, and to motivate his quest for inner religious meaning and experience, within or outside of the church. The Jung family moved down the Rhine in Carl's childhood and schooldays, from Kesswil to Laufen, then to Klein Huningen – a village which has now been swallowed by the city of Basel, which is also on the Rhine. Once his career had found its direction, and he had graduated from Basel University, Carl Jung began his journey in the opposite direction – to work and to live in Zurich and beyond. Dieter Baumann interprets this change symbolically.

> When he had finished his studies, he went again upstream. Namely he went to Zurich, to the Burgholzli [Hospital] not along the Rhine, or one could say along the Rhine for a while, but then it was the Limmat which leaves the lake of Zurich. And then from there in 1908 he had his house built in Kusnacht, which is again upstream, it's on the lake. And later, in 1923, he started to build his Tower in Bollingen which is again more up the lake. And my impression of Jung is that he dedicated his life to going upstream, going against nature, not going with the crowd down the river. It seems very symbolical, and one could say that if you go upstream, he really went upstream, namely to the source, in the direction of the pure source of life and of meaning.

Jung's own 'Memories' confirms the importance to him of living by the water. As a very small child:

> ... the idea became fixed in my mind that I must live near a lake; without water, I thought, nobody could live at all. [*Memories, Dreams, Reflections*, p. 7]

In March 1939, when Dieter was twelve years old, he and his family left Paris and returned to Switzerland. The schools were closed, and for the next three years they lived with his grandparents. His grandfather was then sixty-four, an important and celebrated figure both in Switzerland and beyond. As Dieter Baumann reflects, his own decision to become an analyst was perhaps inevitable:

It is sort of my destiny – I was in almost daily contact with C.G. He was a very strong influence – I was in puberty. He gave me an old book of his on chemistry, and I was always ahead of the teacher of chemistry at school. He taught me lots of practical things like how to sail, and how to cultivate the garden.

To the young Dieter Baumann, Jung was impressive, but human – and in unexpected ways.

He was not that kind of adult who would take an air of authority or superiority. He had an absolutely natural authority. But he also initiated me as a ten year old or eleven year old boy or so, he initiated me to drinking and to smoking. *Ja, ja*, he was that way!

Baumann, who today finds a deep and disturbing rift growing between the conscious life of Europe and its natural environment, considers Jung's upstream journey to be an appropriate metaphor for the effort to revalue the natural psyche, as well as the physical world of nature. Today, he takes long, solitary walks in the woods alongside the Rhine, just as his grandfather did, as a child, about a hundred years ago. At that time, in accordance with his two 'personalities', Jung lived the life of a child at one level and interpreted it with a maturity and wisdom that few adults achieve. What is more, as an adult he continued to have a child's perspective in some matters – in valuing the pure experience of play, giving oneself over entirely to the imagination, to mischief, or to solitude.

As a child, and throughout his life, he had dreams and visions, peopled by characters and symbols which he was to call archetypes. The archetype is a concept so central to Jung's work, which nevertheless appears to defy all attempts to give it definition. To reproduce here the exasperated efforts of Jungian analysts to define 'the archetype' would be more comical than illuminating. For example, when asked, Aniela Jaffe laughed and threw up her hands in protest:

No, please not, no. Archetype is a spiritual instinct, if you want to know.

Jung's use of the term 'archetype' is what has given it wide currency – we talk quite readily of the 'archetypal politician' or the 'archetypal priest' – the ones who conform most completely to a general set of assumptions about the way such people behave or look. In Jungian psychology, the archetype applies not only to images of people – mother, father, child, old wise man, old wise woman, but also to behaviours, to the responses of the psyche to a given situation. In the days of widespread computer literacy, the best explanation might be to call it a kind of psychological program – in the database of the human psyche. One analyst called it 'a kind of unconscious program which is triggered by experience'.

As a child, Jung had a deep susceptibility to the archetypal. His direct contact with the contents of the unconscious was so real to him that in his childhood there may have been times when his ego – the conscious mind – was completely overcome by the unconscious. Many psychologists, both followers of Jung and otherwise, have shown how much closer the world of the child is to the unconscious than adulthood. Nevertheless, in psychological terms, such an occurrence is psychosis. But for him, there was no shame in this 'madness' – his genius was to experience it and to be able to return to conscious reality. He restored it to its rightful place as part of human experience. The underlying assumption of his analytical psychology is to enable the patient to learn and understand himself or herself, rather than to fear and shun the inner psychic life. But for him, it had to be experienced first, before understanding or a systematic explanation could arise.

Jung himself was able to cope with the power of the unconscious images by personifying these different frightening aspects of his psyche. As a boy, Jung comforted or distracted himself with small rituals – building small towns of pebbles, or hiding a carved mannikin, with a painted stone, in a pencil-case on a beam in his parents' attic. Only later did he attribute significance to his games, seeing that they were connected to rituals of religion, to the images of dreams, and to the experience of life's mysteries.

The meaning of these actions, or how I might explain them, never worried me. I contented myself with the feeling of newly-won security, and was satisfied to possess something that no one knew and no one could get at. [*Memories, Dreams, Reflections*, p. 22]

The theologian Don Cupitt suggests that Jung's analytical psychology permitted patients to find ways of spiritual growth from their own inner lives, without any need for reference to 'established religion'. And he incorporated the need for some form of expression of that inner life, which he had experienced, into his therapeutic work with patients. As Cupitt says:

> For example, he must have been the first person in Europe to use dancing and art and things like that as therapy for patients. He took the view that we needed to express ourselves and the works of art, or the little talismans, as he called them, that we produce, are means to our own spiritual growth. You express yourself, you get it out of yourself, and the thing you've made becomes a rung on the ladder of spiritual growth.

Jung was very well aware that alongside the resistance to ideas about the psyche would come the accusation that he was mystical and romantic – particularly in response to his unique ideas about the collective unconscious, and the archetypes of the psyche. Thus while he introduced innovatory ways of dealing with patients, he also underlined the necessity of the scientific basis. This two-pronged approach earns Jung credit for innovation, while at the same time permitting him to retain the status of the rigorous scientist of the psyche.

As a teenager, Dieter Baumann – having read various books which his grandfather had lent him – began to be interested in studying psychology, as his destiny dictated. Jung impressed upon him the necessity of a scientific training for the would-be psychologist.

> Later I started to read his books, when I was seventeen or eighteen, and I used to go and talk to him about philosophy and psychology. I actually consulted him about that when I was eighteen, and he recommended medicine to me, probably because he saw that I was intuitive and needed to get a grasp of practical reality. He said on that occasion that in order to study psychology, you have to get a standpoint outside psychology.

Creatively, Jung's short relationship with Sigmund Freud was both fruitful and destructive. As the younger man, Jung was inevitably cast in the role of follower, and quickly became the heir-apparent in the brand-new field of psychoanalysis. Until Jung's arrival on the scene, psychoanalysis was almost exclusively practised by Jewish Viennese psychiatrists like Freud himself. Jung, as a Swiss Protestant, gave the infant discipline a wider credibility. But he very rapidly saw that his own views and Freud's diverged. At first he attempted to conform to Freud's understanding of the truth about the psyche, and submitted his dreams to Freud's evaluation – though he thought it too narrow. One area of divergence was Freud's negative interpretation of the contents of the unconscious – that it was all repression – and another was that childhood traumas were responsible for almost all adult neuroses.

Andrew Samuels argues that once the two men were stuck in a personal power struggle, all meaningful theoretical debate was set aside.

> I think what we witness in the Freud/Jung split is an outright power struggle, and the results of the power struggle, like all power struggles, are that something of value was lost. I think Jung lost the chance to marry up his ideas about mythology and religion with a solid grounding in the development of the individual human being in the family. In other words, what he became dismissive of in Freud – Jung said Freud's view of psychology was 'confined to the nursery' – was exactly what Jungian psychology needed from the first and still does. Freud lost breadth, he lost the chance to make his psychology into a critique of Western culture. I think what Jung had was this breadth of vision and of knowledge, which Freud lacked, and the Jungian method of amplification – seeking parallels from mythology, fairy-tales, or other aspects of life and culture to illuminate a psychological phenomenon – I think Freud would have found that very useful.

Jung undoubtedly regarded Freud as a major figure, but in the course of only four years of intermittent contact, he found that his own ideas could not be suppressed – they expressed themselves, whether he liked it or not, in his dreams.

> Freud was the first man of real importance I had encountered; in my experience up to that time, no one else could compare with him. There was nothing the least trivial in his attitude. I found him extremely intelligent, shrewd, and altogether remarkable.
> [*Memories, Dreams, Reflections*, p. 149]

I had told myself 'Freud is far wiser and more experienced than you. For the present you must simply listen to what he says and learn from him.' And then, to my own surprise, I found myself dreaming of him as a peevish official of the Imperial Austrian monarchy, as a defunct and still walking ghost of a customs inspector. [*Memories, Dreams, Reflections*, p. 164]

To Professor Freddy Meier, Jung's colleague who was paralysed by the experience of meeting Freud in Vienna, the latter's attitude towards the unconscious could never accommodate the breadth of Jung's vision.

The limit Freud put on the unconscious from the word go was not Jung's 'business'. He [Jung] left everything open and he went much farther than Freud in accepting these manifestations of the unconscious, and trying to understand what they really wanted to say. Whereas Freud from the word go reduced the meaning of such things to a preconceived idea which he had. But as Jung left everything open, he discovered things which existed within the human mind, and in particular within the human unconscious, which could not be reduced to things which we knew already.

With the irrevocable split between Freud and Jung, what the latter might have anticipated as the future pattern of his life effectively disintegrated. He was not to be the crown prince of the psychoanalytic community, after all; Freud's supporters launched bitter attacks on his theories, and later, which was worse, upon both his personal morality and his politics. The ferocity of the mutual enmity between the two schools is worthy of study in itself, and the cause of psychoanalysis – or analytical psychology – has suffered as a consequence.

Jung had faced a choice between a dishonest conformity to the demands of the outer world, and a painful acceptance of the demands of the inner world. It was not a decision taken in a logical spirit at all. He entered into a dangerous battle, played out in his dreams and occasionally in waking fantasies, with his own unconscious. The danger, for anyone, of only living in the material world has perhaps become clear by now, in terms of Jung's ideas of the necessities of the inner life; but there is an equal danger in a total devotion to the inner, for we have to exist in the real world, too. In effect, Jung dived so deeply into the unconscious that he very nearly failed to come back up for air.

When I parted from Freud, I knew that I was plunging into the unknown. Beyond Freud, after all, I knew nothing; but I had taken the step into darkness. [*Memories, Dreams, Reflections*, p. 199]

Dr Adolf Guggenbuhl-Craig is one of a relatively small number of Jungian analysts who, as Jung did himself, works with psychotic and schizophrenic patients, and employs Jungian ideas and attitudes in that work. 'After all,' he says, 'psychotic people have a soul, too – and someone has to look after their soul.' Dr Guggenbuhl-Craig is also particularly interested in the discussion about Jung's 'confrontation' – and its correct diagnosis:

You know when he died, I think there was a leading article in one of the American journals which said he was actually psychotic, or they said he was a man who was schizophrenic and cured himself, and that some Jungians consider to be a great insult. But in some ways it isn't. He was able to go into it and then not be overwhelmed by it. He was closer to the unconscious than most people ever have been and yet did not become – did *not* become psychotic. So the essence was to be at least temporarily very much impressed by it and influenced by the unconscious and yet then be able to deal with it. I can't offer an explanation.

Jung very deliberately began to review the course of his life so far: he was then thirty-eight years old. Jung himself found it difficult to describe the psychic events which dominated his life for five or six years; he called it his 'confrontation with the unconscious'. Jung did more than merely consider the unconscious – he fell headlong into it. What he held at bay as a child, he allowed to overtake him as a man of forty – at a time when he was practising medicine, a husband and father of five children. From 1912–18, he was in a state of near-madness. His house and his head were full of strange visions, over-powering dreams, and mythic figures who dominated his dreams. A series of powerful dreams, which he could not understand, made him more and more uncertain about the activity of the unconscious. As he expressed it in *Memories, Dreams, Reflections*:

I lived as if under constant inner pressure. At times this became so strong that I suspected there was some psychic disturbance in myself. Therefore I twice went over all the details of my entire life, with particular attention to childhood memories; for I thought there might be something in my past which I could not see and which might possibly be the cause of my disturbance. But this retrospection led to nothing but a fresh acknowledgement of my own ignorance. Thereupon I said to myself, 'Since I know nothing at all, I shall simply do whatever occurs to me.' Thus I consciously submitted myself to the impulses of the unconscious.

The first strong childhood memory which arose was of a time – he was about ten – when he had played passionately with building blocks, pebbles, stones and mud, building small houses, castles and villages.

'Aha,' I said to myself, 'there is still life in these things. The small boy is still around, and possesses a creative life which I lack. But how can I make my way to it?'
I began accumulating suitable stones, gathering them partly from the lake shore and partly from the water. And I started building: cottages, a castle, a whole village. The church was still missing, so I made a square building with a hexagonal drum on top of it, and a dome.
[I] asked myself, 'Now really what are you about? You are building a small town, and doing it as if it were a rite!' I had no answer to my question, only the inner certainty that I was on the way to discovering my own myth. For the building game was only a beginning. It released a stream of fantasies which I later carefully wrote down. [*Memories, Dreams, Reflections*, pp. 174–5]

Before long Jung resigned from his hospital job; he was confronted by overpowering dreams and visions; and he struggled to express the images of his own unconscious in painting, sculpture and word. Jung, who was never analysed, now began four years of intense self-analysis. In December 1913, he 'let himself drop'.

An incessant stream of fantasies had been released, and I did my best not to lose my head but to find some way to understand these strange things. I stood helpless before an alien world; everything in it seemed difficult and incomprehensible. [*Memories, Dreams, Reflections*, pp. 176–77]

Jung painted. He produced dozens of pictures, which gave form and colour to images and characters from his dreams. While he was painting to express the 'confrontation', his son Franz would sometimes sit at the other side of the table – he was then about eight or nine years old – making his own pictures.

To the extent that I managed to translate the emotions into images – that is to say, to find the images which were concealed in the emotions – I was inwardly calmed and reassured. Had I left those images hidden in the emotions, I might have been torn to pieces by them. .... As a result of my experiment I learned how helpful it can be, from the therapeutic point of view, to find the particular images which lie behind emotions. [*Memories, Dreams, Reflections*, p. 177]

As Dr Guggenbuhl-Craig observes, it was perhaps Jung's good fortune that he was able to use painting as an outlet for the emotion.

What certainly helped him was his tremendous understanding of images. You can only deal with the unconscious by images and he had a great gift to deal with images. But there is no special method. I mean you could ask was there any special method by which Dante was able to walk through hell and purgatory and heaven. There was no method, he just was able to do it.

Jung himself remembered:

As a young man my goal had been to accomplish something in my science. But then, I hit upon this stream of lava, and the heat of its fires reshaped my life. That was the primal stuff which compelled me to work upon it, and my works are a more or less successful endeavour to incorporate this incandescent matter into the contemporary picture of the world. [*Memories, Dreams, Reflections* p. 199]

In 1922 Jung bought a piece of land on the shore of the upper part of Lake Zurich at Bollingen, which was formerly owned by a nearby monastery. In the following year he began to build a rudimentary house – partly based on the layout of an African hut, but including a small room for meditation and withdrawal as they have in Indian houses. Over the years, the Tower was extended, marking stages in Jung's own inner life, and his need to express his personality's development in a concrete way.

While he described his house at Kusnacht – where he saw patients – as his 'door onto the world', the Tower became the focus of his introspection, his creativity, and his genius. The American analyst Joseph Henderson recalls the impact a visit to Bollingen had upon him.

It's like a little oasis in the midst of an otherwise very crowded countryside. There's hardly a single square inch of land that isn't accounted for and in some way used. There at Bollingen Jung found a piece of land that was really alone and untouched and was not accounted for, did not have the sense of being encroached upon by neighbours. And once you got there it was like being in a different world. It's as though Jung had chosen this place to symbolize and represent his own belief in the integrity of the individual to find his own space.

In later life he immersed himself more and more in his inner life, in the psychic refuge of Bollingen, and identified himself with the landscape of the lake and shore.

I am in the midst of my true life, I am most deeply myself. At times I feel as if I am spread out over the landscape and inside things, and am myself living in every tree, in the splashing of the waves, in the clouds and animals that come and go, in the procession of the seasons. . . . Without my piece of earth, my life's work would not have come into being. [*Memories, Dreams, Reflections*, p. 225]

Jung was of course a fortunate man: one cannot prescribe to everyone that they buy a lakeside plot and design themselves a medieval castle. Carl Jung had the money and opportunity to do it; but in doing so, he himself did as he asked his patients to do. He thought of the Tower in a fantasy form, not logically. He invited his patients to paint or even dance the images that emerged in their dreams, and he painted, sculpted and carved his own. Just as he said 'these houses were all fantasies', so he activated his fantasy in concrete form.

Just as he had carved his two-inch wooden mannikin and painted a stone from the lake to make a ritual object as a child, so in adult life C.G. combined his classical scholarship and the craftsman's skills he learned to produce a series of impressive objects which represent different stages of his psychological development, or major milestones in his life. He carved out the images that he saw concealed in the stones of the Tower walls and gave them inscriptions or mottoes in Latin and Greek. At the age of seventy-five he revived his little mannikin and carved him into the centre of the stone cube which stands beside the jetty at the lakeside of the Tower. The first part of the inscription, which mingles classical sources, represents an indication of Jung's attitudes towards creativity itself:

Time is a child – playing like a child – playing a board game – the kingdom of the child.

Childhood and playing were of lifelong importance to him. It was in childhood that he began to sense the unconscious, to sense the different, deeper life that he was destined to lead; in his psychological crisis he reverted to childhood memories; and his creative life was always based in play and imagination. As the analyst Gerhard Adler observes:

> He played with pebbles and built sand-castles. He had to do it, because it was necessary for him to understand his own unconscious. He had the courage to face it. When he was in the army as a camp commandant he discovered mandalas, and every day he painted a mandala; that takes courage. He obeyed his unconscious; he obeyed the power of the images that came to him. It is utterly rare. I think that needs a great man.

Mrs Dora Kalff, a long-standing friend of the Jung family, lives in Zollikon – the next village along the lake from Kusnacht – in an ancient farmhouse where Goethe once stayed, according to legend. It is another German poet, however, whom Mrs Kalff quotes on the subject of play:

> Schiller says that when man plays, he is completely man. I think you know you can only play when you're really free. You have to be free within.

Dora Kalff is a Jungian, but not a conventional analyst. Her therapeutic method is called sandplay. Just as Jung worked with the dreams that arose from the unconscious of his patients, so Mrs Kalff provides a technique for the unconscious to emerge freely and express itself in concrete pictures. There is a rectangular box of sand, wet or dry, a selection of hundreds of miniature people, animals and objects – and 'a free and protected space'.

> I think what Jung said, that the psyche has a healing tendency, is really shown in the sand pictures, because this healing tendency in a way is able to take over when we are providing this free and protected space. It means that the person who comes here is completely free, is at ease. And therefore whatever comes out of his inner life is displayed outside.

Jung believed in certain psychological necessities – a sense of meaning or religion, honesty with oneself and with others, and respect for the dreams and fantasies produced by the unconscious. He believed in play too.

Every creative individual whatsoever owes all that is greatest in his life to fantasy. The dynamic principle of fantasy is play, a characteristic also of the child, and as such it appears inconsistent with the principle of serious work. It is short-sighted to treat fantasy on account of its risky or unacceptable nature as a thing of little worth. [*Collected Works* vol. 6, par. 63]

Throughout his long life, Jung never lost the capacity to play – letting his mind wander creatively. Dieter Baumann's earliest memory of his grandfather is of his being engrossed in a game with children – and playing like a child.

I was five years old, and he was almost sixty. There was a family meeting, and there was a fountain at the entrance to the garden, with water coming out into a basin. We boys were collecting dandelion stems, and we made a pipeline out of the stems, but the pressure of the water would push it out again. So my grandfather came and saw us playing there and started to play with us. He made a small pipeline, put it into the basin, leaned on the ground and sucked – and then the water came out through the difference of the level – which was of course an absolute miracle to me at that moment. That was my first memory, my first impression of him.

Play is breaking away from the facts that apply at any time, and deciding to re-invent the current realities, so that the individual can transform a situation. It is rewriting the psychological agenda, and play gives the opportunity for people to create symbols that contain meaning for them. For children, the transformation, the immersion in play, is real and absolute, but for adults, it can be a lost art.

In the sandplay room in our own house, our five year old son is always careful that his sandplay scenes be put away before nightfall, because if left overnight 'they become real'. In contrast, adults who visit the sandplay room frequently view it with suspicion and make cynical jokes to relieve the tension its presence alone raises in them.

Even as an old man, Jung still played. He did what his family came to call his 'waterworks'. Alongside the Tower at Bollingen there is a soft mossy bank which is saturated with water, and covered in stones and pebbles. Jung used to cut into the bank and clear away mud and leaves that accumulated at the edge of the lake. By doing so, he could create a clear stream of water which would flow into the lake. He told an English friend that the 'waterworks' were relaxing and left his mind free to work; getting the water to flow, and being by the lake in general, attuned him to the flow of life and ideas. Dieter Baumann, more than fifty years ago, used to help his grandfather to make the waters flow.

> He played all the time. In Bollingen he did his so-called waterworks, namely he dug into the slope by the lake there, which is saturated with water oozing out it. He had a system of rivulets which he connected into a main stream and then that went to the lake, and there was an inner harbour and an outer harbour. Already as a boy, I think when I was eight years old, I helped him there.

As Jung grew older, he spent more time at his Tower in Bollingen, where he withdrew to think, write and remember; to carve, to dream and perhaps above all, simply to play. To this complex man – half Swiss peasant and half world-famous intellectual – play contained images and meaning more real than the concrete world around him. Dora Kalff also recalls the image of the old man who played.

> I remember my son visiting Bollingen once when he was a little boy, because he was a friend of the grandchildren of Jung. And then he came home and he said: 'Oh Mummy, there was an old gentleman and you know he made all those little rivers in the earth.' They were playing next to the lake. And he wondered why he did this.

Jung was quite specific about the importance of play and imagination in creativity; clearly, fantasy was an indispensable aspect of his own creative life.

> We know that every good idea and all creative work are the offspring of the imagination, and have their source in what one is pleased to call infantile fantasy. Without this playing with fantasy, no creative work has ever yet come to birth. The debt we owe to the play of imagination is incalculable. It must not be forgotten that it is just in the imagination that a man's highest value may lie. [*Collected Works* vol. 6, p. 63]

Jung's long life was devoted to the wisdom of the dream and the play of his imagination. No one can doubt the real influence he has had on our age. For most of his life he worked against the popular current of worldly perspectives, bringing unfamiliar ideas and unsettling observations to light – heading upstream. If today the unconscious is a more familiar theme, and has become a reality to many, we owe that largely to the influence of Carl Gustav Jung. Beside the lake at Bollingen, Jung gave a demonstration of the term 'influence' to his young grandson Dieter Baumann.

> In the main stream it was cloudy. There something had been moved. And then a tributary came, very fresh and clean water. We saw that picture of this pure and limpid water going into the cloudy one and it made a special kind of design. And then I said to him 'Look at this interesting phenomenon' and then he looked and he said 'Yes. That is influence.'

5

Encounters with Jung

I have found myself very often in my practice telling stories about him, when they came into my mind, and I have felt it's too bad that this person didn't have the opportunity to meet him personally. That's a motivation to communicate for me. I see people who read his things, and unless they have an experience, that is only looking at the words.
[Dieter Baumann, Jung's grandson; an analyst, Zurich]

Jung's psychology was the result of the way that he lived his own life, and his life was the living-out of his psychology. To an unusual degree, therefore, who Jung was and what he was like is valuable additional material in an effort to understand the analytical psychology which is still tied closely to his name.

Different people experienced him in many different ways, and in the pages that follow, the recollections of those who had personal contact with Jung will portray a man to whom psychological honesty was all-important, even if it meant being occasionally disagreeable or abrupt; a man who had a startling impact on people who were in need of guidance or direction; a man whose solitude and reflection were at least as important as the recognition of his work and fame in the world. To Gerhard Adler, who spent twenty years on the task of editing Jung's *Collected Works* and *Letters* in English, the essential fact was Jung's ability to speak everyone's language.

We went to these legendary events, these morning seminars; there was a lot of laughter. Jung had a terrific sense of humour. After the seminars we would go out together with my friend Erich

Neumann and his wife. 'Today Jung has talked absolutely to my basic problem' one of us would say. And the others would all say the same thing.

Dr Adolf Guggenbuhl-Craig of Zurich recalls a story which was told to him by Jung when Dr Guggenbuhl-Craig was a young resident at the Burgholzli clinic. It is about three women who meet and begin talking about their lives.

The first one says something like this: 'Well you know my life was most unhappy and unfulfilled and I was blanketed in the most profound depression; until I consulted the most wonderful psychiatrist in Kusnacht. Not only did he treat my depression, he has given me the tools to develop a whole new orientation to life, and has helped me to understand the value and meaning of my depression.'

'Well! Isn't that extraordinary,' said the second woman, 'I have also been seeing someone in Kusnacht, but my man is a religious prophet. He has shown me a new way of looking at God and how I as an individual can connect with God and develop a profound and interdependent relationship with him. I have found that this has helped me immensely in my day-to-day life.'

'This is quite unbelievable!' exclaimed the third woman. 'I have also been to Kusnacht, but I have been to see a mystical healer, a modern shaman if I have ever met one. He has helped me to discover the hidden meaning of life and has cured me in much the same way as the Navajo medicine-man, or Asclepius at Epidavros.'

All three women had of course walked down the same tree-lined path to the house at 228 Seestrasse, the home and consulting room of Professor C. G. Jung. Kusnacht is on what is known as 'The Gold Coast' of Lake Zurich – where very large lakeside houses reflect the affluence that is rightly understood to be a feature of Switzerland, and Zurich in particular. Emma and Carl Jung built the house in 1907, and lived there until their deaths, in 1955 and 1961 respectively. The house, and Jung the man, were the focus of many people's hopes – coming to see him, often at great expense, and having exhausted other forms of medical or psychological treatment, in desperate need, or in the midst of an emotional crisis. Others drifted towards Kusnacht, but having arrived, became quite convinced that their fate had brought them into contact with this remarkable man. Personally, he possessed a capacity for almost overwhelming intuitive connection to the individual before him. In many cases, the patient became the pupil, as for example did Jane Wheelwright:

> He always had one foot in the unconscious and the other one in the reality of the conscious. He had a way of just dropping in on the unconscious like that, especially with psychotics. He could just contact them like that, as they were, he just dropped down where the person is.

Jane Wheelwright and her husband Joe met Jung in 1932 – not out of their personal need, but escorting Jane's Aunt Laura to see Jung first, and later Freud. Nevertheless, as far as Joe was concerned, he had met his destiny in Jung's consulting room:

> It took me somewhere between eight and eleven minutes to decide that I was not going to go to Vienna to see Herr Doktor Sigmund Freud, but that this was the man for me. Why I took to Jung in such a hurry? He was very related. He was not hiding behind his beard, and we were *vis-à-vis*, and this appealed to me enormously. We were two human beings, talking to each other. I was just a pimply young man, and Jane was just a pimply young girl, but he paid attention to us, and we really had a connection and a dialogue going.

Physically, Jung was tall, broad, and slim – over six feet, somewhat stooped in later life, but strong and clever with his hands. His country childhood gave him the skills in carving wood which later became such an important form of expression of his psychological images. As a medical student at Basel University, he had a reputation for eating and drinking enthusiastically, and was known in some quarters as 'The Barrel'. Dr Liliane Frey-Rohn remembers Jung's powerful physical presence, allied to his psychological communication:

> When somebody came into the room who was walking this particular way, then one knows that's the great Jung: he had a very, very powerful physical presence. One would know that this man, walking this way with his assurance, with his two legs like an elephant's – that would be Jung. The secret of Jung's genius was that he went to the source of things, he was really perpendicular always, never horizontally interested. He really asked – who are you? what is life? what does my patient really suffer from? what is his outlook? and how can one help him to find himself, to be himself, to follow his own destination?

Jung as a boy.

Group at Clark University, Worcester, Mass, USA *Back:* A. A. Brill, E. Jones, S. Ferenczi; *Front:* Sigmund Freud, Stanley Hall, C. G. Jung.

The view across Lake Zurich from the Tower at Bollingen.

'[At Bollingen] I am in the midst of my true life ... Without my piece of earth my life's work would not have come into being.'

'Time is a child – playing like a child – playing a board game – the kingdom of the child.' Excerpt from the inscription on the stone cube in front of the Tower at Bollingen.

Stone carving in the wall of the Tower at Bollingen. 'The stone I am working on ... gives me inner stability with its hardness and permanence.' (Jung, in a letter to his daughter Marianne in 1956.)

'Fasnacht reveals the true identity of the Swiss in the unconscious sense. The Swiss are really very wild people, but very reticent people' – Dr Gerhard Adler.

Statuettes of Greek actors in masks, from an Athenian grave. Jung used the Latin word persona to describe the psychological masks of everyday life.

Dionysus was the Greek god of wine and religious ecstasy. 'If we don't get our ecstasy in a legitimate way we will get it in an illegitimate way ... by way of alcoholism or drugs' – Robert Johnson.

'He was the most religious man I ever knew' – Aniela Jaffe, co-author with Jung of *Memories, Dreams, Reflections*.

Professor C. A. (Freddy) Meier met Jung when he was sixteen years old. Himself a man of remarkable intellectual range, his deepest impression of Jung was 'his enormous capacity for work'.

'What stuck in my mind was that he talked about a crazy girl who said she was on the moon and talked about it as if it was very real.' Dr Marie-Louise von Franz on her first encounter with Jung.

'I have found myself very often telling stories about him ... and I felt it was too bad the person didn't have the opportunity to meet him personally ... He dedicated his life to going upstream ... not going with the crowd downriver.' Dr Dieter Baumann, Jung's grandson.

The word that recurs in memories of Jung is 'honesty', and many of those people who met him and got to know him well regard honesty as the essence of Jung's psychological approach – accepting the reality of the psyche, rather than pretending it does not exist, and listening to the wisdom of the dream, rather than dismissing 'fantasy' from life's 'realities'. As a young woman, Marie-Louise von Franz was impressed by Jung's directness, unusual among the adults of her experience:

> I met him when I was only eighteen, just before I finished high school, only socially. . . . When I met him I knew, 'That's the man who is really honest,' I was always looking for somebody who is really honest, you know, I knew many people who are honest on the surface, but if you ask them certain ticklish questions about one of these awful themes, like sex or religion! I felt, 'No, that man is absolutely straight, just in the awkward corners, the difficult dark corners.'
>
> He was very sensitive and he had a poetical side, a very impressionable side. It was the same with every human being he met, he was absolutely open and hypersensitive and he let the other have an impact on him.

Baroness Vera von der Heydt first met Jung in 1927, when her marriage had just broken up, and she was 'in an awful mess'.

> And later I realized that of course Jung would have realized this. I was sitting next to him at dinner; he seemed to me to be like an old bird, like a raven, full of wisdom. He never once said to me: 'Why don't you come to Zurich?' He never, or at least as little as possible, ever suggested to anybody that they should have an analysis, they have to come to it by themselves. And that was due to Jung's tremendous respect for the psyche, whosever psyche it was. He didn't say or think that one should be somewhere else, or one ought to be doing this or that. He took you where you were and he gave one the impression that he didn't mind at all whether you were good or bad, as long as you were honest.

Although Jung travelled a lot, he never lived anywhere but Switzerland; his family life and his recreations were all firmly rooted in the Swiss countryside and the spectacular Alpine landscapes which begin at the southern end of Lake Zurich. As a child, Jung remembered in his old age, he and his father had gone to the little village of Vitznau, near Luzern, where a mountain railway climbs to the summit of Mount Rigi, and a spectacular 360 degree panorama of the Alps, the lakes and the countryside stretching north towards Bavaria. Often the mountain-top is stranded above a sea of cloud, and one looks across to other snow-capped islands while the valleys and lakes disappear beneath the cloud. At Vitznau, Jung's father found he didn't have enough money to pay for tickets for himself and his son; so he sent Carl up alone. There on the mountain-top, he felt 'one had to be polite and silent up here, for it was in God's world'. Until late in his life, Jung would drive, or be driven, up into the mountains to places where a panoramic view of the landscape could be seen.

Hardly anyone alive now remembers Jung before the age of forty; by then he was an established doctor, with many patients who came from far afield, including a number of wealthy and influential Americans who cemented his connection with the USA. Because of them, the Analytical Psychology Club was established in Zurich; and because of their interest, Jung made repeated lecture tours to the USA – speaking at Clark University in Massachusetts, attending the Harvard tercentenary celebrations in 1936, or speaking to a large invited audience in the ballroom of the Plaza Hotel, New York. The strong American relationship to Jung's work still exists today; there are more Jungian analysts in the USA than in any other country, and many of the largest American cities have institutes and centres dedicated to educational programmes which disseminate Jung's thought to a wider audience.

Yet what many memories of him underline is that he was 'typically Swiss' – a man with his roots deeply planted in the Swiss soil. According to his colleague Gerhard Adler, Jung was powerfully connected to his environment – Lake Zurich, Kusnacht, Bollingen – in which he cultivated vegetables, cooked rich rustic soups and casseroles, sailed his boat, and carved cryptic archetypal messages into stone slabs.

Jung was a typical Swiss man and a peasant. He was also typically cosmopolitan – that was his strength. He had both his feet planted on the ground. If he hadn't he could not have gone through the discovery of the archetypal unconscious – if he had not been so grounded.

The house at Kusnacht has a small stone jetty, where a sailing-boat was moored; on summer afternoons, Jung would sail on the deep, snow-fed waters of the lake, as he reflected on the patients whom he had seen in the consulting room that morning. His colleagues and pupils remember him for being, in many respects, typically Swiss.

Mary Briner: He was of course a very superior Swiss, and he loved his mountains and he was a great sailor on the lake, and he had the characteristic of commonsense.

Dr Liliane Frey-Rohn: He was Swiss to the tips of his toes: it started with a laughter that he had, a very healthy laughter, and very natural. I would say to be Swiss is to have a certain kind of seriousness, having the feeling of the earth under the feet.

Dr von Franz considers the typical Swiss character to be very much dictated by the mountains, and the rural farming traditions of the landscape – which have psychological consequences, too:

It's an irrational flavour, it's the influence of the earth. Mountain populations have, if you look at Tibet or the Andes, a tendency to want to be free and independent. If you have a little farm in a mountain valley you are cut off in winter by snow, you have no communication with anybody, you are self-dependent. Like when you live in dangerous nature, you are religious in the sense that you know that there are powers which are beyond you, not so inflated as people in the plain; people in the plain think that they can master nature, build roads and walls and so forth. The mountain people are more religious, they are always aware of the irrational powers; you have to be in contact with your own instinct, with your unconscious. You have for instance endless folk-stories, how a man guarding the cattle in the Alps has a dream that snow will come, so he drives the cattle down and the next day the snow comes.

Dora Kalff knew Jung and the Jung family well for many years.

I felt that he was a real Swiss, and that made him stand really upon the earth. He was a very good cook, and he liked good food. I felt that earthy quality in him. Although he talked a lot about the spirit and spiritual development, I still felt that he was very much connected to the earth.

Dr Adler had the good fortune to sample some of Jung's Swiss rural cuisine:

The greatest experience was when you were in his kitchen, and when he was preparing a meal. He was so serious in doing that, it was as if he wouldn't do anything except to be a cook. And he'd taste it, and then he'd go in the garden, and you'd see how he was in the garden – just the same. He was complete in everything he did. He cooked good wholesome country food and he used no recipes – everything was spontaneous and inventive. When he lived at Bollingen, he would drive down to Zurich to get the ingredients for a sauce. And I remember one particular dinner, when he asked 'How many ingredients are there in the sauce?' Nobody knows. He says 'There are thirteen ingredients in that!' Bollingen was primitive circumstances, you know, but he managed to produce everything that he needed.

Jung's early life plays an important role in his personal story; in his childhood he lived in the countryside, before moving to the border city of Basel – which had been the home of his mother's family. Baselers are said to be independent-minded and prone to suspicion of outsiders, due to the geographical location of their city, nestling between hills at the junction of three nations. They are also the people who stage the annual Fasnacht, one of the great European carnivals, in which manners and social proprieties are cast aside, and thousands of people wear masks and wild costumes, have processions through the city streets in the middle of the night, insult each other, and make fun of their political leaders. When Jung was alive, expeditions from Zurich used to make for Basel to join in with the ritual safety-valve for Swiss conventions which Fasnacht represents.

Dr Liliane Frey-Rohn, herself a German-born Swiss, considers the Basel background to be an important aspect of Jung's character:

He was typical of a Baseler in his sharpness, and his critical mind. Persons from Basel are very critical. They have the psychology of the frontiers, they are surrounded by three lands. They have to protect themselves.

In later life, Jung protected himself by giving himself space and a physical environment which offered a contrast to the real but abstract work of his psychological practice. He did it by buying a plot of land on the upper shore of Lake Zurich, by the hamlet of Bollingen. Here, in 1923, he began to build his Tower.

Gradually, through my scientific work, I was able to put my fantasies and the contents of the unconscious on a solid footing. Words and paper, however, did not seem real enough to me; something more was needed. I had to achieve a kind of representation in stone of my innermost thoughts and of the knowledge I had acquired. Or, to put it another way, I had to make a confession of faith in stone. That was the beginning of the 'Tower' the house which I built for myself at Bollingen. [*Memories, Dreams, Reflections*, p. 223]

Jung's breadth of knowledge and scholarly ability was renowned. He spoke and understood many languages, and was able to understand and perceive the hidden meaning of obscure alchemical texts, and modern nuclear physics. He was thorough and completely absorbed in all that he involved himself in. In addition to his scholarly endeavours he painted, cooked and gardened and retreated to the Tower. Gerhard Adler saw him at Bollingen many times: but one particular occasion has stuck in his memory for forty years:

I once went to Bollingen which was extremely primitive – I was shown up by his housekeeper, and I knocked at the door to his study. It was an extremely impressive moment; when he opened it, he was in deep meditation, completely within himself, in a trance like a mystic. The second he heard me, he turned and he was completely with me. He could immediately switch round to the presence of a human being. That was most impressive to me.

Dr Liliane Frey-Rohn knew Jung from her childhood until his death: it was her father who appointed Jung to his professorship at the E.T.H. academy in Zurich. She therefore saw Jung often, even in his Bollingen retreat:

I even visited him there and lived two or three or four days there, and I could really watch him at every moment of the day, when he was swimming, when he was breakfasting, or when he wanted us to be absolutely silent and we would not say one word, not to disturb him. He very often read, and swimming was a summer passion. Bollingen was really like a cloister area, with walls around, it was encircled, and he very much liked to be there, and he liked to watch the lake tremendously.

As Marie-Louise von Franz explains about Bollingen:

It was where he was happy and where he lived the rhythm and the kind of life he wanted to live. He liked to be close to nature, to be quiet, to be introverted, for the scientific and religious concentration of his life. At his house in Kusnacht, he gave himself to the family and to the patients and to the world and to interviewers and to all that kind of life. But that wasn't his true self – he was interested in the world, but then he had a deep need to retire and to meditate and to go into his own depths.

Dora Kalff once went to the Tower in mid-winter:

I think it was on the first of January, you know, when one gives good wishes to people, Franz Jung telephoned and said 'I'm going to see my father today in Bollingen and would you like to come with me?' I said 'Fine.' And it was very interesting because it was the middle of winter, it was very cold, and he opened the door himself and he was clothed in a thing like chain-mail, something that in the Middle Ages soldiers wore under their steel armour. So that was keeping him very warm, and he wore a green apron like the gardeners wear. And it just was always very dark in the Tower but there were little windows around. And then when I entered, you see he was just standing in the light probably of one of these windows, and it seemed that his eyes were so clear. He was really clear, and you could grasp what he was, what he wanted to say. And he was making a fire and cooking there, making a roast (rabbit I think), and then when I looked around Mrs Jung was sitting in one corner, and she said 'I'm freezing,' because it was so cold there you know, and she cannot dress like her husband – it was before the time when ladies wore trousers. Mrs Jung was a very wonderful woman. And of course unfortunately she was a bit in the shadow of a big man. But she was, she took it very well. She was humble but she was a very fine woman.

Jung was devoted to the Tower; to the stability of its structure, to the concrete way in which it represented his inner life, and for the rustic, primitive life he was able, or required, to live there.

Here everything has its history, and I have mine; here is space for the spaceless kingdom of he world's and the psyche's hinterland. I have done without electricity, and tend the fireplace and stove myself. Evenings, I light the old lamps. There is no running water, and I pump water from the well. I chop the wood and cook the food. [*Memories, Dreams, Reflections*, p. 226]

As Jung's secretary, Aniela Jaffe was permitted to come to Bollingen, in particular, when Jung was in his eighties, to take dictation when she was compiling Jung's memories for the autobiography.

At Bollingen, he was in his element. He spoke very little. It was very quiet, and he was feeding the birds and cooking, but he didn't make any conversation. He made his stones – it was a presence, not a conversation. Very few words. It was very, very quiet. Whenever we stood at the lake, it was very funny, when I gave too much bread to one bird, he grumbled. He said 'Take care! let the others have some bread!' So in this way, that was our conversation.

The Jungian analysts of the first generation – those who knew Jung personally, and worked with him as his patients and pupils – associate his psychology with his person and his life. For the second generation, those who began to train from the mid-1950s onwards, there was a reaction against the whole idea of being disciples of the great man – and therefore they worked to make Jungian psychology into more of a scientific system of ideas, and criticized some aspects of Jung's work which didn't fit the scientific model. The third generation of Jungians, starting their work since Jung's death in 1961, have no memory of the man himself, and therefore feel under no obligation to stay within the bounds of the work Jung himself did.

Whichever generation the Jungian analyst belongs to – and the divisions are vague, anyway – the essence of the analyst's practice is the same respect, curiosity and compassion for the patients and her/his psyche which Jung himself demonstrated in his work. Gerhard Adler, for example, defines it thus:

He was related, yes, he was deeply related to himself and to other people. The essence of being a Jungian analyst is of course to be oneself, and in that sense one is truly connected to other people. I always say three 'H's are the essence – honesty, humour, and humility, and they are certainly necessary for work with other people. You give all the time to other people and you have to replenish yourself, otherwise you get stale. I do this work now for fifty-five, fifty-six years, I don't get bored. I wouldn't be without it, and that is because my patients give me something which I can take into myself and think about it. The essence of a Jungian analyst is to be like, to have the same depths of the experience of the numinous which Jung had.

Honesty, humour, and humility are three of the most important
aspects of Jung's own attitude which former pupils and friends recall.
He treated everyone with respect, including children; he had a sense
of humour, and an occasionally quick temper; he had a capacity to
connect with another person at a deep level almost immediately; and
he valued anyone's sense of meaning, or of religion. What is so striking
in talking with the people who knew Jung is how passionately and
devotedly they still want to communicate the experience of meeting
and valuing this extraordinary man, whose genius was not only
scholarly, and psychological, but also was a matter of inspiring love
and deep respect. As Michael Fordham recalled, 'He was enormously
likeable and enormously lovable.'

Gerhard Adler: Other than in the analytical hour he was full of life,
and full of humour. His laughter could shake a house. Jung could
be the most charming and humorous company, and on the other
hand he was most serious. I remember many talks in the garden –
Jung loved to analyse in the garden while he walked, and he was
very serious then.

Marie-Louise von Franz: He had a tremendous sense of humour.
That was very much a secret of his analytical effectiveness, because
you can tell something painful to a patient with a joke, and if the
patient has a sense of humour, you get it over much better.

According to some witnesses, Jung's devotion to honesty could go
beyond normal limits. Wanting to get to the truth about things meant
that Jung liked to play the role of trickster and was always delighted
when something unexpected happened at a party. It is said that he
would get people to drink too much and play wild party games,
insisting that they behave foolishly so that their true nature emerged.

Joseph Henderson's memories of Jung begin in 1929. He had been
a journalist in San Francisco, but at the recommendation of Jung's
English colleague H. Godwin 'Peter' Baynes, and his American third
wife Carey Baynes, decided to head for Zurich. He spent a year as a
school-teacher at his own old school in Lawrenceville, New Jersey, to
finance the trip. He remained in Europe for some years, continuing his
work with Jung and training as a medical doctor at St Bartholomew's
Hospital in London. Returning to California with his English wife (the
daughter of the legendary Cambridge scholar Professor Cornford), Dr
Henderson co-founded the San Francisco Jung Institute with others in

the late 1940s, and maintained his relationship with Jung until the latter's death in 1961.

Joseph Henderson: Jung was very active, both imaginatively and physically. And his interest in people was extremely immediate and very human. He was also a man with a wonderful sense of humour, so that when he was enjoying himself, you knew exactly how to respond, because it was infectious. In a bad mood he could be quite unpredictable and rather frightening, because he had a way of losing his temper about certain things that you had no way of understanding at the moment. But as soon as he had let himself go and expressed his anger or distress or whatever it was, he then immediately got to work to find out what was behind it, and out would come something usually very helpful and creative both for him and for the situation.

Jane Wheelwright: He didn't seem to have bugs, like meanness and pettiness – in other words he very well understood his shadow. He knew he had unconsciousness, he could be mean, and he was sometimes – but he knew it, and so in a way, you didn't feel the projection from that side of him. He didn't look down on you, as he easily could have. I was just a kid, and I didn't know anything. But he took me seriously. He was twice my age and he treated me like an equal. Well, you know, that's quite impressive for a young person.

Jung's humour and delight in the life-long exploration of the mysteries of the psyche communicate themselves clearly in his 'Houston Interview' with Dr Evans. He is almost constantly smiling as he tries to explain, and admits the difficulty of using mere words, the images and patterns that he observed in the personal unconscious and the collective unconscious. Saying anything about man's unconscious, of course, always presented a difficulty:

His consciousness *can* be described, his unconscious *cannot* be described because the unconscious – and here I must repeat myself – is always *unconscious*. it is *really* unconscious, we really don't know it, so we don't know our unconscious personality. We have hints, we have certain ideas, but we don't know it really. Nobody can say where man ends. That is the beauty of it, you know; it's very interesting. The unconscious of man can reach God knows where! There we are going to make discoveries.

Sigmund Hurwitz is perhaps the only man alive who himself had Jung as a patient, although he began his analysis with Jung because of his own mid-life crisis. He was a successful dentist with a practice in Zurich, and Jung came as a patient. Hurwitz recalls one ironical exchange with Jung:

He was a very pleasant patient. He came exactly when I ordered him, and once I asked him 'Why do you always come exactly on time?' Then he answered 'Punctuality is the virtue of kings!'

It would appear, however, that Jung did not take himself as seriously as ultimately the world did: for he was well aware, to refer to two of his important psychological ideas, that a bright light always casts a *shadow*, and that praise and fame are bound to be accompanied by *inflation* – which can lead to an explosion. Aniela Jaffe gave a lecture – to much praise – at the Analytical Psychology Club in Zurich; Jung's response was memorable:

He invited me to Bollingen, and I went there, and he said 'Yes, I heard you suffered this success.' That means it's very dangerous. You are perhaps a bit inflated and then you fall down – you lose your modesty.

Whether Jung was speaking with men, or women, or children, and whatever kind of person they might be, contact with him produced the impression that 'he speaks my language' according to his pupil Dr Frey-Rohn.

Dr Liliane Frey-Rohn: You could find everything you wanted with him: absolutely the deepest seriousness, the greatest humour. In German, we say *allumfassend* [all-embracing]. And therefore, he could speak with everybody, and everybody has a feeling afterwards, 'Oh, he speaks my language.' I've heard this so many times. He went into people, and he spoke out of them. It's extraordinary. So you never knew, who is speaking really – when you were with Jung. He reflected you.

Dr Gerhard Adler: Something which was typical of Jung – he was very silent. He let me talk, and he very often didn't talk to a dream which I told him. I was furious, and he told me some story which was quite unconnected with me. Then this was very very strange, how gradually one realized that the story which he told was in fact the interpretation of one's dream. He had this absolute genius to talk indirectly to one. On the whole he didn't say very much – but what he said was always to the point. He had an incredible intuition.

Freddy Meier met Jung at the age of about sixteen. Jung's daughter Marianne was then his best friend, and she told her father, by way of introduction, that the young Freddy had read *Psychological Types*.

He was quite astonished – I was still a young boy – and he asked me what I made of it, and I said: 'Well, I think you have given a most comprehensive and most complete description of the dynamics of the human psyche.' He stood aghast at this – 'Well, really? That's exactly what I wanted to do but so far nobody else has understood it!'

Dieter Baumann, as Jung's oldest grandson, had a unique experience:

I loved him very much, I also had great respect for him of course, but he also had a very great respect for me. He was not that kind of adult who would take an air of authority or superiority. He had an absolutely natural authority. He had the utmost respect for the personality of other people. I always felt, throughout the time I knew him, that he had a great respect and love for the other person, myself included.

For people whose contact with Jung was only brief, or came at the end of his life, his reputation and sheer presence was perhaps more intimidating than inspiring. It is easy to forget that in the last years of his life – in the 1950s – he was a world-famous figure who was constantly besieged for his opinions about the state of the world, about the future of humanity, about the paranormal, UFOs and life after death. Two of the analysts who first began their work in Zurich during that era, and are now the leading figures of the second generation, recall the difficulties that Jung's reputation posed for them at the time.

Adolf Guggenbuhl-Craig is a psychiatrist who trained in the classical Freudian psychoanalytic school. What he heard about Jung was 'that he was interesting but inclined to seduce people with very esoteric ideas.'

I met him a few times privately, in the sense that his grandson was a friend of mine and so sometimes I saw him. I didn't meet him professionally. My impression was always very ambivalent in the sense that his personality was so strong that he actually scared me or intimidated me. I couldn't have warm feelings for him because I had too much respect; I thought he was a genius, and I was not a genius, and therefore I had very mixed feelings. We, the post-Jungians, are not geniuses any more.

James Hillman reached Zurich by a roundabout route – as 'an early hippy' he had spent some years walking around Africa, and writing, and failing to find his direction in life.

I got into this business because I was a mess. I say the past tense – which is dangerous, because I *am* a mess and because you say the past tense and you distance yourself from it: the mess remains. Jung was so strong a personality that for years I didn't want to see him. I was afraid. I felt that he would bother my compass somehow, put too big a charge in it, and I wouldn't find which way north was any more.

Jungian psychology is not about directing people towards a goal: individuation means that every individual finds her/his own meaning or being as best she/he can. It was one of Jung's discoveries, however, that the inner compass always tended to look for a sense of meaning, or a form of spiritual experience – and this, too, was part of the impact Jung had on those who knew him.

Aniela Jaffe: He was a deeply religious man and very conscious. It began in his childhood. He had experiences and fantasies and dreams, and he was seized by these dreams, and he always knew that there is something beyond – and that's not astonishing because so many of his fathers and grandfathers were clergymen – so the religious problem was in his family.

Professor Freddy Meier is himself a man of remarkable intellectual range, from psychiatry to classics – who, for example, lectured on the theme of Wilderness to the Third World Wilderness Congress in Inverness in 1983 – and who pays homage to the scale of Jung's intellectual and creative powers.

The deepest impression of him was his enormous capacity for work, his absolutely unlimited source of what we would nowadays call libido. The way he produced books and saw people and gave seminars and lectures and also travelled a lot. I never could, even to this day I cannot understand how one single person can cope with so much work. Whenever did he read all this material, whenever did he write all this material, when did he speak and see people, within twenty-four hours a day. I mean it was inconceivable, and it still is to me, still is a total riddle. Whereas I hope I understand Jung as a man fairly well, but I still don't understand how he was capable of all this work.

What is perhaps still more impressive than the reaction of one of Jung's closest followers, is the fact that scholars in quite separate fields recognize the quality of Jung's own scholarship and influence in their own. The theologian Reverend Don Cupitt, and the Celtic scholar Count Nikolai Tolstoi, both respect Jung's work in their own fields:

Cupitt: I think his religious naturalism will prove to be important in the long run, because the belief of theologians like me is that we have to take a naturalistic reading of religion in the future; we have to adopt a multi-faith approach – that Jung pioneered as well – and we also have to pay attention to the shadow side of religious belief. Jung was a pioneer in that as well. He looked at the shadow. Remember, he was one of the first thinkers to be much influenced by modern anthropology, modern religious studies, and the huge increase in our knowledge of other religions that developed around 1900 and thereabouts. This was an obvious challenge to thinkers – was there some sort of universal religious algebra? And Jung's answer was the 'doctrine' of the archetypes.

Tolstoi: Something or other that somebody said about Jung's 'General Theory of Archetypes' just triggered in my mind, and I thought 'Well, that might be worth looking at.' I suspected that it would be a lot of mysticism, I mean in the pejorative sense, and that it wouldn't really tell me about these very solid facts that I was concerned with. But I found – and this is what continues to impress me about Jung – that he is such a scholar, as well as a gifted poetic thinker. The scholarship and the clarity of the writing appealed to me at once. He made a totally new subject instantly accessible.

Jung himself, who was naturally aware of his own prodigious intellectual range and achievements, always tried – though perhaps ambiguously – to retain an air of modesty.

Mary Briner: He was an exceedingly natural person. You never felt that he looked down on you, he treated you as an equal, and he said to me: 'Look, I'm just like all other men, only I happen to know a little more than most men.'

Joe Wheelwright: I made some comment about his encyclopaedic knowledge but that the reason it was so meaningful to me was that it didn't come out like knowledge, he wasn't casting pearls before swine, and he wasn't preaching a gospel and he wasn't doing any of those things; and he said 'The older I get –' and he was a child then of about seventy-five I guess – 'the more I realize that I don't know enough to entirely cover my little fingernail – there could be room for a little bit more.'

Jung's modesty is perhaps not the real point. He achieved a degree of recognition in his own lifetime that is remarkable for any doctor or scientist, and all the more so in view of the nature of his observations. It was of course at a certain price; for Jung speaks in his *Memories, Dreams, Reflections* of being lonely as a child. To Gerhard Adler, that remained a fact of Jung's whole life.

The pioneer is always alone. I was impressed when I first read his memoirs, by the utter loneliness of this man, who was apparently so sociable, so alive. He was really very alone.

The American analyst Dr Edward Edinger observes that in one of the last letters Jung wrote, a sense of pessimism enters into his thoughts.

It's an amazing letter. I wept the first time I read it. One of the passages that struck me most strongly was one where he says: 'I have failed in my foremost task, to open people's eyes to the fact that man has a soul, that there is a buried treasure in the field, and that our religion and philosophy are in a lamentable state.' It gave me a glimpse into Jung's personal experience of what he had to carry, and how he took it personally. He had such broad psychological shoulders that that side of him doesn't show up in any of his ordinary writings.

In Jung's life, the buried treasure was the human soul, was the deeper dimension of the unconscious which could be united with the conscious life and thus help to make a person whole. What Jung considered a failure, we must surely consider an astonishing achievement – of placing that thought before the world in the course of his life's work. Dr Edinger:

> 'I have failed in my foremost task *to open people's eyes to the fact*' – so that's a short-term failure. He has failed, in the short-term. But in the long-term of course it'll be quite different. That's my conviction.

If anyone, finally, can appreciate what Jung's life meant to himself and to the world, it is the members of his own family who observed both from within and without. Franz Jung is now eighty years old. He lives in his father's house and responds to the enquiries of Jungian analysts, writers, and simple sightseers with unfailing courtesy.

> Jung had the quality of giving all of his human attention to everyone who was in contact with him. My father allowed all these people to be in his presence. You can imagine how many patients he had, and they had a life-long connection to him: they came from all over the world and were sustained by him. They came to live here in Kusnacht to be near him. It was a source of life here. My father was able to give all of them this substance of life. But he also gave his wife, his children, his family this life too. We never felt pushed aside.

As the only son of a great genius, Franz Jung has spent his whole life considering his father's legacy. Even at eighty, he simply says 'I am trying to understand the life and work of my father'. To express his attitude, he quotes Goethe's saying: *'Was Du ererbt von Deinen Vätern hast, Erwirb es, um es zu besitzen!'* ('Earn the inheritance from your fathers, So you may truly possess it.')

6

The Secret Life of Relationship - Inner, Outer and Collective

The book on types yielded the insight that every judgement
made by an individual is conditioned by his personality
type and that every point of view is necessarily relative.
[*Memories, Dreams, Reflections*, p. 207]

The testimony of many of Jung's friends and colleagues declares that
part of his genius was for *relationship*. 'He was very related,' says Joe
Wheelwright. There is scarcely anything more crucial to our inner
health, our outer happiness and our worldly success, than relationship.
Yet in an infinity of unhappy cases, relationships between partners,
families, colleagues and friends collapse through misunderstanding
and apparent incompatibility.

Jung's statement 'that every judgement made by an individual is
conditioned by his personality type' seems at first to be a statement of
the obvious; but he uses the word *type* not in its loose, colloquial sense,
but to mean something specific. In the considerable amount of work
which Jung devoted to understanding and describing how people relate
to each other – and how badly they often do it – the most notable
advance was in his definition of two 'orientations' and four 'types'.
The former, the alternative tendencies of *introversion* and *extroversion*,
are widely understood, and have entered into common usage. The
latter, the functions of *thinking, intuition, sensation* and *feeling*, are
harder to grasp, but invaluable reference points in a living diagram of
the psychological encounter between people.

No person is just an introvert, or a thinking type – it is a matter of a tendency, or a bias, towards behaving, or relating to the world and other people, in a certain way. The theory can be used to help us consider how we *will* relate to other people, or to reflect on what has happened already – which is the way that Jung came to evolve it in the first place.

After their theoretical differences produced a division in the infant psychoanalytical profession between Jung and Freud, and indirectly between Jung and Freud's other significant disciple, Alfred Adler, Jung reflected on what had happened. Were the theories incompatible, or the personalities of the men? What would explain such personal incompatibility? The split was as painful to him personally, as it was damaging professionally:

> After the break with Freud, all my friends and acquaintances
> dropped away. My book [*The Sacrifice*] was declared to be rubbish;
> I was a mystic, and that settled the matter.

It took ten years for Jung to produce his first major work. It was called *Psychological Types*.

> This work sprang originally from my need to define the ways in
> which my outlook differed from Freud's and Adler's. In attempting
> to answer this question, I came across the problem of types; for it
> is one's psychological type which from the outset determines and
> limits a person's judgement. My book, therefore, was an effort to
> deal with the relationship of the individual to the world, to people
> and things.

The work became a wide-ranging study of personality types in classical literature, in philosophy, and in the everyday life of Jung's patients. According to people who knew him, Jung was an introvert, and primarily a thinking type, with a strong intuitive bent as well. It may seem an abstract, even a pointless scheme: but if one reviews the way one's friends or relatives behave, how one's own psychological 'way' can grate against someone else's, one quickly finds that the system fits. Jung himself, in his interview with Richard Evans, began by explaining the idea of introversion and extroversion.

> My whole scheme of typology is merely a sort of orientation. There
> is such a factor as introversion: there is such a factor as
> extraversion. The classification of individuals means nothing at all.
> It is only the instrumentarium for what I call practical psychology,

to explain, for instance, the husband to a wife, or vice versa. [Houston No.2]

This is simply practical, because there are certain people [extraverts] who definitely are more influenced by their surroundings than by their own intentions, while other people [introverts] are more influenced by the subjective factor. The psyche has two conditions ... the one is the environmental influence, and the other is the given fact of the psyche as it is born. The psyche is by no means *tabula rasa* [blank state] but a definite mixture and combination of genes, and they are there from the very first moment of our life, and they give a definite character, even to the little child. [Houston No. 2]

At first, just like every other person, Jung assumed that everyone thought and felt exactly as he did himself:

It took me quite a long time to discover that there is another type than the thinking type, as I thought my type to be. There are other people who decide the same problems I had to decide in an entirely different way. There are, for instance, feeling types. And after a while I discovered that there are intuitive types. They gave me much trouble. It took me over a year to become a bit clearer about the existence of intuitive types. And the last, and most unexpected, was the sensation type. And only later I saw that these are naturally the four aspects of conscious orientation. [Houston No. 4]

Jung decided, after much thought, that there were only four functions, and not more; they seemed to him to cover the full range of how people 'get their bearings'. He explained very simply how each function tends to work.

Well, there is quite a simple explanation of those terms, and it shows at the same time how I arrived at such a typology. Sensation tells you that there *is* something. Thinking, roughly speaking, tells you *what* it is. Feeling tells you whether it is agreeable or not, to be accepted or rejected. And intuition – now there is a difficulty. You don't know, ordinarily, how intuition works. So, when a man has a hunch, you can't tell exactly how he got that hunch. [Houston No. 2]

Practical examples help to flesh out the four functions: for example, the sensation type person is very aware of the surroundings and the visual information available. When getting directions on how to find somebody's house, it helps to have the sensation type give the directions; they are aware of the signposts, the landmarks and the traffic conditions. The feeling type will tell you about all the beautiful, or ugly, sights along the way, but you may never find the house at all.

While the sensation type may have what we generally call a 'sense of direction', you may want the intuitive to help you find somewhere 'appropriate' or 'suitable' for a particular occasion – the hunch, or intuition, guides this type in a way no one else can explain – but it works, somehow.

> The intuitive type, which is very little understood, has a very important function because he goes by hunches, he sees around corners, he smells a rat a mile away. He can give you perception and orientation in a situation where your sense, your intellect and your feelings are no good at all. [Houston No. 4]

> We have constantly warnings or hints, that consist partly in a slight feeling of uneasiness, uncertainty, fear. Now under primitive circumstances you would pay attention to these things: they mean something. With us in our man-made, absolutely, apparently, safe conditions, we don't need that function so very much; yet we have seen it and used it. So you will find that the intuitive types among bankers, Wall Street men; they follow their hunches, and so do gamblers of all descriptions. You find the type quite frequently among doctors, because it helps them in their prognoses. [Houston No. 2]

To illustrate the abstract, theoretical system, Jung told Evans an anecdote about two of his patients:

> The man was a sensation type, the woman was an intuitive type. Of course, they felt attraction. And so they took a little boat and went out to the lake of Zurich. And there were those birds that dive after fish, you know, and then after a certain time they come up again, and you can't tell where they come up. And so they began to bet who would be first to see the bird. Now you would think that the one who observes reality very carefully – the sensation type – would of course win out. Not at all. The woman won the bet completely. She was beating him on all points because by

intuition she knew it before. How is that possible? [Houston No. 2]

In such circumstances, in a close relationship, the surprise and mystification could well be followed by irritation and resentment. Everyone has a superior function and an inferior function: the inferior one being the source of difficulties. If the sensation type man has no intuition at all, he will probably be attracted to an intuitive woman, and vice versa. Opposites frequently attract. In marriage, the man may feel he has found 'his' intuition in his intuitive wife; she may feel 'her' sensation has arrived in her husband. They feel like a perfect fit.

But Jung's psychological approach to relationship has a golden rule; one always has to find one's own psychological truth, or experience. Another person can't have it for you. So what may begin in marriage as a source of great happiness, with the inferior function offloaded onto one's partner, soon dissolves into a source of resentment. Opposite types often do not understand each other, and cannot speak the other's language or approach to the world: 'I simply don't understand you' has been uttered in almost every relationship where two people care enough to think that they want to understand.

Another concept originated by Jung which concerns relationships – from the one-to-one to the national or cultural – is that of shadow. The shadow is that aspect of the personality which the conscious mind or ego finds unacceptable. Because the conscious has no patience for the inferior function, so the person tends not to put herself or himself in the position of developing it. Instead she or he will berate a partner for emphasizing its importance. According to Jane Wheelwright, the shadow usually becomes known through 'projection':

Projection is what I don't like about myself, so I project it on you. That's the enemy, you see. Because I have an enemy in me. If just the simple theory of projection could be understood by more people, particularly politicians, particularly people high up in the government and all that, there wouldn't be this danger of war all the time.

The theory of shadow and projection is not original to Jung. As James Hillman points out, it appears in the Bible:

The concept of shadow is an easy one in a way. You can find it in the Old Testament, and find it in the New Testament. You consider the mote in your own eye, you know – what is it that you're seeing in the other person that is yours.

As Andrew Samuels suggests, the most acute conflicts between spouses, or lovers, occur when they each stumble across their own weakness or failing which is manifested somehow in the other person.

I think it is a Jungian contribution to our thinking about relationships that what you find in the other person has to do with you – not necessarily as a projection of bits of yourself you can't cope with, and therefore put into the other person, and beat up in the other person – but as something far more valuable and positive: projections of parts of oneself that, if not projected, one cannot have access to.

Typology is a useful tool for understanding people as individuals; but it can be applied to groups, or even professions, as well. Introverts don't do well in jobs which require a lot of customer-contact; extroverts like to perform and to connect with others. Thinking types are perfect for the rational activities of the courtroom; feeling types suit the caring professions, but not highly technical work. Jungian analysts, according to a fairly scientific study, are mostly introverts; but different functions lend themselves to different aspects of the work. Some are thinkers, and get into the complicated intellectual end of Jung's ideas, like alchemy; others are intuitive and feeling, and are analysts because of the deep personal connection they can make to patients. No one function excludes the others.

Joe Wheelwright, the former actor/musician/reporter is such an extrovert – and such an exception in the Jungian community – that he can make you forget his impeccable credentials, and immense experience, as a Consultant Psychiatrist and analyst. His wife, Jane Hollister Wheelwright, is an undoubted introvert whose upbringing on a Californian ranch – real wilderness country – gave her a life-long fund of psychological self-reliance. Joe declares he is a feeling type: 'People were the thing for me.' Jane is a thinking and sensation type, rational and practical and good with route-directions, among many other things. Both have written studies of typology and relationship; and in many ways they provide a portrait in typology and a life story of its application – for 'it tells you what language they speak'.

Joe Wheelwright: I was really very anxious. To quote George Bernard Shaw, who once remarked that America and England were two countries divided by a common language, it made an impression on me because we were constantly misunderstanding each other; and everybody knows that women feel and men think. I mean that's on page three of any book that you pick up. Well in our family it happens to be t'other way which: I can't think my way out of a paper bag and my wife has an absolutely first-class mind. And also she had a thing called a sensation function, that is she knew very esoteric things like what day it was, or whether she had a dress on, or things that I find very mystical. My strong suit was relationship, I would say. I think ideas are all right if you've got nothing better to do, but what really matters is relationship.

Jane Wheelwright: Women are supposed to feel and men are supposed to think. Joe did the feeling and I did the thinking and so we were upside down. I'm an introvert and I'm a sensation type. Sensation means facts, it's gotta be a fact, you can't fool around with it. You've gotta nail it down, it's gotta be black and white. Then my secondary function is thinking, and for a woman that wasn't allowed in those days.

While Jane's dominant functions were sensation and thinking, her husband's were intuition and feeling. As he puts it:

We're polar opposites. She's very introverted, and I'm *slightly* extroverted! No, *fanatically*! But when I got hold of this type stuff, then it was clear – I had an intuition that reached from Santa Barbara to Hong Kong and back via Buenos Aires. It was quite good.

Jane Wheelwright: I'm one of those types that are probably the slowest to get into the irrational. I'm extremely practical and every time these intuitives would come up with something brilliant, I'd say: 'Prove it', and I wasn't very popular with them. I kept seeing them way up there somewhere, and I wanted to get them down here on the ground, where I could go along with them.

Joe Wheelwright: She has a very strongly developed sensation function as I said. She knew whether I had my trousers on or not; when I used to go to the office, quite often she'd take a look and she'd say 'I suppose you realize your fly's open and your shirt is hanging out?' Well of course I didn't realize any such thing, and finally one day she said 'You know I'm going to let life take care of you, I think it's about time. I don't suppose you'll have a practice left within a week, but it's up to you now to let the slings and arrows of outrageous tiddlypop take care of all of this.'

I've always tried to look a fact in the back of the neck but it was

important to her. For instance, Jane was reading *Ulysses* and all
of these strange things, and Eliot and various people, and I was
busy reading D. H. Lawrence. But she thought that was for the
birds, she didn't like that. But she read Shaw's *Intelligent Woman's
Guide to Socialism and Capitalism*. I read that and it bloody near
killed me – I mean he kept thinking all the time.

Just as sensation types give good directions, they tend to be reliable
drivers. Joe Wheelwright, arch-intuitive, almost put paid to Shaw's
literary career in the Mall – not because he didn't like the book, but
because Wheelwright the driver (with an inferior sensation function)
nearly made contact with Shaw the pedestrian.

One day I was driving in my 1921 Fiat touring car, and I was
bowling along at about twenty-four or twenty-five miles an hour,
on my way to Barts, and I went round Buckingham Palace, doing
my reverse trip from the Mall into the maelstrom of Trafalgar
Square. Anyway, suddenly I saw right in front of me a very tall
thin man in knickerbockers, with a white beard down to his navel,
and it was George Bernard Shaw, and I was about to hit him. So I
switched very quickly, without looking at all, and went up on the
pavement and threaded my way through several pedestrians,
missed a hydrant or two, and finally got back on the road again –
and I looked around, and there was Shaw, and he was shaking his
fist at me. So I've had some connection with the Master – not a
very happy one from his point of view.

It might seem impossible to imagine a more complete mismatch of
typology than Joe and Jane Wheelwright; but it was Jung's observation
that the attraction of opposites is natural, and almost automatic.

For instance, it is very often the case – or I might say it is almost a
rule, but I don't want to make too many rules in order not to be
schematic – that an introvert marries an extrovert for
compensation, or another type marries a counter-type to
complement himself. [Houston No. 2]

The idea of complementarity, however, is often accompanied by the
experience of conflict – and this was the case with the Wheelwrights:

Jane Wheelwright: Lots of conflict. I didn't know what was going on
half the time, with him. And he was baffled by me. We had some
real Donnybrooks.

Joe Wheelwright: We were saying very nasty things to each other and doing an awful lot of misunderstanding – and my relationship to Jane was then, as it has been always, the central fact of my life I think, and so I wanted to do something about it.

What Joe and Jane Wheelwright did was to read Jung's book *Psychological Types*.

Joe Wheelwright: I've never known anything that was as illuminating as that book was. Suddenly we'd got tools to work with, instead of trying to exterminate each other, why we could understand much better why we were the way we were, and why we came on as we did come on and so on and so forth. And it was enormously helpful.

Jane Wheelwright: Oh, it was a revelation. It was absolutely revolutionary in our lives.

In any relationship, it seems, opposites attract, causing the heights of passion and the depths of mutual irritation and distaste. Jung himself made no overwhelming claim for the system in itself:

It is just a sort of skeleton to which you have to add the flesh. It is a means to an end. It only makes sense, such a scheme, when you deal with practical cases.

Over fifty years, the Wheelwrights have had practical experience of Jung's system of typology, and how it can help to give insight and understanding of our own individual character and the dynamics of personal relationships.

Joe Wheelwright: Well it will certainly give your chances of a long-term love relationship, it'll enhance them immeasurably. In fact I don't know how people who don't know something about types manage. In fact there's no question at all that our marriage I think would have probably had to break up if we'd gone on in blissful ignorance. So what really brought me into Jungian psychology was the type stuff, and I've been hipped on it ever since. Everybody dodges me when they see me coming because they know I'm gonna make a speech pretty soon about types.

Of course, the interaction between the type of a patient and the type of the analyst can be an important factor in their relationship. Joe Wheelwright attributed to his intuition the instantaneous connection to Jung that he experienced 'after eight to eleven minutes'. But Jung, more of a thinking type himself, was less likely to respond to an 'intuitive' appeal than to a theoretical argument. Jane Wheelwright suffered from severe depression after the birth of their son in London in the 1930s. According to Joe, she had never fully integrated her wilderness upbringing with a smart boarding-school education; or her roots in 'anything-goes' California with the stuffy social attitudes of between-the-wars London. Joe was convinced she should start her own analysis with Jung. But he was overwhelmed with patients; how could he be persuaded? As Joe tells the story, it became an exercise in typology:

> I came over with her to Zurich, and she stayed with Carey Baynes and I went to see Jung, to bully him or persuade him or seduce him into taking Jane on. I told him a sob story, in my 'feeling' way. I said 'You know it's terrible, we've got two children and this thing is so urgent, something has to happen, it's a tremendous crisis, and you're the only person I know who could take a deep breath and go down into the collective unconscious, which is where she's residing at the moment, and take her by the hand and bring her back so she can rejoin the rest of us – and so if you can't take her it'll be a real tragedy.'
>
> Well, he had a way of letting you know when you were working with him, how things were going. He has a little round brass thing – he smoked a pipe continuously – and he got hold of an infernal pipe, which had little aluminium circles on it, and all the spit collected in these circles, and if he was bored, he'd pull his pipe apart and pour spit into this thing – and then you knew things were going very badly and he was bored out of his skull. He began pouring a lot of spit, and I thought 'Oh God, Oh Jesus, now what shall I do?' Then I thought 'I'll hoist him with his own petard.' So I converted, and I presented the problem to him in theoretical terms – the problem of the very primitive stuff in the archetypal world, and the orderly world outside, and the personal unconscious. My first mushy one, where I'd done it out of a feeling function, speaking feeling language, he'd said 'I might be able to see her for an hour in a month or so.' I said 'Oh but it's urgent!' No good. More spit. But when I did *this*, he interrupted me after about five minutes, and he said 'Come on, let's go downstairs to Marie-Jeanne Schmidt (she was his secretary). I'll see her tomorrow morning,

I'm sure she can shift people around' – and so he did.

About six months later I came back for a short visit – I got a break in medical school – and I went to one of his seminars, and after the seminar he said 'Wheelwright, I'd like to talk to you' and so I touched my forelock and said 'Yes sir!' and he said 'Well I suppose you think you're pretty clever, don't you?' And I said 'Who, sir? Me, sir?' He said 'Yes, sir! You, sir!' 'Oh,' I said, 'You mean all that type stuff?' 'Exactly,' he said. I said, 'Well, it worked, didn't it?' He said, 'Sometimes I wish I'd never formulated all that stuff. Well, you know, it's really all right, as a matter of fact it's going very well. But I really had to let you have it, because I was afraid you were getting inflated, and thinking you really had twisted the old man's leg, and you didn't.' But I said 'Didn't I?' And he said 'I mean, *you did!*' He was marvellous. That was one of his engaging things, he could hear something from a pipsqueak and take it.

John Beebe is another San Francisco analyst who is hipped on types – and on movies, too. As a life-long film buff, he likes to employ Jung's psychological concepts to understand the dramatic tension of a film. In the popular 1988 movie *Broadcast News*, directed by James Brooks, three principal characters, all TV news journalists, represent a typological love triangle of infinite complexity. To John Beebe, psychological types really make sense on screen:

All this typology seems kind of grey and drab until you go to a movie like *Broadcast News*. There you see a rather clear example of an extroverted thinking type woman [Holly Hunter] who is a high-powered television news producer. She is pushing her principles to people who are not really relating to what she's saying, and she's losing her audience. She doesn't have the touch that it needs. Who does she fall in love with? The William Hurt character, a news presenter who is brought in to increase the ratings by his charming good looks. He's about as clear an example of an introverted feeling type as you'd want on film – a very quiet, reserved man with a hidden gentlemanliness and a kind of grace – and a real insecurity about his thinking. So that they become an immediate love-match.

Yet on the side there's a third character [Albert Brooks] – who is an introverted thinking type. He's a brilliant man who can parse out sentences and work crossword puzzles backwards in his mind and do all kinds of pyrotechnics of thinking in an introverted way, but has no grace. And as soon as he gets before a camera, he is dour and sweaty and difficult and completely lacking in extroverted feeling. To Brooks, William Hurt, the introverted feeling type, is just the devil. To Holly Hunter, the extroverted thinking type, Hurt's an absolutely marvellous man – until he disappoints her by not acting exactly according to principle. He decides there's nothing wrong with putting a tear in his eye, after the fact, because he felt like crying anyway. For her that's faking the news. She completely sacrifices her feeling relationship for a principle; he sacrifices a principle for the sake of feeling – and they never get it together. The opposites are so different, they can't come together, and that's so like life.

Besides typology theory, another major plank of Jung's work which refers to relating and relationship is the idea of *animus* and *anima* – the 'contrasexual inferior archetype' within each person. We know that gender is not a black-and-white, absolute question – that biologically every person has a mixed genetic inheritance of both male and female genes. But almost everyone is clearly masculine or feminine; Jung's inquiry was to consider how, in psychological terms, the feminine psychological bit of a man, or the masculine psychological bit of a woman, expresses itself and influences her or his behaviour – particularly towards members of the opposite sex. In Jung's own words:

The anima is an archetypal form, expressing the fact that a man has a minority of feminine or female genes. That is something that doesn't appear or disappear in him; that is constantly present and it works as a female in a man; therefore already in the sixteenth century the humanists have discovered that man has an 'anima' and that each man carries his female with himself, they said. So that is not a modern invention. The same is the case with the animus; that is a masculine image in a woman's mind which is sometimes quite conscious – sometimes it is not conscious, but it is called into life the moment that woman meets a man who says the right things, and then because he says it, it is all true, and he is the fellow no matter what he is. Those are particularly well-founded archetypes, those two. And there you can lay hands on the basis as it were, of the archetype. They are extremely well-defined. [Houston No. 1]

The British analyst Andrew Samuels is one of many who has wrestled with the practical implication of what the animus and anima really mean:

> It is not about a man having a little woman in his head and vice versa – only at the most simplistic possible level is that what it's about. What it's about is this: each of us has difficulty in gaining access to our full potential – it's in some sense foreign to us, other to us. What more profoundly psychological and symbolical way of meeting up with what is 'other' to you than doing so with that other represented by a being with another anatomy? So that the woman represents for the man what he isn't yet, but could become; and the man for the woman stands for her potential, expressed in symbolic form.

Using the everyday meaning of 'archetype', the anima in a man is an archetypal woman – a kind of template for all the women he encounters, which will be heavily influenced, whether he likes it or not, by the most influential woman in his life: his own mother. A great deal of the conflicts which arise – whether real or imagined – between wife and mother-in-law revolve around the invisible partner in the equation: the anima. This feminine image also tends to dictate the style or language in which a man is capable of behaving in ways which are other than stereotypically male. And he will project on to his girlfriends, or wife, or his mother herself, all sorts of psychological assumptions which may be more true of his own inner life than any aspect of theirs.

> *Robert Johnson:* Dr Jung felt that the anima in a man was the feminine minority of his character, which is much larger or occupies a greater percentage of a man than he's generally comfortable in acknowledging. The anima generally in a man consists of a softer, feminine, generally more feeling side of his nature.

> *Bani Shorter:* The animus to me is one of the most significant concepts that has arisen in Jungian psychology. It speaks of the function that connects a woman with her deepest self and personhood, her creativity, the unformed that's forming as she ages. Her work, her word, her ideals, her self, her person.

Jane Wheelwright: The animus is a male complex in the female psyche, and it appears in dreams as a man, as a male animal or whatever is male. And, it's an asset in its right place. But the old traditional idea of 'Men know best' has somehow geared women not to trust their own opinions or trust how they see things – they're scared away from that.

A woman with courage, a woman who's adventurous, a woman who speaks her mind, is supported by the animus. But if the animus gets out in front, then she's a headache, she's just miserable. The whole point is that the female ego has to be in charge of the animus. Now that's not a generally accepted idea because of the old hangover of, 'You lean on men and men'll somehow make your life interesting.' And you just lose all your own ideas, or innovations, or creativity. And I think a lot of women are scared out of being who they are and doing whatever is important to them still. You see a few that are kind of daring. They sometimes end up alone, because men are not used to that kind of competition.

Andrew Samuels: A general example would be the whole question of a woman's relation to her aggression and self-assertion, and the difficulties she might have in that because of our culture and her upbringing. If she comes to me, the analyst, and says 'My partner is assertive, aggressive, domineering' – or even more likely, 'You the analyst are assertive, aggressive, domineering,' then it's possible over time and sensitively to enable her to take back that projection, to see that there is a self-assertion and aggression in her, that it's not bad, it's not masculine either in the sense of something that men have and women don't. It's absolutely, inalienably part of her as a woman. But for the reasons I've given – her background and upbringing and the way our culture does these things, she has to leave it in the man.

In the opening scene of the Alfred Hitchcock film *Notorious*, Ingrid Bergman is surrounded by a crowd of photographers, reporters and plain-clothes policemen in a courtroom where her father has been convicted as a Nazi spy. Every single person other than Bergman is male. John Beebe interprets the film in part as a drama of the animus; played out in the conflict between one woman and many men.

I think Hitchcock was busy creating an emotional effect with imagery, and that he knew with his feeling function when the image worked and when he had what he wanted.

Notice the way the woman is badgered by a series of men. All the people holding cameras are men, and all the people who speak to her are men, and so you immediately get the image of a woman in a vulnerable position, badgered by a group or a series of men. Now there is the perfect image of what Jung means by the animus, the way the animus attacks the woman and the way it's often symbolized by a multiple figure or a crowd, and the way it moves in on the woman and judges her.

Now the camera is on the lower left-hand of the screen. Now that's the view through which we see her. Then gradually we realize that in the lower left-hand, there is now one man whose viewpoint we have, and he's a dark kind of unknown figure. And he's the very image of all this criticism, all this suspicion, all this anxiety. And look at the way she keeps looking at him as she drinks, and wondering – she's half attracted to him, half suspicious of him, wonders is he a policeman. The policeman, by the way, is a very common image in dreams of the animus – the man who's kind of investigating the woman.

This is the experience of so many women, of constantly being under an attack – Do I look OK? Is my reputation OK? The camera turns and finally he becomes a personality in his own right. Indeed he's Cary Grant. And so suddenly this anonymous critical collective perspective takes on a human personification, and actually an attractive personification. So that the very critic, the very thing that's most attacking the woman is also somehow the thing that's most erotically exciting, and the most interesting, and the most energetic. And there in a nutshell you get the problem of the animus.

Just as typological opposites attract each other, so perhaps the embodiment of the critical perspective within ourselves is the image of our perfect partner. Certainly Jung himself was well aware that the force of the archetype – when embodied in a human form that answers roughly to the right description – can blind us to the realization that 'Mr or Ms Right' is the last person on earth we should become involved with.

You see the archetype is a force. It has an autonomy and it can suddenly seize you. It is like a seizure. Falling in love at first sight is something like that. You see, you have a certain image in yourself, without knowing it, of woman, of *the* woman. Then you see that girl, or at least a good imitation of your type, and instantly you get a seizure and you are gone. And afterwards you may discover that it was a hell of a mistake. So you see a man is quite capable, or intelligent enough to see that the woman of his choice was no choice – he has been captured; he sees that she is no good at all, that she is a hell of a business, and he tells me so, and he says, 'For God's sake doctor, help me to get rid of that woman' – and he can't, he is like clay in her fingers. That is the archetype; that is the archetype of the anima, and he thinks it is all his soul, you know. [Houston No. 1]

The concept of animus and anima stands alongside the system of typology as a way of understanding both the pain and the delights of relationship.

Marie-Louise von Franz: Love at first sight is generally full of illusions. And I've heard couples confess to each other, now we are married twenty-five years but we don't know or understand each other at all.

Robert Johnson: Man insists upon making some outer figure, generally a flesh and blood woman, bear his anima for him. That is, he mediates the outer world by way of his anima, instead of using her inside, where she belongs. This produces more suffering and more upsets and more pain than any other single thing that I know about.

Adolf Guggenbuhl-Craig: What happens in analysis, is that two people face each other. But in marriage, you *really* face each other. You are bound, you have no way to escape. You might have, if you're lucky, forty years to face each other and that's of course a tremendous confrontation with yourself, facing another person for forty years. It really means that you face yourself too, that both psyches face themselves in all the depths and all the heights, and therefore it's one of the most concentrated, one of the most intense ways to be able just to find yourself.

Robert Johnson: Hardly anybody in our world knows the difference between loving someone and being in love with someone. We have the language for it, but we don't have the concept for it, collectively speaking. To love someone is to draw close to that person as a human being. To be in love with someone is to make a divinity out of one's beloved, which neither he nor she, nor oneself, can ever live up to.

Ultimately, psychological theory – whether Jung's or anybody else's – is of purely academic interest unless it directly approaches and describes the reality of how people experience life, both consciously and unconsciously – in the street, at work, and in their dreams. Typology, introversion and extroversion, animus and anima all have a tinge of the theoretical about them; but the testimony of many people indicates that they are also real, true, and useful. Jung claimed nothing for his work other than that it was the product of his efforts to help people out of their psychological pain and into an understanding of themselves and of their relationships and difficulties. As Andrew Samuels concludes:

> I believe that this contribution of Jung's, animus and anima theory, is not only of immense use in understanding relationship difficulties – and the joys and richness of relationships, but it's actually something, as with all the best ideas, that people, ordinary people, are doing anyway. That's a real acid test of all psychological theory. If it really turns out to be a description of what's happening, it's good theory. And I think men and women know, often know quite consciously, that they are finding and retrieving bits of themselves in their relationship with the other person.

Jung's view of relationship did not only concern the way individuals related to each other. He was also interested in the way the individual related to the inferior aspect of his own personality and, at the other end of the spectrum, the way in which a society or culture as a whole relates to its collective, inferior side. Thus the questions of how a patriarchy treats feminine values, and how both men and women integrate their feminine or masculine inferior aspects, both arose for Jung.

Although today Jung is credited with being a sort of pre-feminist thinker, in ascribing importance and value to a vaguely-defined 'feminine way', it appears that his consideration of feminine psychology was by no means voluntary – at least according to Dr von Franz:

> He told me that when he was very young he thought women to be something very strange. To his horror eighty per cent of his patients were women – and he found out that he didn't understand the ABC about women and they were just strange animals. Then he

took the trouble, he said 'If they all come to me, that's a sign of fate, against my taste I have to understand.' He had dreams that he should become a woman – that is the old archetypal dream of the shaman who wears woman's clothes, to integrate the other sex and descend into the other world. So he assimilated his own femininity. That naturally took him out of any patriarchal one-sidedness.

It was Jung's view that masculine, patriarchal values have produced a Western culture – both secular and religious – which neglects the soul, and the balancing influence of the feminine psyche. Andrew Samuels:

Jung intuited an imbalance in Western culture in favour of one whole style of psychological and behavioural functioning, in favour of analysis, in favour of logic, in favour of external achievement, in favour of social hierarchy and so forth. He asked: What happened to the other side? If you like, to the other cerebral hemisphere and all that it deals with. Holistic ways of perceiving things. Being rather than doing. What happened to 'Love thine enemy'? What happened to 'Turn the other cheek'? Those are feminine things in a way, if you'll pardon my using a word I don't like. What Jung is struggling to do, and I think it's a kind of political project with him, is rectify an imbalance – and unfortunately his project is marred by the thoughtless; less conflation of the kinds of qualities that one might list as being 'feminine', with the word 'feminine' as referring to women. I think the feminine stands against organization, for example against organized religion. It stands against hierarchy, for example class systems. It stands against an overdependence on logic and rationality, so that the hard sciences are challenged. It stands against an excessive dependency on technology and so it espouses natural issues, an interest in ecology, in the environment. In other words, the feminine principle needs to be understood not as some kind of neutral discovery of Jung's, but as a political movement of the unconscious, with a programme, just as any other political movement has a programme.

The twentieth century has seen the rise of an overt political move-ment, in the form of feminism, or the 'women's movement'. When Jung began working with patients, questions of women's role in society, and of their getting the vote, were only beginning to reach public consciousness. It is interesting to note that Emma Jung predicted the dramatic effect birth control was to have on women's changing role in society. Bani Shorter, an American analyst who lives and works in London, sees Jung's attitude in the light of the influences of the times in which he was living:

> He entered into reflection both conscious and unconscious at a time when culturally the role of women was changing and shifting, people began to protest and wanted the vote and so on. So he contributed to something which has become a movement of our times.

It is her view that Freud's case-load – a high proportion of women suffering from hysteria – was equally a sign of the times.

> They symbolized what I think was woman's inability to adjust herself to the demands that were being made upon her at that particular time, and a portent of the future, actually, because they could not embody that which they felt was needed, or demanded of them, as women.

Jungians argue that Jung's major achievement has been to reinstate the neglected aspects of the human psyche – the inner, the shadow, the feminine, and the physical body itself. This is not a contest – it is a reinstatement, a restoration of balance. Mrs Shorter considers that the deepest underlying difference between women and men can be expressed as a contrast between 'process' and 'goal'. The masculine-dominated, patriarchal, materialist society is about doing, acting and achieving; and it ignores and oppresses the invaluable 'feminine' ways of being, processing, and enabling.

> We women embody life. You men act upon life. That resonates psychologically, which means that we are constantly working with it in terms of our aims, our ideals, our understandings and perceptions of what it's like to be ourselves now and in life. We as women are attuned to process by way of our own bodies. Rhythmically and constantly. And what we later act, we conceive and generate appropriately, in tune with our natural rhythm. Whereas a man goes forth to meet and to act upon whatever comes to him. I think there has been a tremendous gift of women to our times and the future by this very awareness of process that we have contributed; that goal is not foremost, but process is continual, and in the process itself we discover our meaning.

Baroness Vera von der Heydt expresses the idea thus:

I think that Jung was instrumental in showing the value of the feminine way of thinking, or the moon-thinking, as a complementary factor to the more direct and searing intellects of man.

Dr von Franz points out that as patriarchy undermines the feminine ways of being, so it is alien or uncomfortable for the archetypal man to adapt to the feminine way:

It's terribly difficult for a man to be confronted with problems and not to have the masculine reaction that one has to do something about it, and instead to have the 'Chinese' reaction – let it happen, and watch.

One of the events which most impressed Jung was the declaration by the Vatican in the mid-1950s of the Doctrine of the Assumption of the Virgin Mary – adding a long-neglected feminine aspect to the masculine trinity of Father, Son and Holy Ghost. As Reverend Don Cupitt comments:

He thought the scientific materialist self had lost touch with its symbol-making, its intuitive, its more feminine side. He thought that scientific industrial man suffered great psychic distress and frustration because the religious side of our nature was repressed. Jung was trying to speak to that. To that extent he saw himself as a religious teacher or a sage for industrial civilization. He was trying to show us a new way to religion.

Jung studied both history and anthropology with an appetite which defies belief. He therefore was able to observe the yawning gap between modern Western culture's attitude towards the feminine, and that of earlier times or other cultures. In historical terms, one unchanging aspect of the feminine is women's physical and cultural involvement in what can be called 'life's mysteries' – from birth to death.

In one traditionally feminine activity – weaving – one may observe an allegory of what women do, psychologically. By keeping a firm grasp on the different threads or strands in their life and intertwining them, all the different roles and tasks – mother, worker, wife, friend, lover – can be given their rightful place in the creation of the overall pattern of life.

In Navajo culture, in Arizona, the women weavers inherit their designs, based on healing sand-paintings, from their own mothers and grandmothers. The designs are never drawn, because it is somehow the expression of the weaver's feminine role – not something to be taught or overtly learned.

More unexpectedly, in the Zurich apartment of a Swiss psychotherapist, Dr Anne-Marie Klingler, an immense loom stands alongside the chairs where she and her patients sit. Dr Klingler weaves dramatic, oversized garments with archetypal titles: 'Earth', 'Mist', 'Rage', 'Night' – which present different appearances and impressions to different observers. She says it has become:

> ... an absolute necessity for me. When I can't weave, and I don't have an idea what to weave, I get depressed. Weaving is like breathing for me. All of a sudden I get an idea or an image of what I would like to weave, and first I carry that around in me for a while, and all of a sudden it's ready to go on the loom, and I do it. And then afterwards I find out why I did it.

For Anne-Marie Klingler the process of weaving seems to be as important as the finished product. In fact, one feels that the beauty of her finished work is attributable to her respect for the products of her imagination and the act of weaving.

> When you embroider or when you paint, you can go in every direction. You start somewhere, you can go up or down or right or left. When you weave you can absolutely not do anything but build up. You start at the bottom and you build up and somehow for me that sequence seems to be important.

Anne-Marie Klingler and Bani Shorter are close friends; the latter wrote the notes for an exhibition of Anne-Marie's cloaks, at a small gallery in Kusnacht. Referring to Jung's ominous view that 'the world hangs on a thin thread', Mrs Shorter argues that it has always been woman's work to weave, and to continue weaving the thread of life into rich patterns.

Another woman analyst in Zurich, Dr Sonja Marjasch, sees weaving as a form of folk art which has always been undervalued – because it is woman's work. Nowadays, however, such work has become 'collectable', as one can see from the exorbitant price tags on the patchwork quilts and primitive American folk art which is for sale in a shop up the cobbled street from Anne-Marie Klingler's studio. Dr Marjasch believes that people are buying folk art as a compensation for the sterile materialism of much Western life – in order to possess the feminine time and care put into a product which displays the process. Dr Marjasch feels however that this somehow misses the point. When a woman sews a quilt:

> ... it not only satisfies the need of the woman for a blanket, but also it becomes a vessel to carry her emotions. There are beautiful descriptions of women who worked for months, maybe years on a certain quilt, and then years later she tells her grandchild what emotions went into that quilt. These patterns hold all the hate and the love and the upset and they are really like a vessel where things can be transformed. When I studied the history of quilts I was astonished to discover that in Cleveland, the first speech for women's right to vote was at the church quilting-bee.

Jungian analysts who examine cultures other than the European, or American, find no lack of examples of women (and the feminine) representing a quite different role. The San Francisco analyst Donald Sandner, who has studied the Navajo Indians in Arizona for more than fifteen years, has observed a strong and authoritative role for women.

> In Navajo culture, of course, one of the things that strikes you when you enter it is the great power that women have. It's really what you call a matriarchal culture. There are two primary deities – the sun, which is masculine and Changing Woman, and certainly she is right up there with the sun, if not a little higher, and she's a woman. And she represents all the seasons, the changes of life. She represents all of nature and life that holds you. And, in general, the powers of women are derived from her.
> Navajo women have animus energy, but they also have great femininity. I mean the feminine is powerful and contains the animus. You have no doubt about that, their power, their effectiveness, and yet it's contained within the great feminine. It's not a kind of imitation of a man, it's a woman, but it's a powerful woman. The minute you meet women in that culture, you get a different feeling from them. There's a different sign or body language. They don't do anything submissive, they don't make the submissive gesture. They make the prideful and equal gesture.

In the widest span of human mythology, the world of nature is associated with the feminine; and just as Jungian analysts follow Jung's lead in seeking a feminine balance in the patriarchal world, and in the psychology of the individual male, so they tend to be concerned about the materialistic rape of the environment – a conflict of imposed goal over natural processes. As Dr Dieter Baumann, Jung's grandson, complains:

> I've nothing against extraversion: but against that conquering greedy extraversion of wanting to dominate and exploit matter.... In other words, a lack of religious attitude towards the Great Mother, and matter is not considered as a part of the divinity.

Using a quite different frame of reference, John Beebe argues that one can find evidence of the undervaluation of the feminine way not only in general psychological patterns of society, but also in the prevalence of violent, criminal attacks on women. In movie terms, the shocking portrayal of such incidents – for example, in the shower scene of the Hitchcock film *Psycho* – expresses for him an allegory of the tragic destruction of the feminine in the world.

> Hitchcock's a sort of Aeschylus who looks at the human condition and isn't afraid to show us the dark stuff, and I think what he's showing us is what a bad time the feminine has had in a patriarchal society and how the feminine is regularly cut down, not just by her own shame and guilt, but by a tremendous psychotic attack. He wants us to see this injury to the feminine and to the anima and I think he wants us to be shocked by it, to see it and to be unable to forget it. It's a kind of guilt we can't wash away. Our guilt is very complicated because we're also fascinated with the process. Of course we've been watching the feminine cut down as trees get cut down and rivers get polluted and everything gets injured and bureaucratized that's feminine – for a long time in a passive kind of fascinated way. Just as we watch that film, horrified, but feeling impotent, that we can't do anything, and caught in the grip of a kind of depressive apathy, while we watch a paranoid scenario.

If it is a sign of real influence for a thinker's work to become not just a part of the intellectual currency of the age, but to become a cliché, then the deep concern of Jung to consider and reflect upon relationship and relatedness is another clear sign of his stature in late twentieth-century culture. Whatever the medium, from quilts to movies to marriage, relating stands at the heart of a useable psychological system.

7

Travels in Time and Space

For the visitor fortunate enough to enter Jung's library in Kusnacht, the bookshelves bear witness to a massive intellectual and cultural journey through the religions, mythologies, fairy-tales and fantasies of a multiplicity of cultures. C. G. Jung read the psychological history of mankind in half-a-dozen languages; and when he had read enough, and dreamed enough too, he began to travel in search of evidence for the connections he had detected in all humanity, regardless of culture, location or period. His discovery of 'the collective unconscious' began with the dream in which he found himself descending through the floors of a house, reaching older and more primitive scenes the further he went.

He felt that he detected a deep and hidden truth about the human psyche: that its functioning was essentially according to patterns which were ultimately *human*, more than they were distinguished by any other feature – male or female, primitive or sophisticated, European, Oriental or African. To pursue the analogy of the psyche with the computer, one might suggest that the word processor on which this is typed somehow contains information which no one has put into it: and of course, it does – it has been manufactured to behave as a word processor. The collective unconscious, perhaps, manufactures each individual to behave as a human: to react to particular circumstances according to a basic set of psychological instincts and attitudes.

If this were to prove true, it would be necessary to find evidence for the identity of psychological patterns, or images, or behaviours, in a variety of different cultures. Jung called these patterns 'archetypes'. We use the word freely, to mean something rather stronger than 'typical'. The Greek word, which Jung puts into common parlance, meant the 'original pattern or stamp'. In his studies and his travels, his journeys in time and space, Jung established that the archetypes do repeat from culture to culture; that people dream of images which 'belong' to another continent; that religions at opposite ends of the globe attribute the same powers to the same animals or human symbols.

The collective unconscious represents a psychological database that is common to the basic matters of human existence. According to Robert Johnson, whose 'old man's dream' concerned not the imagery of his native Oregon, but a succession of Buddhas, the theme is central in Jung's work.

The concept of the collective unconscious is absolutely essential for understanding Jung. I can't say it was his invention, but it was his discovery. The collective unconscious is that set of building blocks from which human reality is made. It's as if there is this great reservoir outside of time and space, patterns or energy – from which everything is drawn or everything is made. Reality consists of patterns made upon this gridwork, and like a gigantic spider-web, if you pluck one part of that web, other parts of it respond. One could call the collective unconscious that web, the stuff from which reality is made. Jung discovered it in the unconscious of his own patients and in his own extraordinary experiences, or dreams and visions and also in the mythology which fascinated him – the fact that mythology from every part of the world carries so many elements in common fascinated him. He is the first to say that none of this is new to him, but he takes credit for having presented it in language assimilable to a twentieth-century citizen.

Jung revived for a modern audience the meaning and value of archaic wisdoms – from myth and legend. He read about these themes at first; then he travelled. Observing the lack of a sense of meaning in the lives of so many of his patients, he wanted to get beyond his Swiss, European homeland to gain first-hand experience of cultures where meaning was still connected to daily life. Such connections are about the place of ritual in social life; the importance of a myth by which people live, and the negative consequences when the myth loses its hold. In all these strands of cultural, anthropological and psychological research, Jung saw the archetypes as a common feature – reminding him of the basic hypothesis of the collective unconscious, which he described to Richard Evans in the 'Houston Interview'.

You know what a behaviour pattern is – the way in which a weaver-bird builds his nest – that is an inherited form in him which he will apply. Man has, of course, an inherited scheme of functioning. You see, his liver, his heart, all his organs, and his brain will always function in a certain way, following its pattern. You and I have a great difficulty seeing it because we cannot compare. There are no other similar beings like man that are articulate that could give an account of their functioning. It is a fact that people develop in their psychical development on the same principle as they develop in the body. Why should we assume that it is a different principle?

The dynamic energy of the archetype – an image, an instinct, a pattern of behaviour – can perhaps explain the force of a 'big dream', a mythological story, the symbol of a snake or a serpent, or the universal impact of a work of religious art. For Dr Joe Wheelwright, the American analyst, an experience of the collective unconscious occurred at the National Gallery in London, in the 1930s.

They had on loan an El Greco – one of those greenish Christs either just getting up to be nailed or just being unnailed – and I was totally engrossed in this painting, just entranced. And suddenly the most frightful waves of garlic began to pour over me, and it wasn't coming from below me, it was coming from over me. Well I'm not used to being breathed on from above, at six foot six, and so I looked around and there was a Sikh, eleven feet tall approximately, with a mauve turban which made him that much taller, and he was liberally laced with garlic. He was transported. He was just as hooked on this thing as I was. And I thought my God, that's strange. It got him too. And then I looked around, and there was a Chinese couple, and there was a German couple, and there was an Italian couple, and there was a smattering of Americans and British. And I thought, if anybody wants proof that there's such a thing as the collective unconscious! They didn't know the difference between Christ and a hollyhock, and cared less, many of them. But they were absolutely held. That's why El Greco was so good. He was painting at a level that was not only below the personal and below the cultural, national level, but was even deeper, it was a universal language. The idea of the collective unconscious became very real for me.

The collective unconscious is illustrated not only by the universal impact of a single image – but also by the recurrence in different cultures and conditions of similar themes or images. Almost every mythological tradition has a classic story of a hero confronting dangers (and often dragons) – or a half-human, half-animal 'trickster' to whom life's irritating flaws and confusions can be attributed. In the most technological areas of modern life, it is commonplace to hear of the 'gremlins'; and all our computers have 'bugs'.

Jung's travels were explorations into unfamiliar psychic territory. Distance and the difference in cultural patterns gave Jung a sense of perspective on the civilized Western psyche. When he first travelled outside Switzerland it was to the USA, 'the land of unlimited possibilities' as he called it. It was here that he first encountered non-European patients, and began to explore his inklings of the collective unconscious. The dream of the house with successive, older levels took place during his first trip to the USA, when both he and Sigmund Freud had been invited to give lectures at Clark University in Worcester, Massachusetts. Jung had many American patients in Zurich, some of them wealthy and influential, and their support for his ideas introduced him to the medical-intellectual community of the East Coast.

In 1912, Jung returned to the USA for a trip which began with a far from successful public lecture in the impressive ballroom of the Plaza Hotel – one of New York's most exalted venues. An enthusiastic. but incompetent volunteer undertook to operate the slide-projector to illustrate Jung's lecture – and the audience became increasingly restive as slides appeared out-of-order, upside-down and back to front. One of his professional followers in the American psychiatric community was Dr William Alanson White, then Superintendent of St Elizabeth's Hospital in Washington D.C.

In 1913 White and a colleague inaugurated a *Psychoanalytic Review* of which the first five issues published Jung's 'The Theory of Psychoanalysis' in instalments. But a year earlier, Dr White invited Jung to come to Washington. St Elizabeth's was the principal federal psychiatric hospital of the USA – until 1987, when it passed into the jurisdiction of the District of Columbia. Jung accepted the invitation to meet and examine Negro patients immediately. He wanted to discover whether black patients there had the same sorts of dreams as white Europeans – a question no one had ever asked before.

The patients at St Elizabeth's today, exist in a quite different culture from that of seventy-five years ago: many of their psychiatric problems are intertwined with drug-addiction, alcoholism and sheer poverty. The 'insane' patients of 1912 had never been asked about their dreams, but when Jung talked to them, he found that the dreams, fantasies and artwork of Negro patients contained images that matched those of his European patients' dreams, and even the symbolism of one ancient Greek mythological text. It was here that Jung heard a striking remark by a woman patient:

> I cannot forget that crazy old Negro Mammy who told me 'God is working in me like a clock – funny and serious.' By 'clock' seems to be meant something precise and regular, even monotonous; by 'funny and serious' compensating irrational events and aspects – a humorous seriousness expressing the playful and formidable nature of fateful experiences. [Letter to Father Victor White, 10 April 1954]

It was the contact he had with patients at St Elizabeth's which gave rise to Jung's later conclusion about the collective unconscious:

> In all probability the most important mythological motifs are common to all times and races; I have in fact, been able to demonstrate a whole series of motifs from Greek mythology in the dreams and fantasies of pure-bred Negroes suffering from mental disorders. [*Collected Works* vol 6, par. 443]

Jung did not fail to mark his gratitude to Dr White – both for publishing his work, and inviting him to meet the patients, and to see some of their artwork, at the hospital in Washington. Some years later, he sent him a gift which indirectly referred to the 'mythological motifs'. The handsome bust of a Greek goddess, shipped from a studio in Munich, now stands in the hospital museum at St Elizabeth's.

This was the first of many important encounters with different cultures: Jung repeatedly returned to the USA, and in 1925 accompanied a Swiss friend to Tunis, visited England and then embarked on his longest adventure into the psychological Dark Continent of Africa. Later he visited India and Ceylon. His assumptions about the people he would meet in tribal societies were very much those of a nineteenth century man: he was meeting, in Africa, 'primitives' whose lack of 'civilization' Jung regarded as an asset for the purposes of his research. The American analyst James Hillman puts these journeys into the perspective of Jung's intellectual expectations:

Remember Jung always has a theory in his actions, and the theory was that the cultural overlay disguises archetypes more than it reveals them. So he doesn't talk about Shakespeare, he prefers to talk about Africans – because his theory is that the more archaic or the more primitive or the less developed a place is, the more the archetype will show itself naturally and freely. Therefore in the same way – this is all part of nineteenth century thinking in a way – the crazy person reveals the archetype more than the sane person with a cultural overlay. It's a questionable idea, but I think that was part of what Jung was doing with his travels.

Jung expressed highly innovative ideas in the languages of his time – which sometimes failed him by seeming simplistic, or to today's ear, naive. He referred to 'primitive' Africans – but held the primitive in high respect, as it was primitive man who was most intimate with nature and instinct. He regarded the loss of this connection as a part of the collective tragedy of the Western world. Jung's cross-cultural research was unscientific; but he attributed great importance to his travels and encounters with other races, which moved him deeply, and enabled him to look back upon the European psyche, and his own, as if from outside.

We always require an outside point to stand on, in order to apply the lever of criticism. This is especially so in psychology, where by the nature of the material we are much more subjectively involved than in any other science. [*Memories, Dreams, Reflections*, p. 246]

In travelling to Africa to find a psychic observation post outside the sphere of the European, I unconsciously wanted to find that part of my personality which had become invisible under the influence and pressure of being European. [*Memories, Dreams, Reflections*, p. 244]

Through my acquaintance with many Americans, and my trips to and in America, I have obtained an enormous amount of insight into the European character. [*Memories, Dreams, Reflections*, p. 247]

The travels gave him empirical evidence – from the reality of the psyche of other races and his own inner identification with them – that the collective unconscious truly existed, transcending racial, geographical and temporal boundaries. Attempts to define the collective unconscious vary – it is not an observable entity which can be described. It is said to be, for example: 'intimately bound up with the symptomatic behaviour of all people, irrespective of their personal idiosyncrasies and cultural conditioning'.

While some Jungian analysts concern themselves principally with the 'personal unconscious', others find the comparative cultural range of the idea of the collective unconscious stirs their greatest enthusiasm for Jung.

Andrew Samuels: It's the relation of past, present and future, but specifically in terms of ideas. I think what I get from my reading of Jung is that in a way all new ideas are old ideas. This linking up of the cutting edge of psychological investigation with archaic thinking, with a kind of mental archaeology, is fascinating to me, and it's important – because it does away with the hubris or inflation of there being lots and lots of breakthroughs. And because the continuity of human ideation, thought, culture, seems to me very important, particularly in our age which in every sense is atomizing. We need to know that we're not actually different from what we were hundreds of thousands of years ago.

Joseph Henderson: Right away the thing that spoke to me most strongly was what he said about the nature of the collective unconscious and the archetypes – archetypal images. That spoke to me immediately, even before I had met Jung, and that was the magnet that drew me to Jung originally. It gave me the feeling that there was this deeper level of the unconscious that Jung had discovered, and in it were many different archetypal images that could be understood as part of a timeless and universal language, quite different from the personal unconscious.

Nikolai Tolstoi: It would be very hard to explain, it seems to me, the universality of certain myths, which repeat themselves – and very often in strikingly similar detail in very different cultures and societies – I don't see how that can be explained unless there's something springing up, universally, within man, which Jung gave this term, the collective unconscious.

Don Cupitt: Jung was quite happy to interpret the dreams of patients in Zurich in terms of the Tibetan Book of the Dead. That's to say, Jung thought there were world-wide patterns of myth and symbolism which were in everybody, in all cultures. Jung believed that his archetypes were a kind of universal symbolic vocabulary, that belonged to the whole human race.

Robert Johnson: One learns a profound fact, which is that I belong to a great collective or a matrix or a ground of being which includes all mankind. Christianity has called it the communion of saints, or the body of God, or the family of mankind.

Marie-Louise von Franz: Certain fairy-tale motifs repeat all over the world from Japan to the Amazon to Europe to Mongolia – everywhere. Though there has been a lot of migration and cultural exchange, it cannot be explained purely by that. So it seems to point to the fact that there is a similarity of the human psyche, a structural similarity. This is a proof of Jung's hypothesis of the collective unconscious and the archetypes, that always the same fantasy structures appear. In similar situations the same fantasy comes up, without cultural influence.

In January 1924 Jung was again in the USA, travelling across the continent by train. His companions included Fowler McCormick, a Chicago industrialist who remained one of his closest friends until his death: McCormick visited Zurich often, and in Jung's old age would drive him up into his beloved mountains for the views and the fresh air. Another was the scholar of native American Indian life and culture, Jaime de Angulo, who was then married to Godwin Baynes's future third wife Carey.

On my next trip to the United States, I went with a group of American friends to visit the Indians of New Mexico, the city-building Pueblos. [*Memories, Dreams, Reflections*, p. 247]

The Pueblo Indians' oldest settlement is Taos Pueblo, in New Mexico. They are one of the many tribes of the Anasazi culture, whose original homes are now ruins, like the White House in the Canon de Chelly in eastern Arizona. These oldest inhabitants of north America are farming peoples whose history, mythology, religion and calendar are interwoven. Their tradition is one of living close to the earth and the elements, attuned to the seasons, related to their gods. For them, the earth is Mother, and the sun, Father. When Jung arrived in Taos, he was anxious to hear about their religious and cultural traditions, and encountered a man who was able to tell him.

Joseph Henderson: He was very impressed by a man he met there, called Mountain Lake, and he always liked to repeat what

Mountain Lake had said – 'That the Americans were all crazy because they think with their heads instead of with their hearts, the way the Indians do.'

Edward Edinger: Mountain Lake shared with him the Indian religious view that their rituals helped the sun to come up every day and, that without their help, the sun would stop coming up. And that piece of information and the meeting of a living embodiment, a representative of such a way of life, struck a very deep chord in Jung.

Mountain Lake was the English name of Ochwiay Biano, a Pueblo elder who talked to Jung about the tribal life of the Taos Indians, and about their traditional religion. As far as can be determined, Jung was in Taos for only one day – but it made a profound impression upon him. The meeting with Mountain Lake has taken on the status of myth: there are those who regard the encounter as exaggerated, and allege that Mountain Lake was a gas station attendant, and others who romanticize the tale, claiming that Jung's encounter was with a medicine-man or a chief – 'shaman to shaman'. But in Taos it is possible to establish who Mountain Lake was, and even to hear first-hand memories of him. His granddaughter Martha Suazo still lives in Taos, and she remembers her grandfather – and the impact of Jung's visit upon him – very well. She has even preserved copies of letters which Mountain Lake wrote to Jung later.

My grandfather was Ochwiay Biano, Blue Mountain Lake, also known as Antonio Mirabal of the Taos Pueblo tribe. He was a member of the Taos Pueblo council, and he lived here until he died. He did a lot of talking for the tribe, way back in the twenties and thirties. He was sort of their spokesman, since his English was so good. He only went to third grade in school, but as he was in contact with so many non-Indians, he spoke like a college graduate. I've always been impressed with my grandfather because he corresponded with a lot of people and, as a child, I was always over at his house and I would see some of the letters that some of the people would write to him. Sometimes, he would be sitting there – he had a big table, it was a dining table, but he used it for a desk and he had all his boxes of paper and whatever. And he would be sitting there sometimes writing letters to people.

Mountain Lake was the spokesman for the tribe in the 1920s, as Martha's husband Gilbert Suazo is today, as secretary of the Taos Pueblo Tribal Council. Sixty years ago, Jung was one of the many intellectual and artistic visitors to the Taos community; in 1924 he might easily have bumped into D. H. Lawrence, who was resident nearby, and whose essays on New Mexico help to communicate both the landscape and the spiritual experience which so impressed Jung too. Today, tourists pour into Taos, not least because the buildings which Jung saw – two groups of pueblo houses of adobe brick, up to five storeys high, and divided by the fresh stream which flows down from the nearby sacred mountain – are unspoilt and timeless. After a century of efforts to commit genocide on native Americans, white America – the 'Anglos' as Indians call them – has more recently recognized the cultural and historical value of the continent's original inhabitants.

Jung and Mountain Lake climbed up the rough wooden ladders on to the roof of the pueblo, and talked about the Pueblo religion, about the Anglos, and about 'the Father Sun – nothing can be without the sun'. Mountain Lake confided something of the daily ceremony that the Pueblo Indians perform. Their mythology indicates that this ceremony enables the sun to cross the sky each day, and that they are doing it not only for themselves, but for the whole world. Jung saw this as 'a valid reply to the overpowering influence of God'. The idea that a people had such a clear sense of their role in the world struck Jung as a powerful contrast with the 'Anglo' world of European and Western civilization.

The Indian religion is supposed not to be discussed; but in their conversation, Mountain Lake told Jung that their religious rituals were essential to the survival of the world. As Martha Suazo recalls:

My grandfather did say that if the Taos Indians give up their Indian religion, if every last thing about it goes, then give or take ten years, then the world is going to end. It's our religion that's keeping this world going. I really don't know maybe to what depth he told Jung but, he made an impression on him and Dr Jung made an impression on my grandfather.

In Africa two years later, Jung was to recall the force and simplicity of the Pueblo Indian's religious role.

My old Pueblo friend ... thought that the *raison d'être* of his pueblo
had been to help their father, the sun, to cross the sky. I envied
him for the fullness of meaning in that belief. [*Memories, Dreams,
Reflections*, p. 256]

Mountain Lake also poured scorn on the 'Anglos' – people who
'think with their head, not with their heart'. It is an idea which still
seems familiar to his granddaughter, Martha Suazo.

We do feel with the heart or think with the heart. There was
something that my grandfather said about the white man. He
never really trusted them, you know. He said: 'Indians really don't
trust the white men, you look at them and they have narrow beady
eyes, you just can't trust them. I'm sorry to say that!'

As Jung recalled Mountain Lake's remarks, he said:

Their eyes have a staring expression; they are always seeking
something. What are they seeking? The whites always want
something; they are always uneasy and restless. We do not know
what they want. We do not understand them. We think that they
are mad.' [*Memories, Dreams, Reflections*, p. 248]

Jung travelled in order to get an outsider's view of the European
psyche – here it was, in unadorned, direct language. He said of this
journey:

I understand Europe, our greatest problem, only when I see where
I as a European do not fit into the world. [*Memories, Dreams,
Reflections*, p. 247]

For the first time in my life, so it seemed to me, someone had drawn
for me a picture of the real white man. This Indian had struck our
vulnerable spot, unveiled a truth to which we are blind. [*Memories,
Dreams, Reflections*, p. 248.

After Jung had returned to Europe, he wrote to Mountain Lake to
ask for more information about the Pueblo Indians' religious traditions.
On 27 April 1926, Mountain Lake replied – partly discussing the
difficulties the tribe was facing over both agriculture and the actions
of the Federal Government, and partly reiterating the ideas which he
had expressed to Jung at their meeting:

My dear friend Jung,
I received your always welcome letter, indeed I am very glad to
hear from you. What I told you the day we was top the roof, you
understand me correct. And also I will tell you more that you can
write in that book. Ten years after our religion is destroyed the
whole world will see that we been working for the whole world. As
I told you our great father the sun is the one who support the whole
world. And that's our duties to help our great father the sun. [*Sic*]

It is not known whether Jung replied on that occasion – though he
rarely failed to do so. But six years later, Mountain Lake wrote again
(see Fig. 2):

My dear friend Dr Jung,
Many moons gone by since I hear from you. I been thinking of you
many times to write to you, but I lost your address. . . . I
accomplished many important matters for my peoples since I see
you. You know I was in poor health when I meet you, but now I
am intirely well again. [*Sic*]

Dr Jung replied by return of post:

My dear friend Mountain Lake,
It was very nice of you indeed that you wrote a letter to me. I
thought you had quite forgotten me. . . . I often thought of you in
the meantime and I even talked of you often to my pupils. Are your
young men still worshipping the Father Sun? Are you also making
occasionally sand-paintings like the Navajos? I am busy exploring
the truth in which Indians believe. It always impressed me as a
great truth, but one hears so little about it. All you tell me about
religion is good news to me. There are no interesting religious
things over here, only remnants of old things. I was glad to hear
that you are in better health than when I saw you. I'm sure your
tribe needs you very much, and I wish that you will live still many
years.
As ever your friend,
C. G. Jung

In 1963 Jung's grandson Dieter Baumann, also an analyst, was on
a lecture tour in the USA, travelling by Greyhound bus. As the guest
of some friends in Santa Fe, about sixty miles south of Taos, Dr
Baumann sent a message to ask if Mountain Lake was still alive, and
if he could meet him. A few days later, he followed in the footsteps of

ANTONIO MIRABAL
TAOS PUEBLO
TAOS, NEW MEXICO

Oct. 7-1932.

My dear friend Mr. Jung

Many moons gone by since
I hear from you. I been thinking
of you many times to write to you
but I lost your address. and I didn't
had any way of getting your address
until Mrs. Schevill came to see me
last week in from Berkeley Calif.
The first thing I done was to ask
her your address, and got it. I learn
she was in Switerland and see you. I
accomplished many important matter
for my peoples since I see you.
you know I was in poor health
when I meet you, but now I am
interelly well again. I can fight
This will be all for this time
with many good wishes to you
I am hoping to hear from
you

Respectfully your friend

Antonio Mirabal

Fig. 2   Mountain Lake's letter to Jung, 7 October 1932.

his grandfather, to Taos, to meet the elderly Indian who had had such an impact on Jung.

> It was very moving because forty years before when my grandfather had met him, and he could remember very well, he showed me that they had talked there on the roof with each other. I found him a very fine man, a very special man. He was very intelligent and he had a very soft face – profoundly human. I think he had a very deep feeling.

Mountain Lake died in the early 1970s as a very old man, well into his nineties. To Dieter Baumann, he was a representative of a culture whose myths, religion, rituals and ceremonies were united with the environment and the reality of their daily existence.

> The main message from the Indians was for me the respect for the earth, the religious attitude towards the earth. They are really touched with the spirit of the earth.

Visitors to Taos can today witness performances of the Indian ceremonial dances like the Eagle Dance, the Shield Dance or the Intertribal Dance. To the Pueblo Indians, the eagle and the buffalo are both sacred animals. Religious traditions dictate that eagle feathers must be used in ceremony and ritual – so the tribe thanks and honours the bird by imitation. Mary-Esther Winters. a Pueblo Indian who participates in the dances, explains the purpose and meaning of the Eagle Dance:

> It depicts the way the eagle soars high in the sky, with its graceful movements, and at the end of the dance, when his wings come together, it shows how he flies in for the prey, to kill his prey. It's also a dance of respect that we give towards the eagle for the Indians being able to use his plumage for our ceremonial dances.

Nature and religion are intertwined, as they always have been, in the culture of the native American Indians. Their survival has always depended on their crops and herds, on water and sunshine – therefore their religious ceremonies worship Mother Earth, and Father Sun, and the blessings of rain and snowy rivers. What Carl Jung and Dieter Baumann both encountered was a culture whose religion, history, rituals and mythology are fully integrated. In the traditional crafts, like pottery, nothing is used which is not natural, nothing which does not consist of the four elements in the tribe's traditional homeland.

Lilly Salvador is a traditional Indian potter of the Acoma tribe in New Mexico, who grinds pottery shards on a stone which was handed down by her mother and her grandmother before her. The potters, and the traditional designs – all done from memory, and never drawn on paper – are a female inheritance in the Acoma tribe.

The shards are from in the hills, when we take a hike we find them and we bring them back, because they're used back into our clay, used as a temper. So it's an old and a new pot put together. The new clay is found at a secret place. Only the potters know where to get it, and there's no road to it, so we just have to carry it on our backs. The paints are from natural rocks or clay and they're found around here, up in the mesa and in the mountains. I don't think if anybody else like the Anglos or anybody else, if they learned how to form the pot, they wouldn't have that feeling of the clay or just the touch of our ancestors there.

The pots themselves are not merely decorative; they tell the history of the Acoma tribe's search for their promised land, the high mesa of Acoma known as 'Sky City' and claimed to be the oldest inhabited settlement in the USA. The story of the long journey to the Acomas' tribal home is passed down the female line – and the women potters give the story expression in the traditional form.

The design here represents how our people have travelled a long time ago. It was taught to us that they had travelled in a circle, always looking for a place that was ready for them. In our language Acoma means a place that was ready, or the promised land.

The myth of the Acoma people reflects the everyday reality of many of the Indian tribes. Wherever there is rain, or water of any kind, there can be agriculture, food and survival. But the tribe is not only at the mercy of the elements; its traditions also bring the elements into harmony. Lilly Salvador's pots require the clay earth, and fire to set them hard. But they also need the life-giving water and air as well.

After I finish making a pot, I'm told to blow into them to give them a heart, or their own spirit. And down at the bottom, where we draw our first line, we are told not to close it completely, and that brings in the spirit. The spirits of my ancestors are there.

Joseph Henderson: For the traditional Indian, mythology is part and parcel of their whole social system. They don't just believe in myths – the myth *is* their culture. Their way of life is their myth.

Dr Henderson is one of many Jungian analysts who have combined anthropology with analytical psychology to study the similarities between Jung's approach to the psyche and the collective unconscious with the tribal life, and healing rituals of American Indians. The Indian ceremonies intended to cure the physically sick and the psychologically distressed present a number of significant parallels. Just as in analysis the patient brings dreams, so in Navajo healing, for example, it is essential that the patient understands the mythological background to the curative process, and believes that it will work.

Traditional tribal people recognize the importance of retaining their religions and staying close to their myth. Jung recognized Mountain Lake's idea that the Pueblo Indians think with the heart as a source of psychological health. In eastern Arizona, the Navajo Indians have their reservation. Their religion is based on a system of healing cere-monies or chants, intended to cure illness or to bring members of the tribe back into harmony with the tribal traditions. Sand-paintings illustrate the stories and symbolism of tribal mythology – created by hand with naturally coloured sands.

Navajo religion is based on healing rituals: the medicine-men are both doctors and priests. Healing consists of bringing the psyche into harmony with the natural and supernatural forces that surround it. Cultural symbols help to give a context for whatever suffering afflicts the patient, by allowing her/him to identify with a mythical personality who suffered the same affliction.

Many Jungian psychologists have followed Jung's footsteps to visit the Indians of New Mexico and Arizona. For Donald Sandner, President of the Society of Jungian analysts in San Francisco, the interest is in the Navajos. During a fifteen-year period he has studied their cere-monies and drawn certain parallels with Jungian psychology.

If you wanted a place to look for corroboration of a lot of Jung's views, particularly the ones about archetypes and the collective unconscious, you could do no better than to look in to the Navajo symbol system – where it's all there. It's all put together from the collective unconscious. You could say that in the Navajo system there is a myth behind every chant. And behind every chant there was a story, and if you had a certain illness, for instance, let's say you had what they would call joint pains, swelling, arthritis or rheumatism, you would say, what hero or what heroine had that disease. So you might say that you would be identifying already with her. So you would choose that chant.

The chant is a recitation of part of one of the epic mythological stories about the gods and the early history of the tribe, and the sand-paintings in the ceremony illustrate the story symbolically.

Then the patient comes in and he identifies by sitting on some part of the sand-painting, he identifies with that power in the sand-painting. It would be roughly paralleling the myth – although the myth is not told, is never told. It's assumed that you know it already. That power is put on the patient, and at that moment the patient takes it in. He identifies with the medicine-man, with the power in the painting and with the hero or heroine of the whole chant. And he himself inwardly goes through the process of being healed by that identification. In the Navajo, they say that the patient has to not only believe but actively concentrate on what's going on.

Andy Natanobah is a Navajo medicine-man who is on call to a vast tract of the Navajo reservation in eastern Arizona. He also teaches the cultural and mythological background to the healing tradition at the Navajo Community College in Tsaile, about fifty miles north of Window Rock. He illustrated the basic plot of a healing ceremony, and made two sand-paintings that would be used in such a ceremony, on the floor of the hogan – a round hut with a central chimney, and a floor of earth – as the March winds blew fresh snow across the plateau outside.

That patient wants to get well, and get back on his feet. That's what it is. So it's really up to the patient.

In analytical psychology, the patient shares responsibility for the cure. Jung said 'If the problem is to be solved, the mystery has to be lived,' and the Indians do just that.

Donald Sandner: The symbolism, the images have to enter the patient's mind, and he has to do that in Jungian analysis also. It's the patient – if there are no dreams, we can work with other things, but the patient must produce the symbolism in order for it to be worked on.

Healing ceremonies are known as 'chants' because the medicine-man chants the long, mesmerizing narrative of a mythological story as the process unfolds. Chants can last as long as nine days – involving many sand-paintings which portray, in symbolic form, the characters and images of the myth which is invoked to effect a cure. A nine-day ceremony begins with purification of the patient, by administering herbs which produce vomiting and sweating. The second phase consists of the arrival of the gods – as they are represented in the sand-paintings. The third phase is the ceremonial renewal of the force of the myths, by the chant taking place, and the curative process.

Sand-paintings are made with immense care and skill on the floor of the hogan, and despite the vivid colours in many designs, all the materials used by Andy Natanobah are entirely natural.

> For these sand-paintings we get the colours from our mother earth, it's the natural colours like white, and so is the black, so is the yellow, so is the grey colour. The natural colours come from our mother earth.

Sand of different colours is funnelled between the thumb and fore-finger into exact and formal patterns – which represent a whole pantheon of symbols, animals, gods and mythological figures.

> You have the black stars and grey stars and yellow stars and white stars, and the five-pointed diamond shapes; the lightning-tip of the arrow-heads, and then you have the sacred mountains around the sand-painting. There's a rainbow that surrounds it, green and red, that's the path of the rainbow that is to cure the patient. In the Mountain Way chant you've got the bear claw, the footprints, and arrow-heads – one a female, the other a male. Then you've got four lightnings in a square, and you've got the snakes – black represents darkness, and the white, daylight people. The bear is to protect us – people live here out on the mountain, they live with the bear. The bear represents our grandparents. And the snake's the same way. The snake's to protect us.

Some symbols recur in almost every sand-painting. Lightning flashes, rainbows, and the warrior gods and star gods are the most common. They are found in many different cultures, and Jung recognized these symbolic strands as archetypes. It was the visual impact of the sand-paintings which first drew Donald Sandner into his years of studying Navajo tradition.

It was the symbolism that really grabbed me. As a Jungian, that was the main thing. That symbolism then led on and on, as I read into it, and found that the symbolism really spreads out in all directions, until you have a whole symbolic system – the kind of thing Jung talked about all the time.

The rich Navajo symbolism is not confined to healing chants and ritual: it provides the decoration of the Navajo arts and crafts, like weaving, as well. As Joseph Henderson observes:

The Indians' ceremonies come from the rightful use of archetypes in the unconscious.

The Hopi, Navajo, Pueblo and Acoma Indians all shared a participation in making life meaningful, not merely being the recipient of God's meaning for man. The Pueblos help the sun across the sky for the benefit of the whole world. The Hopi migration myth states that they went to a high plateau where they would not lose the need to rely on their Creator. The Acoma tribe went around in circles until they found 'Sky City'.

When the force of the archetypes in a culture, or the life of its myth, begins to wane, both the community and its individual members can crumble. Medicine-men today are in short supply, and are now being trained formally, while in earlier times it was a treasured inheritance among the tribe. Indians who drift away from their tribal myths and places tend towards rapid decline in the inhospitable Anglo culture. As in Africa, they succumb to alcoholism among other ills. The Indian reservations are all 'dry' – alcohol is banned, because alcoholism had reached such proportions among people whose heritage had been destroyed by the 'civilization' of compulsory schooling in English-speaking boarding schools, the withering of traditional religion in the face of 'conversion', and the concrete pleasures of consumerism. Liquor stores proliferate in all the towns which lie just outside the reservations; and, of all things, bingo is the biggest single economic activity on the reservations – as they have no gaming laws. As Jung said in a speech he gave to the Oxford Congress in 1938:

If you break up a tribe they lose their religious ideas, the treasure of the old traditions, and they feel out of form completely. They lose their *raison d'être* ... all the meaning goes out of their life. It does not make sense any more because we infect them with our own insanity.

Jung's encounter with Indians was short, but lasting. A year later, he set off for a far longer adventure: the B. P. E. or 'Bugishu Psychological Expedition'. In October 1925, Jung and his two companions – the English psychiatrist Godwin Baynes and George Beckwith, an American game hunter – sailed from England and after four weeks disembarked at Mombasa. From there they began their journey into the African interior. Together, Baynes and Jung filmed their expedition in search of psychological discoveries. Jung and his party trekked for weeks through the highlands of Kenya towards Mount Elgon. Their African destination was an extreme contrast from the Europe of the 1920s.

Here again, Jung encountered tribal societies for whom mythology was the religious explanation of their life and origins, expressed in story and ritual. Jung was quite sure that man is not complete without a living mythology – or religion. Unlike his European patients, tribal people had a sense of meaning to their lives. As the theologian Don Cupitt expresses the idea:

> He thought that scientific industrial man suffered great psychic distress and frustration because the religious side of our nature was repressed. According to the Jungian tradition, our religions are produced something like folk art. Religion is the heart and centre of culture, and it's through religion that we work out a common vocabulary of rituals and symbols that together makes up a kind of house of meaning that we dwell in – our particular vision of the universe, of human life, of human personal relations and so on. and so on.

Among the Elgonyi, as if to confirm the hypothesis of archetypes and the collective unconscious, Jung witnessed an attitude towards the sun which was very like that of the Pueblo Indians. As Gerhard Adler recalls:

> Mountain Lake told him that through their ritual, every morning they made the sun come. And then if they didn't come the sun wouldn't rise any more and it would be the end of the world. And he realized that people have to live their own myths and it was important to him that they were related to something important. A similar experience he had with the Elgonyis, they had a ritual every morning: when the sun rose, they went and spat into their hand. Spit of course was the soul, or spirit. They didn't know why they did it. They just did it. Jung realized that people have to live

their own myths and it was important to him that they were related to something greater than themselves, and that is all that matters. He found similar instances with them and with others and this made him believe in the all-presence of the collective unconscious.

Jung defined the term 'archetype' in different ways at different times: but to call it 'the psychological expression of an instinct' is helpful in the circumstances of mythology and tribal life. A man or woman has an inborn tendency to function in a certain way – and this tendency is given descriptive expression, in a dream or a mythical story, by being characterized in a personality, or an animal, or a bit of plot or action, as if from a script. In Africa, as Jung told Dr Evans in 1957:

The way in which a man should behave is given by an archetype. That is why primitives tell the stories they do. A great deal of education goes through story-telling. For instance, they call in a palaver of the young men and two older men *perform* before the eyes of the younger all the things they should not do. Then they say 'Now that's exactly the thing you shall not do.' Another way is, they *tell* them of all things they should not do, like the Decalogue – 'Thou shalt not.' And that is always supported by mythological tales. For instance our ancestors have done so-and-so, and so you shall too. Or such-and-such a hero has done so-and-so, and that is your model. Again, in the teachings of the Catholic Church there are several thousand saints. They show us what to do, they serve as models. They have their legends and that is Christian mythology. In Greece there was Theseus, there was Heracles, models of fine men, of gentlemen, you know, and they teach us how to behave. They are archetypes of behaviour. [Houston No. 1]

The sense of perspective Jung sought, and achieved, by putting distance between himself and his normal surroundings, did not improve his opinion of the modern Western world. As we have earlier seen, he preferred the 'primitive' existence.

Our camp life proved to be one of the loveliest interludes in my life. I enjoyed the divine peace of a still primeval country. Never had I seen so clearly 'man and other animals'. Thousands of miles lay between me and Europe, mother of all demons. [*Memories, Dreams, Reflections*, p. 264]

Jung duly returned to Europe, to wrestle with the demons of his patients; it was his clear view that the long-standing myth of the West, that of Judaeo-Christian religion, had lost its force in a rationalistic, materialistic modern age. People had become lost, and the twentieth century faced the tragedy of searching for a new myth to make sense of its own existence. Europeans, in their modern city lives, had lost what American Indians still preserve – that they live where their gods also reside. As Jung said in 1957:

> We think we are able to be born today and to live in no myth – without history. That is a disease – absolutely abnormal – because man is not born every day. He is once born in a specific historical setting with specific historical qualities, and therefore he is only complete when he has a relation to these things. [Houston No. 4]

However, Jung well understood that myth did not exist only in the remote, inaccessible places where a non-European, non-Christian atmosphere gave him a sense of perspective. Every culture has its myth or myths – the danger is in losing touch with them. As the author and scholar of Celtic mythology, Nikolai Tolstoi, suggests:

> A myth is a story which, to those who told it and who heard it, was a believable story and a real event that actually took place. But it is in fact an exemplary story. It illustrates or exemplifies essential factors in human existence, or it accounts for things like the creation of the world or of certain human situations, but told in the form of a story.

The Arthurian legends have survived in Britain, and they too drew Jung's attention. His wife Emma was writing a book about the legend of the Holy Grail, which was completed upon her death by Dr von Franz. While many school-children, and some adults, are aware of the stories of the Knights of the Round Table, and may have seen the table itself in Winchester Cathedral, Arthurian mythology narrates the creation and early history of Britain as a whole.

> It is a British myth, it's *the* British myth – 'The Matter of Britain', as they call it, but it was called 'The Matter of Britain' on the continent and it has been accepted the world over. Arthur is, of course, the archetypal king. He later became a figure who was believed to be sleeping beneath a mountain in a cavern surrounded by his Knights to be called again in the hour of need. The idea of

retiring into the heart of a mountain and living on there is I'm sure his descent back into the unconscious.

On a visit to England – probably the one they made in 1920, visiting the Baynes family – the Jungs made a point of seeing Glastonbury, one of the most evocative sites of British mythology. In doing so, they did as many tourists do – who are drawn to a site which has only vague mythological connections. Underneath Glastonbury Tor, legend has it that the Holy Grail is buried, the object of the constant quest of King Arthur and his Knights. King Arthur's supposed grave – or one of them – is in the grounds of the nearby Glastonbury Abbey. Count Tolstoi observes:

> It is fascinating that these places draw people, and they don't just draw them because they're beautiful – I mean the Tor is very striking – but it's the strikingness I think which is probably the key. It looks different, it feels different, and that's how it occurred to early peoples, and so they invested it with this numinous quality.

The same could be said of Tintagel Castle in Cornwall: it has been almost conclusively proved that the castle dates from a far later period than the supposed era of King Arthur. Yet Tintagel beach is regarded as the location where Merlin discovered the infant king-to-be washed up on the shore; and the town of Tintagel today has King Arthur's Tea-room cheek by jowl with the Merlin Arms. Nikolai Tolstoi argues that the 'truth' of a myth is really irrelevant to the force it has for people – myths don't operate at the factual level, at all.

> In the case of Tintagel, there isn't really any very good evidence to link it with the story of Arthur. The fact is that people simply do invest these places with a numinous quality, without knowing and it's not necessary really to know the true story of what lies behind it. In a sense, you can say the facts are dispensable. There must, one would suspect, be a need, and this is certainly the case with myth, that all societies certainly, until quite recently, lived by myths, and we have our own maybe distorted myths, and, where we don't have them, probably our state reflects that.

There is a danger that the modern, technological world has invaded all the mysteries and mythologies which previously gave humankind its roots. Progress has enabled us to know how everything works, while forgetting the importance of understanding what something means. The modern age has conquered all the heights and even invaded the heavens. The dwelling-places of the gods and spirits have been demystified. Thus modern people strive to retain a connection with the 'numinous' places which somehow embody the old myths and mysteries.

It is not known whether Carl and Emma Jung visited Tintagel, besides Glastonbury. It seems likely, as the first seminar Jung ever gave outside Switzerland was at Sennen Cove, near Land's End, in the summer of 1920; and his next, three summers later, was at Polzeath in Cornwall, only a few miles from Tintagel. But almost twenty years later, in 1938, Jung had a vivid and elaborate dream, all about the quest for the grail, which took place on 'an unknown island, presumably situated not far off the coast of southern England'. Jung appears to be describing Tintagel when he refers to 'a medieval castle', 'on the rocky coast'. In India, Jung's dream referred to England and Europe; when in Africa, he mostly dreamed about scenes from home. It was as if the unconscious balanced the overwhelming foreign impressions with its own roots in Jung's native environment.

But during his trip to India, Jung was immersed in another field of study – an investigation not into a new geographical milieu, but an intellectual and spiritual concern of the European past. Alchemy represents decidedly the most difficult example of Jung's efforts to revive and revalue human psychic history into accessible, meaningful ideas for the twentieth century reader.

Alchemy has been assumed to be the origin of chemistry. It emerged from medieval mysticism with the first scientific revolution, in which matter began to fall under the practical influence of man. The legendary goal, of making gold from base metal, through the agency of the philosopher's stone, of course failed.

Jung recast the alchemical saga in psychological terms. The gold was the human wholeness of individuation, and the processes of *calcinatio, separatio, conjunctio* and so forth corresponded to psychological changes in the psychoanalytic process. As Gerhard Adler describes alchemy:

It is psychological and mythological. It is of course not alchemy
in the chemical sense that people make gold. But the best
alchemists knew that they were aiming at the gold in themselves.
In all the writings of these alchemists there is the clear indication
that the aim is the self. Jung himself said that alchemy was somehow
the mirror-image of psychology.

It was Jung's achievement to make sense of the alchemists by treating their work and ideas as real and true because they were mythic; the literal approach had dismissed them because they didn't 'make sense'. The contemporary pattern of the developed world has robbed vast numbers of people, and aspects of life and history, of meaning – by the domination of fact over fantasy, and reality over intuition. Myth, and fantasy, may be 'unreal' – but still they have symbolic meaning, as Gerhard Adler suggests:

Symbolic meaning – through amplification of myth and legend, dream and story – restores to individual life the numinosity it has largely lost.

The two analysts who have been brave enough to follow Jung deeply into the topic of alchemy are Dr Marie-Louise von Franz and Dr Edward Edinger.

Dr von Franz: What fascinated Jung were the illustrations of alchemical books firstly, which reminded him of patients' pictures – mysterious fantasy images which he couldn't park anywhere. Then he discovered what is really very understandable, that those people who cooked chemical matter in the Middle Ages and in antiquity had no idea what they were cooking. Suddenly it stank and poisoned them, or it exploded in their face, or it changed from a red to black colour, suddenly developing a tremendous heat. We know now that that is the concomitant process of what we call chemical reactions, but they didn't know that, they just wondered and so they said: 'Iron loves the rust!' And when there was heat developed in a chemical connection, they said 'They loved each other passionately!' – that was the heat of love developing, when the two substances met. So involuntarily they fantasized into the matter. They (as we would say) 'projected the unconscious fantasy' into matter.

As Aniela Jaffe expresses it:

What the alchemists experienced as the properties of matter was in reality the content of their own unconscious; their psychic experiences appeared as the special behaviour of the chemical substances.

Jung (centre) with George
Beckwith and African
tribesmen on the Bugishu
Psychological Expedition,
1925.

'It's our religion that's
keeping this world going.'
Mountain Lake (Ochwiay
Biano), the Pueblo Indian
Jung met in Taos, New
Mexico, in 1924.

Andy Natanobah demonstrating the 'Great Star Chant' sandpainting in a healing ceremony. 'The patient wants to get well and get back on his feet. So it's really up to the patient.'

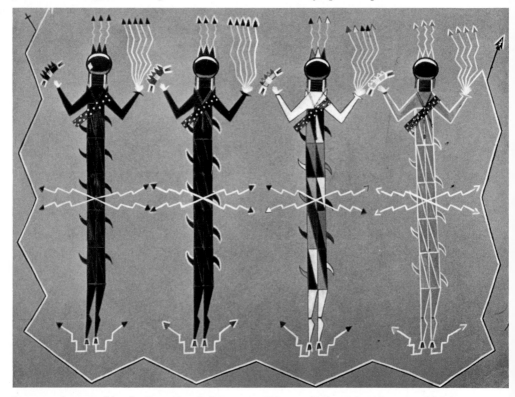

Jung was fascinated by the American Indian way of life, in which myth, religion and healing are intertwined. Navajo sand-paintings illustrate the stories and symbolism of tribal mythology.

Navajo medicine man Andy Natanobah. Healing ceremonies or 'chants', which last as long as nine days, are passed on from memory and never written down.

Dr Joseph Henderson (left) and Dr Harry Wilmer during filming of interviews in Salado, Texas.

Taos Pueblo. 'I went with a group of American friends to visit the Indians of New Mexico, the city-building Pueblos.'

The rooftop where Mountain Lake and Jung conversed in 1924. 'This Indian has struck our vulnerable spot, unveiled a truth to which we are blind.' [*Memories, Dreams, Reflections*, p. 248]

The Pueblos' Eagle Dance. 'It depicts the way the eagle soars in the sky ... It's also a dance of respect we give towards the eagle ...'

(*Above left*) Mrs Dora Kalff, expert on sandplay therapy. 'You can only play when you are really free. You have to be free within.' (*Above right*) Dr Adolf Guggenbuhl-Craig. 'When I was young I hoped that one day I would understand what's going on. Then all of a sudden I woke up and I was old myself, and I wasn't a bit wiser.'

Opposite psychological types often attract, but they don't speak the same language. Joe and Jane Wheelwright, the 'polar opposites' who have been married for over fifty years.

(*Above left*) 'Hardly anybody in our world knows the difference between loving someone and being in love' – Robert Johnson. (*Above right*) 'The idea of getting high is directly connected to the experience of an altered sense of self. Cocaine is the drug of choice of the puer aeternus culture' – Dr Jeffrey Satinover.

'A woman with courage, a woman who's adventurous, a woman who speaks her mind, is supported by the animus.' Jane Wheelwright (left) with author Merrill Berger.

Science and science fiction are our modern myths. Is the search for extra-terrestrial life really the search for the inner self? (Voyager encounters Saturn and its moons – NASA simulation.)

'I learned a lot of psychology from Hitchcock. He is just as much a pioneer in imagery and the undiscovered self as Jung' – Dr John Beebe. [Alfred Hitchcock, Cary Grant and Ingrid Bergman on the set of *Notorious*.]

Edinger: What he demonstrates is that the whole phenomenon of alchemy is a vast collective chemical fantasy, extended over many centuries. There's something about this fantasy that's very gripping. The alchemists were working on their own psyches. Matter was completely unknown to them. It's completely different for us now; we've got a good notion of what matter is. Matter was a complete mystery to the alchemists: and into that mystery they projected yet another mystery – namely, the unconscious psyche. They had no realization that the psyche could contaminate their external observations, and so out of that innocence, their writings lay out naively the workings of the transformation process of the archetypal psyche.

Dr von Franz: We had these fantasies as so-called superstitious nonsense, and developed chemistry – till Jung discovered that what has been discarded as superstitious nonsense is the prehistory of the science of the collective unconscious. So now we have alchemy as the mother of two sciences, of depth psychology and of chemistry.

Physical experiments upon matter, and the impressions the alchemists had of what was going on, could be read as a symbolic description of a person's analysis. First, there is the *prima materia* – 'a little piece of chaos' in Edward Edinger's phrase. It has to be heated up – as if by an emotional crisis – and changed from one element to another. What is earthy has to become airy – as the excessively rational person needs a bit of flighty fantasy to help his/her unconscious to take off. There is a separation of different aspects of the material, or of the psyche – the personal, the cultural and the collective, for example. There is a death and a rebirth – like the seasons of the year, perhaps – and finally a meeting, or marriage, of two paired aspects of the material, or the psyche; symbolized, in alchemy and in dreams, by a pair of animals, a king and queen, or a sun and moon. This is the *conjunctio*, creating the 'philosopher's stone', which is the goal of alchemy; the integration of the conscious with the unconscious, the process of 'individuation', which is the goal of analysis.

It is no coincidence that 'analysis' itself is a chemical term. But it should not be forgotten that the term was coined by Freud, whose approach was to break problems down into their component parts, to find their origins; according to Edward Edinger:

Jung quite early on pointed out that this was not an adequate description of the therapeutic process, and he said it should be complemented by the term 'synthesis'. So that analysis and synthesis would correspond to the alchemical terms of *separatio* and *conjunctio*.

Dr von Franz, Mrs Jaffe and Dr Edinger represent the first and second generation of Jungian analysts. But the interest in a subject as admittedly obscure as alchemy is not confined to the immediate disciples of Jung. John Beebe, the analyst and film-critic in San Francisco, is very much of the younger, third generation. To him, the symbolic value of alchemical concepts can be applied very readily – in his favourite medium.

When I think of *Casablanca*, I really think there is something mythic about the way Bergman and Bogart come together, and there's something about the play of opposites between the two; the male and the female, the sweet and the sour, the blonde and the dark, all those things come together to create a tremendous energy that has the sense of freshness. If we look deeply into it, there's a very basic mythological motif – the motif of the *conjunctio*, the coming together of male and female opposites, which creates a sense of wholeness, a sense of the self.

In his physical journeys, and his travels of the mind, Jung kept a massive task in mind: to revalue the symbolic life and revive archaic wisdom, to reconnect modern people with the deeply necessary roots from which they have largely been separated by the progress of the twentieth century. As Donald Sandner says:

Why we're interested in this is because, in a sense, we've lost it and we're looking for it back another way. We can't go back to tribal life, but through psychology and through Jung's psychology especially, it's a way of bringing us back to a certain extent.

Gerhard Adler: Most of all in his journey both to the Pueblos and to the Elgonyi he learned to look at the Europeans – at the white man we may say – from outside, and he saw that it was quite wrong to believe that the white man had all the truths.

As Jung wrote to a correspondent only a year before he died:

Old Mountain Lake said to me: We are the people who live on the roof of the world, we are the sons of the Sun, who is our father. *We* help him daily to rise and to cross over the sky. We do this not only for ourselves, but for the Americans also.' He correctly assumes that their day, their light, their consciousness, and their meaning will die when destroyed by the narrow-mindedness of American rationalism, and the same will happen to the whole world when subjected to such treatment. [Letter to Miguel Serrano, 14 September 1960]

8

The Inner World of the Outer World

Strangely, in setting foot upon Moorish soil (Tunisia), I
found myself haunted by an impression which I myself
could not understand: I kept thinking that the land smelled
queer. It was the smell of blood, as though the soil were
soaked with blood. This strip of land, it occurred to me, had
already borne the brunt of three civilizations:
Carthaginian, Roman and Christian. What the
technological age will do with Islam remains to be seen.
[*Memories, Dreams, Reflections*, p. 239]

The inner life is not confined to inner processes: the psyche displays
itself and shows its existence in the built environment, the pastimes
and interests we pursue, the cultural and commercial activities which
dominate 'everyday life'. The landscape bears the imprint of the collective history of mankind which has been acted out upon its surface.
Although, as one analyst is quick to point out, 'Analysis is real life,
too,' the Jungian psychological approach addresses itself in a unique
way to the outer physical aspects of 'real life' and practical matters in
human affairs.

With the assumptions, or discoveries, that Jung made – the reality
of the psyche, the creativity of the unconscious, and the collective
roots of human psychology – both he and his many followers and
successors are taking psychological ideas and observations, and in
effect measuring them up against facets of life that superficially have
nothing to do with psychology. The 'inner world' of the 'outer world'
touches upon landscape, architecture, science and science fiction,

cinema, money and stock-markets, the rich and the royal. In all of these spheres, the relevance of the Jungian psychological approach is in seeing that no creative or intellectual act today occurs in a vacuum – each one has a context, and a pre-history.

Mankind creates its own environment – making the buildings which reflect practical needs, social aspirations, and reflections of the image of the people. In the early nineteenth century an American architect named Ithiel Towne, from the village of Thompson, Connecticut, saw the newly-arrived Elgin Marbles in London. Inspired by the beauties of classical architecture, he returned to America and began to build pillared porticoes on elegant clapboard colonial houses. Towne was the man who began the 'Greek Revival' school of American architecture – which produced many of the nation's most celebrated public buildings, including the Lincoln and Jefferson Memorials in Washington.

Ithiel Towne's village is where the analyst and author James Hillman lives today. This is the New England of the Puritans, Shakers and Quakers where outer simplicity and austerity house spiritual depth and a humane, imaginative spirit. According to Hillman:

> Places themselves have a psyche and the psyche speaks through how a place displays itself. There's a darkness in the soil here. New England has the dead Indians and the dead witches and the dead Puritans. You know, we're walking over the dead here really. They give the soil, or the psyche of the soil, much more sadness. This sense of the soil having blood in it, gives depth to, and gives soul to a place.

James Hillman, who has written and edited a great many pages on the Greeks and their myths, is a Greek revivalist like Ithiel Towne. But his interest in myth is for the reality it holds; what myths tell us about ourselves that we have forgotten to learn in other ways. The practical application and thoughtful widening of psychological ideas to make sense of daily life, is the distinctive feature of Hillman's very wide range of essays, articles, and criticism. Today his image is that of a rural gentleman-scholar in the Connecticut Yankee style. Behind his big, white clapboard house are chickens and geese and a muddy paddock occupied by a neighbour's old horse. White lime dusts the soil which needs sweetening to grow more grass before it can sustain any more horses. Hillman is a wiry, humorous, plain-speaking man with a sharp eye and nose and a tall, lean body. This all houses a personality which recognizes 'the mess'. Acknowledging his own mess, the inevitable messiness of life, means that there is room for other people and their mess – their human nature, including its imperfections. He first got involved with Jung's psychology in this way:

> I got into this business because I was a mess. And I say it past tense, which is dangerous, because I *am* a mess, and because you know you say it 'past tense' and you distance yourself from it. The mess remains. But I got into it because I had been an early hippy, you might say. I was walking around Africa and the Sudan and the Congo in the early fifties and then went to India, and then did some writing, and a lot of things like that. And one day it didn't work any more, and eventually I came back to Zurich, I came down to Zurich – came down to Zurich – from the heights!

Hillman's first impression of the Jung Institute was negative – but he stayed for twenty-five years, training as an analyst, writing, setting up a publishing company for Jungian books (Spring Publications) and becoming Director of Training at the Institute. In the early 1980s he returned finally to America; but between Zurich and Thompson, Hillman lived in a very different environment – that of Dallas, Texas. Here he observed and experienced the modern city, in its purest form – and was appalled by its lack of humanity and its insensitivity to human needs.

> Dallas is a modern city and is not for people, it's for business. You drive in from the suburbs, you drive your car underground, put it in the garage and you don't come into the street at all. And then you go up the elevator and that's it. You walk up and down the halls, you could be in any kind of office building, and it's nothing to do with people. Take the climate there. All those massive buildings have what they call 'air' – they don't use the word 'air-conditioning', they have 'air', you turn on the 'air'. The 'air' means that twelve months of the year a machine is using energy, electricity, to make a temperature, a climate inside the buildings. Six months of those years, if they opened their windows, they wouldn't need any of that – at least six months, the weather is so good there. [The effect is] to provide a contained, closed world which is not flesh and blood.
>
> Now they are beginning to realize that the interiors are full of poisonous gases and exudations from the furniture. It is also the way the room is lit, with a light coming straight down on you that casts no shadow, windows that can't be opened. You're in a little

prison room. So of course you're going to have illnesses inside offices, and psychological breakdowns, because the places of work, the materials you work with, the sound when you drop a pencil on a plastic table, or whether you drop it on a wooden table, are completely different. All of that affects every moment of your life, which you can't just clarify by going to an analyst once a week.

Hillman believes that the psychopathology of the modern city's buildings is self-evident. Just as a person displays himself through the way he walks or dresses, buildings similarly reveal themselves – and reflect us and our self-image.

The thing about Dallas, the thing about the psyche in the world or what I've been calling *anima mundi*, the soul of the world, is that it's in the world. It isn't 'What do we see in this building?' but 'What is this building displaying itself as?' So that it has to have no openings on the ground floor for people, but just repelling walls? What is it for a building to be absolutely skinny and bare-boned and stretching way up and empty on the interior with an atrium? I mean that's an anorexic building. The clinical language can be moved from just talking about people to talking about buildings.

James Hillman has even directed his psychoarchitectural attention to the specific feature of ceilings; concerned that while man has traditionally looked up, raised his eyes to heaven to make contact and spiritual connection to God and gods, today our line of sight is obstructed by heating ducts, 'air' pipes, fluorescent lights and all the paraphernalia of the artificial environment.

Nobody looks up any more. It's too horrible. The ceiling is repressed, you look at architects' drawings, you don't see the ceiling.

As Hillman writes in his essay 'On Ceilings':

If looking up is that gesture of aspiration and orientation toward the higher order of the cosmos, an imagination opening to the stars, our ceilings reflect an utterly secular vision – short-sighted, utilitarian, unaesthetic.

One does not need to be an analyst to see something psychologically significant in the fate of Dallas today: the city which a television series made into a synonym for money and power now represents how badly the drive for money and power can go wrong. Making money in itself is clearly a highly psychological business, too.

Adolf Guggenbuhl-Craig is a Swiss analyst of the second Jungian generation – now into his sixties, he wears a moustache-less beard and looks the image of a stern elder of a Mennonite or Amish church. Despite the Swiss solidity of his panelled consulting-room, and the calm, almost austere atmosphere. Dr Guggenbuhl-Craig has displayed a persistent fondness for the provocative or the unlikely psychological idea. 'Marriage is never simply happy and shouldn't be only happy,' he asserts; or indeed 'the old wise man is a one-sided propaganda gimmick of older people to dominate the younger ones.' Turning the obvious on its head, he regards the urge to make money as an archetypal experience.

Most people think that dealing with money is a rational activity. We want to become rich, we want to have money to buy things and so on. What one doesn't realize, is that money in some ways is like one's gold in alchemy, a symbol of the life-force. In Western Europe I think most people don't want to earn money only to afford certain things, but because money symbolizes something. Speculators, people who really only deal with money, they don't really deal with money as a thing to buy something with, but they deal with money because they want to get more gold or they want to get more *soul* in the end. I think the speculators speculate as they think that they can get a life essence by having more and more money.

Let's say you win at the Stock Exchange – then you are close to the gods. A philosopher can say something, and he might be right or wrong, nobody can prove it. But when you deal with money, you really know if you are right or wrong. You lose or you win, there's no argument, and it might give you then an elated feeling, that you were on the right side, that you were so much in touch with the gods that you actually won.

In late 1987 the financial world was shaken by a spectacular crash in stock prices, which reverberated through all the major stock-markets, ruined major individual fortunes, and destroyed the hopes and expectations of thousands of people whose livelihood depended on being in touch with the gods of money. The world financial markets seemed to be on a permanently upward trend – but why? Was it only because the collective wish was that they be so? And did the crash come, not for economic reasons, but because of a crack appearing in the psychological illusion? According to Dr Guggenbuhl-Craig, the stock-market crash is pure psychology:

> Jungians talk about the personal and the collective: so they have something to say about the crash. In the stock-market, people try over and over again to get systems to predict it and they claim they know what is going to happen. In reality the human psyche cannot be predicted, and therefore nobody ever can predict what will happen in the stock-market. Because the stock-market is the mood of the collective, and people might be inflated, and then they buy and buy, or they all of a sudden might get scared, a depression takes over – not an economic depression necessarily, but a psychological depression – and then they become sad and want to sell. The stock-market is a beautiful expression of the collective mood, and is not an expression of economic indicators.

Dr Guggenbuhl-Craig's explanation may be just as viable as any of the others offered after the October 1987 crash – which was marked by a general sense of mystery as to why shares did drop so low. Some people in Britain, jokingly, linked the crash to the hurricane which battered southern England a couple of days earlier.

If the financial world puts us in touch with the gods, Dr Guggenbuhl-Craig also sees the modern media of television and cinema as a means of giving us a sense of other powerful archetypes.

> Let's take a series like *Dallas*, which obviously fascinates a lot of people, and lots of people say it's rubbish and nonsense, but you know that's not the way to deal with it, because it has a big impact on people. There you have a mythological figure, in J. R. Ewing – it's an attempt to present evil mythologically, and to show it to you in an image. This man is not just a bad invention of a bad writer, but it means to us something we have in us – this kind of evil, destructive, false, scheming mind. He's a devil, a modern devil, and I think it's not bad that you have the Devil in a modern television play. Because otherwise the Devil is no longer there anyhow. He's smart, he's elegant, and the characteristic of the Devil is that he's always hidden.

The television series is not only rich in archetypal characters and plot; it also reflects the realities of its city. 'South Fork' ranch is so-named because the three existing forks of the Trinity River, which enabled Dallas to be established as a town, are North, East and West

Forks. Dallas is a stereotypical frontier town which originally based its economy on cotton, and then on oil. More recently, the oil money brought in massive property speculation. But when the oil price crashed, so did the property market, and Dallas today has dozens of spectacular, speculative, and empty office buildings and condominiums. Banks which lent money to fuel the property boom have themselves gone bust; only the lawyers kept afloat. As James Hillman argues, the story reflects the American psyche of boom and bust:

> It's sad, a part of our American tradition. We had that before with Florida: boom and bust. We had it in California, in San Francisco. There have been many booms and busts. That's the psyche of the country – manic-depressive, you know. Keep depression away at all costs, and when it comes, it's wiped out.

In Dallas the vast, sheer-sided towers of mirrored glass reflect each other, but reflect nothing of a human scale; there is an overreaching, a hubris in the scale, a mania in the freeways which throw a ring of steel and concrete around the downtown towers, and a narcissism in the mirrors everywhere. As Hillman says of the mirrored buildings:

> What are mirrored sunglasses telling us? You certainly can't look into the soul of the person, into his eyes or her eyes. It's that paranoid perspective of 'I can see you but you can't see me.'

After five years in Dallas, he has retreated to the peaceful, forested Connecticut countryside. Was it important for him to live in a place which is very beautiful?

> Yes, but I wouldn't want to limit beauty to a beautiful place, in the sense of old trees and old fences or stone walls. I don't know what beauty is, but I do know that people are extremely moved by it, and that therapy has left it out, and that ordinary therapy takes place in small cellular collective state rooms, as if talk could do it. And there's much more that moves people than that. The longing for beauty and being moved by beauty, I see it in people I work with, that the thing they tend to flee is being caught in their own depth of feeling for something beautiful, and their longing for it. And until that gets activated, they remain cramped in some way. So the longing for beautiful movies, beautiful music, beautiful paintings fills us. It's not merely nature.

Hillman is one of the relatively few Jungian analysts whose reputation as an intellectual critic and essayist is respected beyond the field of analytical psychology. As something of a maverick thinker, he says that nowadays he is temperamentally more a Freudian than a Jungian, the former being the more critical thinker; but in speaking of beauty Hillman fulfilled the Jungian tradition of 'the poetic observer'. There is the same paradox as existed in Jung; on the one hand he claimed he was an empirical, medical scientist first and foremost and yet this professional identity contained one of the twentieth century's most creative and sensitive minds. Hillman said of Jung:

> I think he drew conclusions from his observations the way a poet does. A poet writes from his observations of people and trees and birds and chickens and so on, and his feeling states, and Jung drew conclusions from those things.

There is an unresolved debate among Jungians about whether to claim Jung primarily as a scientist, or as an exotic hybrid of scientist-poet-mystic. The latter identity tends to undermine the essentially practical discoveries he made, and the lifetime of work in healing patients. Analysts argue whether analytical psychology is a science, or an art: whether it relies on technique, or on empathy above all. John Beebe, the San Francisco analyst, believes that it is dangerous to limit the ideas to a single category:

> If you think it's an art, then you think that you can do anything you want, and it's poetic, and you have licence, and you're free. But you're *not* an artist if you're a doctor. It's actually a practice of healing in a very old tradition, going all the way back to Paracelsus. Jung was trying in all kinds of ways to be the wrong kind of physician. He tried to be Bleuler's assistant as a *psychiatrist* [at the Burgholzli Hospital], he tried to be Freud's assistant as a *psychoanalyst*, and it took him quite a bit of time to catch on to the kind of physician he was – neither a scientist like Bleuler, nor an artist like Freud, but something else – some kind of bombastic healing personality, like Paracelsus. He was in effect some kind of alchemist. There's a perfectly good long tradition in all this – what we try to do in our training is to bring a little bit of art on the one side and a little bit of science on the other side to keep us honest, so that we don't become inflated healer personalities, or sellers of 'snake oil of the unconscious', but actually try to check our work. The empathy for me is the most important thing – but even that

shouldn't be made the whole principle. I always feel that I am checking all those fantasies I have about what's going on in the patient against the hard data of their actual dreams. If you want to call that scientific, it may be. It's at least empirical.

Andrew Samuels, a London analyst who stands at the intellectually-critical end of the Jungian spectrum, believes that the scientific credentials of Jung are perfectly valid, but often overshadowed by the apparently outlandish interests and researches that Jung undertook. He argues, in characteristically direct language, that Jung's clinical, scientific work must lead the reader – or patient – into the esoteric psychological material.

If you can start to see Jung as a reliable mainstream shrink, then you have to look at his nuttier ideas – alchemy, mythology, mysticism, religion – in a different way. Because the problem for the Jungians is to get the guy's clinical credentials established. Then all the things we hold dear in his more esoteric and arcane interests, get re-evaluated.

The answer must be that analytical psychology is not exclusively art or science; but that it is a new kind of science; a science, perhaps, for the age of relativity, in which facts have ceased to be objective, and every judgement, as Jung explained personality types, is conditional. Jung knew all about the Age of Aquarius. The New Age movement, to the unease of many Jungians, claims him among others as a central thinker in their tradition. They may indeed be entitled to do so; for example, in August 1940 Jung wrote in a letter to his former assistant and friend Godwin Baynes:

My dear Peter,
This is the fateful year for which I have waited more than twenty-five years. I did not know that it was such a disaster. Although since 1918 I knew that a terrible fire would spread over Europe beginning in the north-east, I have no vision beyond 1940 concerning the fate of Europe. This year reminds me of the enormous earthquake in 26 B.C. that shook down the great temple of Karnak. It was the prelude to the destruction of all temples, because a new time had begun. 1940 is the year when we approach the meridian of the first star in Aquarius. It is the premonitory earthquake of the New Age.

James Hillman confirms that Jung has a connection to the New Age – with reservations:

The ideas that he started in the twenties are foundational for the New Age, absolutely foundational. He wrote the first introduction to Zen Buddhism, he began the rediscovery of Greek mythology; gods, goddesses and myths. He was concerned with the American Indians, he visited them; and he was interested in synchronicity, he was interested in astrology and he wrote on all these subjects and had lots of good things to say about them. So of course he's one of the pioneers or buttresses of the New Age. But the New Age tends to pick up only the so-called good or positive stuff. You know we carry the same ideas and go on repeating them in new dress every few years – that's our Western curse, or maybe it's history. So the New Age loses its own vision by being swallowed by our history. Now Jung always remembered our history and that's a big difference. He didn't think that you could leap over the history of Western culture, or that you could get out of the mess that this culture has produced in the world.

Jung didn't forget history – and he didn't fail to look at contemporary life with the eye of the historian, or the social anthropologist examining our own Western, contemporary culture as if it were the strangest phenomenon. He put distance between himself and his familiar surroundings, and the psychological patterns of himself and his patients, so that they could become less familiar – only then could the realities begin to appear to his eye. To Jung, myth was a way of expressing the truth of a culture – he knew that every culture needed its myth, so that it could explain itself. According to Hillman, Jung's travels helped him to see through the 'cultural overlay' which disguises the inner life of any nation.

Hillman is one of three American analysts who have arrived at the same view of modern society and its contemporary 'myth' – which reveals the truth about our collective psychology. For, just as the Jungian community itself is concerned to establish the 'scientific' credentials of Jung, so our Western culture has attached itself completely to the idea of science and technology as our foundation, our future, even our salvation. Science has become our modern myth: we like to believe that it will answer every question and cure every ill – that scientific progress will solve all our self-inflicted problems, and even answer fundamental questions about the nature of human existence.

James Hillman: The modern man had lost his myth, had lost his sense of myth. But you see we've moved that. Now we realize that technology is our myth. The myth is always the thing you're in and don't know it's a myth. We've lost certain ancient myths, or connection to the world as mythical, but we're still living myths. We can't ever step outside of a myth. We're in one now, television is a myth.

Robert Johnson: Mythology is always present. It's like asking 'Is matter present in today's world?' A much more difficult thing to say, and antagonistic to many ears, is that science is our present myth. Science is our 'as if'. For most people science is their religion. When a patient comes and says 'I will have nothing to do with all that medieval trash of beliefs and saints and the like,' I will say 'All right, tell me your beliefs,' because everybody has a belief. I can presume that everybody has a belief in the same sense that I can be assured that he has a liver and a heart and a gall bladder and a spleen – that's simply human equipment. Often a modern person, trained in scientific thinking, will seize upon this, and reproduce a wonderful myth in scientific terms, and often finds out that he has recapitulated traditional Christianity in new language.

Edward Edinger: Science is man's current authority. It's the one thing that is believable now. It's our reality and we can't escape that. That's why Jungian psychology is and had to be a science, because the new level of awareness must be born out of our best reality, and our best reality is science.

One does not need to look very far to see the irony in humankind's modern dependence upon scientific research and technological progress. We had begun to think that leaving our human environment on earth was not really dangerous, until the NASA *Challenger* Shuttle blew up in January 1986. We had become accustomed to the eradication of diseases by medical research until AIDS brought the very word 'plague' back into use. And the by-products of our research, progress and scientific discoveries have offered humanity the doomsday choice of destroying the planet at a single stroke with nuclear weapons, or slowly with the destruction of the whole ecology of the earth. When Jung spoke of the world's fragility, he said it hung 'by a thin thread' – the human psyche:

Nowadays we are not threatened by elemental catastrophes. There is no such thing [in nature] as an H-bomb; that is all man's doing. We are the great danger. The psyche is the great danger. What if something goes wrong with the psyche?

It seemed to Jung, as to many people who join pressure groups and Green parties, that something had already gone wrong. As long ago as 1924, in a Tunisian oasis town, he watched an elderly Arab ride by him on a mule. Jung was overwhelmed by the calm dignity of an essentially medieval figure, as he remembered later in *Memories, Dreams, Reflections*:

> The European is, to be sure, convinced that he is no longer what he was ages ago; but he does not know what he has since become. His watch tells him that since the 'Middle Ages' time and its synonym, progress, have crept up on him and irrevocably taken something from him. ... He compensates for the loss of gravity and the corresponding *sentiment d'incomplétude* by the illusion of his triumphs, such as steamships, railroads, airplanes, and rockets, that rob him of his duration and transport him into another reality of speeds and explosive accelerations. [*Memories, Dreams, Reflections*, p. 240]

In the 1980s, astronauts step off the planet in a routine which is now intended to be as commonplace as setting sail on a moderately choppy sea. We even send our spacecraft beyond the solar system: the *Voyager* craft has a panel of coded and illustrated messages from earth, to offer some image of ourselves to the beings who may one day find it. But why has science itself embraced the central hypothesis of science fiction? Have we got ourselves into such deep trouble that we are looking for help? And if the psyche is the great danger, are we doing the right thing by looking outwards into the stars – where we used to see the gods – instead of looking into ourselves? Space exploration ironically underlines the idea that humankind cannot after all rely on the intellectual, conscious life alone. If science is our present myth, science fiction is the myth of the future: it contains our hopes and fears about who and how we will be, rather than what we are now. Dr Edward Edinger sees science fiction as an expression of psychological need:

The psyche is taking the phenomenon of science and spinning fantasies, fantasy stories out of it, and what comes out of it is very interesting, because it's a modern mythology. And I think it's safe to say that science fiction – in all its various forms and variations – does have one basic recurring theme. It's the theme of extra-terrestrial intelligence in one form or another. It has a multitude of forms, but that's the basic idea. And that's highly significant psychologically because it demonstrates that the second centre of the psyche, the self, is all ready to be discovered.

A stylish example of the theme, occurring not in outer space but in domestic Californian suburbia, was seen in the Steven Spielberg movie *E.T.* – as John Beebe observes:

'E.T.', the extra-terrestrial himself, is a botanist and seems to operate in an extremely ecological way that goes so much against the kind of science that we see from the NASA scientists. The film is playing with another dimension. I think if *E.T.* is about anything, it's about empathy. It's about the enormous need for empathy which is somehow a different model from the scientific model. The myth of science, the myth of the heroic knower, the great heroic consciousness, whether we call that consciousness Darwin or Einstein or Freud or Newton, a whole myth of the modern age is the myth of heroic consciousness. We realize that if we go on with that period style, past its time, it won't work and besides it led us to the brink of destruction. The emerging myth in our time is the myth of empathy – that capacity to somehow vicariously experience what another person is experiencing.

To many modern people, the idea of myth is foreign: yet the modern media are the exponents of myth. Cinema is the purveyor of mythic stories, and the creator of mythic, archetypal figures – whether in falsifying real people, in the process of creating film stars – or in giving expression to existing heroic archetypes of cowboy, policeman, astronaut, Rambo. It is no coincidence that the most beautiful film actresses like Marilyn Monroe became known as 'screen goddesses'. And though the election of a film actor to the Presidency of the USA must be seen as an exception, both Presidential candidates in 1988 were seeking the public endorsement of performers such as Cher, Robert Redford, Sally Field and Arnold Schwarzenegger.

Film-makers like Steven Spielberg and George Lucas have drawn deliberately on myth and archetype to make their movies: hero archetypes and their quests, and grand dramas in confronting the shadow side of life. The Lost Ark (of the Covenant), the Temple of Doom, the Last Crusade, Star Wars, 'The Force' all evoke deep associations of good and evil in our cultural history. To San Francisco analyst John Beebe the massive appeal of science fiction films like the *Star Wars* trilogy or *E.T.* comes from their mingling the archetypal fantasy of extra-terrestrial life with characters which represent our own contemporary culture, and its myth.

> If you think a myth is something in the mind's museum that gets replayed again and again, you can say 'Well, *Star Wars* is a recreation of the hero myth' and so forth. That seems to me a little less interesting than to see myth as something that's happening all the time, that myths are being made all the time. It's interesting when a movie becomes not a kind of updated depiction of an old myth but creates its own new myth. To me the movie [*Star Wars*] comes alive because it has so many of the elements of our culture, all scattered around through it. The princess is a little bit like a rather pert but nevertheless American, women's lib kind of princess. Then of course we have R2D2 and the butler [C3PO], as a kind of Laurel and Hardy; and of course we have the Cowardly Lion [Chewbacca] and you have the young kind of sparky, spanking clean young hero [Luke Skywalker]. You have the wise old man [Obi Wan-Kenobi] and you have all these loose archetypes of the culture.

One cannot be surprised that Jung himself commented on film as an art form and a source of archetypal images; he allegedly analysed 67,000 dreams during the course of his life, and there can be few aspects of human experience which did not arise, somehow. In the volume of the *Collected Works* that was compiled from a series of his seminars on dreams, he is quoted as having said:

> The movies are far more efficient than the theatre. They are less restricted, they are able to produce amazing symbols to show the collective unconscious since their methods of presentation are so unlimited. [*The Seminars*, Vol. 1, p. 12]

The film-maker, above all, is not restricted to reality: and John Beebe is particularly interested in a scene in *Star Wars* in which the myth comes to life.

At a critical moment on the Death Ship, one finds them in the
garbage compacter, and so to speak all this cultural garbage is
gradually being compacted and suddenly Luke Skywalker is
grabbed by one of his legs and taken down into the sort of primal
slime – it's some kind of peculiar serpent has grabbed him. Down
he goes, and then he comes up spluttering, and it's as if just at
that moment the life in the material grabs one of the characters,
and when he comes up, the whole thing is now a living myth. The
whole thing has a kind of joyous energy. I think it was that joy in
rediscovering the mythic dimension that makes that such a
wonderful film. In other words, the unconscious got interested in
what the film-maker had done.

To John Beebe, the movie experience is vividly psychological:

The Freudians have it that going to the movie is like having a good
feed at the breast – you know, the curtains part just exactly the
way the mother unbuttons the blouse. . . . As a Jungian – we always
clean things up a little bit – I feel that the issue with the movies is
the hope that a bit of truth will be captured and that in some way
our consciousness will be raised. Whenever you see a film in a
dream, someone is watching a film or going to the movies, that's
a not uncommon dream image, I think it means that we're looking
at a situation that has been thoroughly studied, it's been cut and
edited and homed in on, and presented for us, and it's a completely
understood situation now, and if we just watch it through, we will
have a complete sense of what it is. In our own individual life we
only get a chance to see perhaps one little piece of a whole
archetypal pattern, but in a movie we can have the whole pattern
laid out for us in a couple of hours. and in a great enough film,
there's really a sense of having been translocated from one's own
personal experience and the little bit that one has experienced, to
something truly universal, and I think that's what the archetype
can do. It's sort of a ticket of admission to a broader perspective.

Of all directors, the one whom John Beebe most admires – and for
him presents the widest psychological canvas – is Alfred Hitchcock.

Hitchcock often complained that there were so few people in
Hollywood who understood anything about imagery, and I
consider him one of the great masters of imagery of the twentieth
century. He gets more done per unit time than any director I know.

And then of course all his films are about psychological development, and all of his films are a kind of emotional or if you like, psychological autobiography, which is why I think he walks through each one of them, as if to say 'This is me, this is my psychological process.' And through the fifty-three films you see his individuation, and how many things he had to bump off to get on with his life. Of course late in his career, in *Marnie*, he actually has one of the characters, played by Sean Connery, give Tippi Hedren, who plays Marnie, Jung's book *The Undiscovered Self* to read. Film-makers tell you what they've been reading or noticing, they put a little homage in, and that was a little homage to Jung. But the point was in the title – *The UNDISCOVERED Self*, because the self isn't a known thing, by Jung or anyone else, and Hitchcock is just as much an explorer and a creator and a pioneer in this area as Jung. I learned a lot of psychology from Hitchcock.

Through the flickering light from the projection room, a film drama can enable us to project ourselves, by fantasy, into the situations that present themselves in the film. No individual can truly experience the full range of human possibilities – but she/he can 'project' what other possibilities might be like for her/his own life. There can be physical limitations, which are easy to understand, or the limitations of one's personality type, or any other psychological aspect. The wild cheering of audiences that greeted the screening of *Rambo* and *Top Gun* suggests that for the passive spectators the idea and experience of even a caricatured battle between good and evil, or might and right, can provide something psychologically necessary.

Robert Johnson is an analyst and author whose simple and direct books on the psychology of men, women and relationships – succinctly titled *He*, *She*, and *We* – draw on mythological stories to identify unchanging truths of human life. Johnson is a tall and broad, tanned man who walks with a limp and talks slowly, quietly, one word at a time. He has a meditative and almost monastic manner which in fact reflects not only his psychological reality, but also a certain physical limitation, which creates a need for projection.

I was born in Portland, Oregon, the north-west corner of America. It's left on me what I choose to call a 'lumberjack' part of my personality. It's lumberjack land. It's forest, it's roughness, it's an unsophisticated part of America. It forms a considerable part of my character. But it's very difficult for me – because I was very badly injured in an auto accident when I was eleven years of age, and have done very little sport, so I've not made much use of my body, in my lifetime. So that rather primitive lumberjack quality hasn't had much expression in my life. It lives largely in projection to this day in my character. I can't do much of it, so I have to surround myself with people who are proficient in things like that.

Such things form a great deal of one's character. Life has a cruel dimension to it, in that we're born with a wide range of characteristics, choose some of them to live, and have a residue of unlived life, no matter how we have lived, and that unlived life is very demanding in one. If you have married, it's the bachelor or the monk in you which remains unlived and makes demands on one later in one's life. If one has not married, then it's the family man in one which intrudes and makes such incessant demands upon one later in one's life. Life simply isn't long enough or broad enough to live all of the capacities which one brings to it.

We cannot live out all the archetypal possibilities personally, so we project: on to other people, known to us or otherwise, who live out the bits of the psychic pattern we do not ourselves have – thus we may marry the opposite psychological type for compensation; or have quiet, rational, chess-playing friends if we are loud and emotional extroverts. This pattern offers one explanation of the phenomenon of 'fame' – that the undistinguished mass of people, who are 'ordinary', are absorbed and fascinated by those whose achievements, wealth, beauty or talent are 'extraordinary'. Projection is the fate and burden of movie stars, political leaders, and royalty – as the British royal family knows only too well. Robert Johnson was staying with friends in London when he witnessed the force of the 'royal archetype':

The housekeeper came in one afternoon and she was completely overwhelmed, because she'd seen the Queen. There was no dinner possible that night because the housekeeper had seen the Queen, and she couldn't focus on anything, she couldn't boil a kettle of water for tea. So we had to do something else. That household moved to America, and five years later – same housekeeper had been brought along – she came in totally out of commission, because she had seen Clark Gable, and there was to be no dinner and she couldn't boil a kettle of water. I was in near tears because England offered a queen as a repository for the greatness and the majesty of an archetype which exists in all of us, and the best that America could do was Clark Gable.

It is Johnson's view, however, that in recent years the necessary majesty of the British royal family has somehow been undermined.

England has its royal family, not doing particularly well with them at the moment, but they're there and the very fact that they draw so much attention from so many people means that the archetype of royalty is still alive and fully functioning in the British people. But the English royalty is not accorded the dignity, or the majesty which that archetype is worthy of. Ask a man what he thinks of his king or his queen, and you'll ask him what he thinks of himself, basically. We don't have a king or a queen to bear such images, so we have to go to Hollywood for it.

Hollywood movie stars do have a mythic dimension, but they cannot truly replace the archetype of royalty – which requires that one be born to the inheritance. Yet our inheritance of dreams, the collective unconscious, makes us aware of all that unlived potential for psychological experience, which somehow we need to bring to consciousness. As Robert Johnson points out:

The collective unconscious is too big to live out personally. It's like asking someone to cope with 100,000 volt power in a high tension line through the 110 volt wiring of the house, to live out the collective unconscious himself. Much of it has to be lived by projection. So we assign the great heroic 100,000 volt archetype so to speak to someone else, some place else, some thing else. If one tries to take them personally, he's quite likely simply to burst into a psychosis and be burnt as badly as if 100,000 volts had come through the wiring of his house.

The object of our projections and fantasies can be burned, too. The film critic and analyst John Beebe points to the archetypal screen goddess, Marilyn Monroe:

I think there's no question that the person involved can get quite confused with the archetypal image that's being portrayed, and that can confuse people on both sides of the screen so to speak. The famous example is Marilyn Monroe and in a dream which she apparently reported to someone and was written down, she was standing naked in a church, and all kinds of people were coming and worshipping her there. Of course simply said, this is the love goddess, but in its religious aspect. It seems to me that her education and her consciousness and the amount of security she had in her early background didn't give her a strong enough ego or strong enough personality, to stand up to an archetypal image like that, and criticize it and say: 'Well it's as if in some way, my image is terribly important to people and has religious significance, and no wonder, there's so little of the goddess in our culture, no wonder that they would use me in this way.' I think there the person gets swallowed by the image.

Woody Allen's film *The Purple Rose of Cairo* made an overt comic plot from the confusion of screen star and real individual. A downtrodden housewife (Mia Farrow), whose only escape from the drudgery of her life is found in the fantasies of the movie theatre, is astonished to find that the matinée idol on the screen begins speaking to her directly and then steps right out of the screen into her life. John Beebe adds:

That's all because people don't have an imaginative space to let this live inside themselves, and that's really what Jung could open up for us, which is the right way to take these movie images, and that right way I don't think is exactly literally, but rather to give them a kind of reality in the imagination.

What we do imaginatively in the darkened space of the cinema, we do more fully and whole-heartedly in travelling to other countries and cultures; where our own understanding, customs and feelings may prove to be very inadequate equipment for relating to the people and places where we find ourselves. Equally, we may visit a new country and find ourselves overwhelmed by a sense of ease, that 'this is where I belong'. We project ourselves into another culture; and in doing so we find that the way people act, think, and relate can be generally typical of that culture – and we discover that the same is true of our own, when we get the distance to observe it objectively. What is 'typical' describes the 'type' of the culture or the nation; and Jung's system of typology appears to work, in a fairly generalized way, for nations as well as for individuals. Switzerland, competent and rooted, is introverted and sensation type – related to facts. The USA appears to be mostly extroverted, and thinking type, as Jung himself observed in speaking to one of his American friends:

In America you blow across your country, there's no limit to its space, anybody can go any place, but the Swiss are held together, enclosed by our mountains, we can't blow around, we have to stay grounded.

When we travel we feel different: we may not smell the blood in the sand, as Jung did in Tunisia, but we detect an atmosphere that belongs to the people. Robert Johnson, an introverted feeling type, regards himself as ill at ease, and untypical, in extroverted can-do America. But on his first trip to India, he had 'come home'.

I was born in the typology of introverted feeling, which occupies only one per cent of the American populace. America's an extroverted thinking nation, and I had the good fortune/medium fortune/bad fortune of being born into a typology one hundred and eighty degrees opposite to my own. My attraction to India is that it is an introverted, feeling society, and I am immediately at home in India. My first trip there – I'm not a very heroic, audacious person – was a frightening event to take on. I arrived alone at four in the morning, had been in the air twenty-four hours, was dreadfully tired, my luggage was lost. A swarm of Indian taxi drivers seized upon me, but I was at home, and I knew it. Relationship in India is light years ahead of ours in consciousness. That is their speciality – feeling and relatedness is their differentiated faculty, and it's a joy for me to be in a society which has introverted feeling as its differentiated faculty. Just as it might be an enormous relief to an Indian of a different typology to come here and have things clean and on time, and working mechanically.

The use of type to describe nations or regions can easily be over-loaded and stretched too far – like all psychological observation. In the outer world, we are wrong to think that life is purely material, for the human psyche is the source of all imagination, creativity and thought – whether its product is 'all coming evil' in Jung's phrase, or the compassion and humanity which can save an endangered planet. Equally, there are aspects of the outer world which have nothing much to do with the psyche, and everything to do with practical necessities. The outer world of the everyday does have an inner dimension, which we can observe, consider, and possibly even understand.

Jung was always interested in the way the psyche made itself known in the outer world. He had an instinct for finding it in those things which ordinary people found fascinating, rather than that which medical science deemed worthy of investigation. He always maintained that he was a medical doctor and empiricist first and foremost – but he wrote about spiritualism and seances, UFOs, Picasso and James Joyce, astrology, alchemy, fairy-tales, Gnosticism, and the doctrine of the Assumption of Mary. In it all he saw a reflection of the human psyche.

9

A Meaningful Life

For Jung, the inner meaning was the real meaning,
especially under modern conditions. As Jung would put it,
in the Middle Ages, it was all out there. You looked up at
the night sky, and you saw heaven and those stars *were*
living beings and so on. But since Galileo, it's all got
internalized within the self, so the things that used to be up
in the sky are now in our hearts. That's how Jung would
put it.
Reverend Don Cupitt

In his long career Dr Jung, the psychiatrist, did more than treat his
individual patients. By the end of his life, he felt that he had diagnosed
'the crisis of man in the age of science and technology.' This crisis, he
felt, derived from the decline of formal religion, the development of
man's capacity both to create life and to destroy it all, and the psychological evidence of an increasingly desperate, often despairing, search
for meaning in the world of everyday human experience. When
Andrew Samuels attributes the cliché of 'meaningfulness' to Jung
himself, he is reminding us of the fact of our times that however much
we know of the causes of life and events, we increasingly lack a sense
of the meaning of life.

The Swiss dentist, later an analyst, Sigmund Hurwitz, who became
Jung's patient in the course of his mid-life crisis, recalls that in his
childhood, he needed to ask profound questions:

When I was a boy of about twelve years, I went once to the forest
together with my brother, who was ten years older than I, and I

asked him 'Tell me, what is the meaning of life?' He hesitated a
moment, and then he laughed and said 'The meaning of life is life
itself.' I was not satisfied and I thought 'I don't know the meaning
of life now, but later on I must find that out.' And I found it out
by my analysis with Jung. Now, towards the end of my life, I know
that the meaning of life is to get a relation to the unconscious, to
ripen, to grow, and to come to the inner nucleus of the personality.
What Jung calls the Self. Through analysis, normal as well as
neurotic people get this relation to the unconscious and come in a
process of ripening and growing to nearer their inner centre – and
that is the way from the ego to the self in Jungian terminology.

The search for meaning, at an individual and personal level, underlies Jung's psychology and the method of analysis. He observed that
for the majority of his patients in the second half of life, the question
of religion was the crucial aspect of psychological difficulty. He did not
define religion narrowly, in the sense of 'organized religion' or 'the
church'. It was the individual's capacity to have a real spiritual experience, and to feel a sense of personal meaning. It might come in the
structure of the church, but it might not; and Jung was sceptical
about whether the church and its adherents necessarily had anything
essentially religious about them. Baroness Vera von der Heydt is a
Jungian analyst in London, who first met Jung in 1927. A German
Catholic, with an unhappy marriage behind her, the Baroness spent
some years teaching Jungian psychology to youth leaders in Edin-
burgh.

He was interested in me because of my being an ordinary Roman
Catholic. And he asked me many questions about it, and yet when
I had religious experiences in Zurich, when I went there, he never
touched the essential experience, he left it alone. Whether he was
pro- or anti-organized religion depended on the individual he was
seeing, and whether they had in fact experienced what they
believed. That is to say whether dogma, doctrine, rites, ritual, was
a meaningful, helpful, opening for them and their psyche or not. As
soon as he saw or thought that he encountered dishonesty, then
that was out.

It is almost inevitable that Jung should have been drawn to consider
the religious dimension of the psyche; his father was a Protestant
minister in the Swiss Reformed Church, who struggled – perhaps
unsuccessfully – to retain his faith. Carl Jung himself never professed

to be a believer – but religious imagery presented itself in his dreams; his patients dreamed of him as a kind of God; his pupils dreamed of being initiated as priests; one of them had a dream that he and Jung's other followers were toiling to build a massive temple – a task which would take them six hundred years.

In his travels, in mythology, in the archetypes of the collective unconscious, he was always finding religious material which helped to make sense of the psyche; and at home, religious atmosphere was both deliberately and coincidentally present. At Kusnacht, where the two largest buildings in the village are the Protestant and Catholic churches, he had stained glass windows built in his study, where he saw his patients; at Bollingen, which became a kind of sacred retreat for him, there lived a famous spiritual healer who healed animals and villagers alike; and a few miles away, near the Black Madonna cathedral at Einsiedeln, was the refuge of the religious healer-hermit Paracelsus.

Baroness von der Heydt sees Jung's attention to religion as being an extension of the concept of the 'reality of the psyche':

> I think that he minded not having the charisma of faith. He very much minded that his father was unable to go further than the actual dogmatic teaching he had received, and that he died prematurely because he was unable to deal with his doubts, that he saw his suffering and heard his father pray – he says that, he writes that. And he writes that he would not have been able to continue his research into religion and might have lost all his religious sense if he had not discovered the importance of experience. And from early childhood on he had so many religious experiences, which he comments upon, and so much of his knowledge came from his experience, that he was unable to give up the idea of the spiritual perspective of man. For him religion was really *religare* – the binding back to the roots of one's self.

The crisis of modern man is to have lost his soul, or become rootless; but at the same time to have become godlike in the ability to manipulate birth, death, and the potential destruction of all known life. We understand almost all the technical causes – but not the meaning. It was the pervasive, even oppressive, absence of meaning in the lives of his European patients which drove Jung to consider Europe from the more objective distance of non-white, non-European cultures. In New Mexico, Jung felt that the civilized Western white race – the 'Anglos' –

suffered from having lost their true myth, unlike the Anasazi tribes whom one can encounter even today.

The Acoma people, for example, repeat and illustrate their 'Exodus' story in their everyday crafts – which sell to tourists and sustain them directly. The Pueblo Indians perform, for themselves and also for tourists, the ceremonial and ritual dances which relate them to the gods and the natural world which sustains them. And their everyday ritual of greeting the sun and assisting it across the heavens, gives a dignity to the tribe, and establishes a relationship between humanity and deity. Jung observed:

> That man feels capable of formulating valid replies to the overpowering influence of God, and that he can render back something which is essential even to God, induces pride, for it raises the human individual to the dignity of a metaphysical factor. 'God and us' – even if it is only an unconscious *sous-entendu* – this equation no doubt underlies that enviable serenity of the Pueblo Indian. Such a man is in the fullest sense of the word in his proper place. [*Memories, Dreams, Reflections*, p. 253]

Thus he found – despite the modernity of his chosen field of psychology and psychiatry – that the eternal aspects of religion were inescapable as a psychological experience. Dr Adolf Guggenbuhl-Craig observes that this in itself was a contradiction of prevailing scientific thinking:

> In the nineteenth century, one even tried to have a psychology without soul, and he was courageous enough to face soul, because the human soul is something very frightening, and what made him was that he was maybe frightened too, but able all the same to face it, to face psyche. You cannot be a psychologist without taking the religious into account. We all have a religious side and it was one of Jung's courageous statements saying that we cannot deal with the human psyche without having to deal with religion. He always insisted he's not a theologian, but in reality of course, in his writings, there are many theological statements, and some people even thought he was really rejuvenating modern Christianity.

The Reverend Don Cupitt *is* a theologian, and is Chaplain of Emmanuel College, Cambridge. While by no means agreeing with all of Jung's ideas and observations about religion, he acknowledges that Jung has influenced the modern way in which religion is perceived – as an inescapable psychological reality independent of church, dogma, and confession.

> Jung was a non-realist about religion. That is, he didn't think of religious objects as beings out there, he thought their true and most vivid meaning was within the psyche. So for example the real encounter with God is the encounter with your own unconscious. Religious experience was the psyche's own struggle towards integration. It was in effect the process of psychic growth. Jung was a religious naturalist, that's part of his originality. That is to say he takes it for granted that religion is produced from inside us. He doesn't accept any metaphysical or supernatural account of where religion comes from, and on that I agree with him. I sometimes provoke my fellow believers by saying that if the idea of God hadn't been produced from inside us, it wouldn't be of any interest to us. What is more, the gods that people worship quite obviously tell us a lot about the people who worship them, which is surely evidence that our gods come from inside ourselves.

The reality of religion, to Jung the doctor, was a fact because of what could be observed, objectively, in the life of the patient. Don Cupitt explains with a surprising example:

> For him, religious realities were realities because they have effects, they bring about events in our psychic life and so on. It's perhaps easier to understand his meaning if you take another case, like that of say the Loch Ness Monster. Now for Jung the Loch Ness Monster was a real thing. It was an event in our psychic life. So when people start having visions of the Loch Ness Monster, what this means is that some kind of eruption is taking place within the unconscious of our age. For him, stories of monsters and flying saucers are genuinely interesting stories about human spiritual life.

Seven months before he died, Jung summarized the religious emphasis of his life's work, in a letter to an English correspondent. Not included in the *Collected Letters*, but later published, in part, in an article by the editor of the Letters, Dr Gerhard Adler, this was the letter which made such an impact on the American analyst Dr Edward Edinger.

> It's a rather lengthy letter, of several pages, but the passage that struck me most strongly was one where he says 'I have failed in

my foremost task – to open people's eyes to the fact that man has a soul, that there is a buried treasure in the field, and that our religion and philosophy are in a lamentable state.' It's the human soul, that's the buried treasure.

Jung's recognition of the treasure is not universally shared, and this alone is his failure – though such pessimism is exceptional within his published works and letters, and many of his followers find it impossible to accept that he could have written or spoken of his own failure. But in our modern existence, instead of finding the treasure, we search for pleasure. The pursuit of pleasure has become manic and obsessive; and in the form of drug-addiction and alcohol-abuse, the most debilitating symptoms of that mania are now beginning to be considered in the context of Jung's ideas about religion, meaning and the soul. Indeed, Jungian psychology has a history of relationship to alcoholism: Jung himself had as a patient the American alcoholic who became the founder of Alcoholics Anonymous. Dr Jeffrey Satinover, the psychiatrist and analyst in Stamford, Connecticut, is specializing in the treatment of both addiction and senility in his new clinic:

> Basically the motive for starting Alcoholics Anonymous came out of a patient of Jung's experience, and Jung's communicating to that patient the idea that essentially he was not going to ever successfully get over his alcoholism if he did not find God.

The official history of Alcoholics Anonymous traces the group's origins to Jung's diagnosis of the incurable alcoholic known only as 'Rowland H.'. In a public lecture, given in 1958, one of the founders of Alcoholics Anonymous, 'Bill W.', gave this account:

> Few people know that the first tap-root of A.A. hit pay-dirt some thirty years ago in a physician's office. Dr Carl Jung, that great pioneer in psychiatry, was talking to an alcoholic patient.

The patient, Rowland H., had exhausted all other medical possibilities in the USA, and was treated by Jung for a year. But within a short time he was drinking again, and returned to Jung, who told him that medicine had nothing more to offer in such a severe case of the neurosis. But he added, according to Bill W.:

> 'Once in a while, alcoholics have had what are called vital spiritual experiences ... and a completely new set of conceptions and motives begins to dominate them. Ordinary religious faith isn't

enough. What I'm talking about is a *transforming experience*, a conversion experience, if you like. I can only recommend that you place yourself in the religious atmosphere of your own choice, that you recognize your personal hopelessness, and that you cast yourself upon whatever God you think there is.'

The patient chose the Oxford Group of that day as his religious association and atmosphere. Terribly chastened and almost hopeless, he began to be active with it. To his intense joy and astonishment, the obsession to drink presently left him.

Three years later, in a letter to William G. Wilson, the author of the official history of Alcoholics Anonymous, Jung wrote of Rowland H.:

His craving for alcohol was the equivalent on a low level of the spiritual thirst of our being for wholeness, expressed in medieval language: the union with God.

The only right and legitimate way to such an experience is that it happens to you in reality, and it can only happen to you when you walk on a path which leads you to a higher understanding. You might be led to that goal by an act of grace or through a personal and honest contact with friends or through a high education of the mind beyond the confines of mere rationalism.

You see, alcohol in Latin is *spiritus* and you use the same word for the highest religious experience as well as for the most depraving poison. The helpful formula therefore is: *spiritus contra spiritum.* [Letter, 30 January 1961]

Jung's approach, now taken up by Dr Satinover and others, was that the alcoholic craving was an inappropriate and dangerous expression of a valid, indeed necessary, craving – for a sense of meaning, for elevation above the mundane and material world; for the things which traditionally have been thought to arise in religious experience. Dr Satinover explains:

What people seek in addictive experience is something which in and of itself is normal – that is to say, the craving is normal, the craving for certain kinds of elation, for a certain specialness, for heroism, for cessation of pain, and underlying all of those really, ultimately, and most powerful, is the seeking of a sense of meaningfulness. The capacity of drugs and alcohol to induce transient illusions as it were, of life being filled with meaning, is probably underestimated. We don't look at drug and alcohol experience from an introverted point of view, saying 'What is it that the person is really experiencing and craving?' When you do that, you understand that drugs and alcohol provide a crude substitute for other kinds of experience that are much more difficult to achieve, but are also much more profound and long-lasting when achieved.

Dr Satinover treats both alcoholics and drug-addicts; and in the abuse of drugs, some doctors are evolving a theory that the drug of choice reflects crudely the type of psychological problem, or the aspect of meaninglessness, that the individual suffers. He explains it thus:

From a more medical point of view, you could say they're treating an illness, crudely. From the more psychological point of view, you could say that the illness is in fact a lack of certain emotional experiences and they're attempting to induce those experiences through the use of exogenous substances. A lot of research is beginning to show that there are correlations between the drug of choice and the underlying need. So that depressed individuals tend to seek drugs like cocaine, whereas extremely anxious individuals will tend to seek alcohol. And this is why *heroin* got its name. Individuals are seeking in addiction to many substances a *heroic* experience. Cocaine probably does that more than any other.

I think it's probably fair to say that cocaine is the drug of choice of the *puer aeternus* culture. That's a Latin term that Jung introduced, referring to a collection of gods of antiquity that remained eternally young. The *puer aeternus* simply means eternal boy – the ancients recognized that the craving for eternal youth is a universal one, and that it's best to worship that craving in the form of a god out there, than to simply enact it in one's life. We live in a culture now where enacting the myth of the *puer aeternus* is so widespread that it's almost become the norm, and it's not surprising that cocaine would be the drug that goes along with that, because more than any other drug, cocaine induces the sense of eternal youthfulness, eternal capacity, endless capacity, lack of limits, no boundaries, the capacity to fly – without the restrictions of mundane life.

What we hope an individual will gain from the psychotherapeutic dimension of substance-abuse treatment is a way of finding meaning in their lives again. Because as Jung correctly recognized, ultimately, the key motivating factor in the beginning of an addiction is the seeking of spirit.

In referring to the gods, and the ancients, Dr Satinover reminds us that the human need for a sense of meaning and validity is an archetypal quest, which is more often expressed in mythology and legend than in factual history or everyday life. The Greek god Dionysos, whose name has become inaccurately connected with drunkenness, was originally the god of religious ecstasy. Robert Johnson argues that Dionysos offers an insight into the modern epidemic of alcoholism:

> If you dethrone an archetype from Olympus, it immediately turns up as a symptom. As we lose mythology we gain neurosis. The Greeks had a Dionysian vision which was pure ecstasy; and the Roman world degraded it considerably into Bacchus, the drunken one, and Bacchanalia which was Bacchus's festival, was banned in the year 152 or something by the Greek Senate and has not been seen in polite society since. So the Dionysian quality turns up now in the thrills which we get and the drugs which we take, and, maybe worst of all, in alcohol. Dionysos was not the god of drunkenness, he was the god of ecstatic vision. He was a god of wine, but that was the wine of religion, not the wine of drunkenness.

Johnson draws on mythology for fables of psychological reality. His most recent book *Ecstasy* (referring also to the 'designer-drug' of the same name) explores the myth of Dionysos as a metaphor of modern life and its deep need for meaning, for emotional highs, and ecstasy.

> It is basic, and if we don't get our ecstasy, which is an archetypal quality, in a legitimate way, we will get it in an illegitimate way – which accounts for much of the chaos of this culture now. We have to have an ecstatic dimension of our life. If it doesn't come in legitimate ways, then we will get it by way of alcoholism, or drugs, or the thrill and the kicks of violence in movies, on television and the like. If we don't get a particular archetypal quality legitimately it will, so to speak, pop up somewhere in its symptomatic, that is, its compulsive form.

In all ancient cultures, the heights of the mountains and the heavens have been identified as the place of the gods: Moses received the Ten Commandments from his God on the mountain-top; the Greek gods dwelt on Mount Olympus; the Pueblo Indians live close to their Father Sun on the 6,000 foot high plateau of New Mexico. The phrase 'getting high' is purposeful slang, as Dr Satinover observes:

The metaphor of height applied to a mental state is universal. You could be on top of a mountain, 'I'm at the peak of my form,' 'I'm sitting on top of the world' – the idea of getting high is directly connected to the experience of an altered sense of self. And when an individual seeks the experience of getting high, the implication is that they chronically, or as a matter of course do not feel high.

Technological advances of the modern age have physically conquered all the heights and even invaded the heavens. Thus we have eliminated the mystery and the meaning of powerful archetypes. Jung himself was dismayed:

> The gods have become diseases. Zeus no longer rules Olympus, but rather the solar plexus and produces curious specimens for the doctor's consulting-room or disorders the brains of politicians and journalists who unwittingly let loose psychic epidemics on the world. [*Collected Works* vol. 13, par. 37]

The far-flung community of Jungian analysts is a group for whom a sense of meaning is an everyday reality – either as something to be discovered gradually, and in retrospect, or as an experience bordering on revelation. Many analysts describe their finding Jung, or Jung's work, as a moment of illumination in which their destiny became apparent. Baroness von der Heydt is one of those who, in encountering Jung, met her personal destiny.

> I didn't want to become an analyst, I knew I was. I had been working with a man who did hand-analysis. He was a Jungian, and he was the man who pointed his finger to Jung and told me that I should have an analysis. At the time it was impossible for me for financial reasons, but I was able to read; and I read my first book – it was *Modern Man in Search of Soul* – and for the first time I did not mind that I understood what I was reading. Because I always thought that if I were to understand what somebody wrote then it meant that the man was an idiot just as much as I was an idiot. And for the first time Jung really spoke to my condition and really spoke a language which I could understand and which I could follow, and I knew that it was the right language for me.

The survivors of the first generation of Jung's followers are now at the end of their lives: through their work and that of the now-ageing second generation, the matter of ageing itself has become a focus of attention. They are able to reflect on their own experience, of how dreams are fewer but 'bigger', more archetypal, and often more important. More elderly patients are entering into analysis, it seems, and for women there seems a new turning-point, at about sixty, where a need arises to find new meaning. Jung's work began with his own inner life, and for these elderly analysts – almost all still working, writing and seeing patients – the arrival of old age and the approach of death is an opportunity to observe what the unconscious has to say. Many of them find that the permanent human search for meaning can only be fulfilled in looking back. Dr Joseph Henderson, the San Francisco analyst who first met Jung in 1929, offers this reflection on Jung's theme of individuation, the personal psychological fulfilment which can be expressed simply in the phrase 'meaning in life':

> In the second half of life, I think individuation – not for everyone, but for many people who grow and develop and become conscious of themselves – it becomes part of a way of life. And the end of it is death and they know it, and they have to get somehow ready for that occasion. But not in a gloomy way, simply as a part of life which has its natural end, and along the way a new philosophy of life usually emerges which is able to meet that.

As theologian Don Cupitt points out, Jung's idea of psychological development included the whole of life – even unto death – and thus contradicted evolutionary theory which argues that human, or animal, development ceases after the point of procreation.

> It doesn't seem to me to make sense to suppose that the process of psychic development Jung describes as going on all our lives could have been produced by biological evolution. For example, Freud thought that when we raised our children, our psychic development must come to an end because nature has use for us only as long as we've still to pass on our genes. Once our kids have grown up, nature's finished with us. Whereas Jung thought we went on developing right up to death.

Colleagues and pupils of Jung face their old age with a striking calm. Jung believed that death is a part of life, rather than an end to life; and many of them are apparently living that idea in their old age and, in some cases, ill health. Dr Marie-Louise von Franz, *'diese kleine Genie'* ('this little genius') as Jung called her, continues to work on alchemical texts despite what she considers a terminal illness. But her commitment to the reality of the psyche is undimmed:

It is only now, that I have dreamed that it is finished, and I've done my work, that I see the pattern. In old age, one turns away from outer activity more, and one begins to reflect and to summarize whatever I have done up till now and what for and has it any meaning or was it meaningless, and a certain fear of death which makes one prepare to be concerned with death. And then one begins to be less concerned with detailed questions – but more with overall questions: what is life, what is the meaning of life, why have I lived, what have I lived for, was it worthwhile. One *reflects*, which means one *bends back* into what happened, to make a summary.

Aniela Jaffe, who worked alongside Jung as pupil and secretary for more than twenty-five years, also considers a sense of meaning as the product of reflection.

What is meaning? We create meaning and that's so important. Afterwards, when I look back on my long, long life, there were things which were very difficult for me. But later I saw the meaning, I created it. If you try to understand your dreams and your fantasies, then perhaps you can find meaning, in looking back, as Jung saw, in reflection.

As an example, Aniela Jaffe quotes her own brief marriage, at the age of twenty, to a fellow-student in Berlin. Aniela is Jewish – and that apparent mistake probably saved her life.

I was married. We were very young – twenty and twenty-one – but it didn't last very long, so we divorced and I thought what can that mean? It was ridiculous, two students marrying, then splitting up. The meaning for me was: this marriage saved my life, because I got a Swiss passport – he was Swiss – and so I could go to Switzerland, and I came to Jung. These are the detours, you see, which life creates which one doesn't understand. But decades later one understands.

Dr Joe Wheelwright, who was born in 1906, has filled his life with adventure, travel, amusement, extroversion and story-telling, and a deep feeling for his patients. Both he and his wife Jane retreat for up to half of every year to a ranch on the California coastline – part of Jane's original family property – where the peace of natural surroundings sustains the reflective mood of old age. As Joe says:

When one is preparing for death, which is what I've been busy doing for the last ten years – it sounds lugubrious, but at my age, it isn't. I've had an incredibly rich life. I call God 'Albert', and if they threw the switch on me tomorrow and I had time, I would scrawl: 'Dear Albert – thank you – Joe.'

Jane Wheelwright: I no longer dream about houses or walls or anything like that. Sometimes there's a little suggestion of a wall, which is like saying – this is a house. But that's all. Because it's all nature now. I think old age leads right in to nature. It came out of nature, it goes back to nature.

These elderly analysts have spent their lives in the attempt to fathom the realities of human psychology, and in their old age they appear to embody a wisdom and calm. The archetypes of the 'old wise man' and 'old wise woman' appear in mythologies, religions and dreams everywhere; many people enter analysis in the hope of absorbing some wisdom, insight or meaning from an older analyst. Dr Adolf Guggenbuhl-Craig, however, has written a book with a very different attitude to old age – called simply *Old Fools*. He argues that the 'old wise man/woman' archetype is incomplete, idealizing, and dangerous – and that it needs to be balanced by an understanding that in old age, people can and do become foolish or incompetent – and that they can enjoy their lack of responsibility or authority. He quotes a Japanese ceremony in which people reaching the age of sixty-one or sixty-two get dressed in children's clothes; and the Buddhist saints who laugh absurdly on the mountain-sides – the fools on the hill. King Lear, he suggests, was the real, tragic fool – unable to see who loved and protected him; while the 'Fool' spoke the truth. Dr Guggenbuhl-Craig explains:

The old fool is a reaction against the old wise man or the old wise woman. When I was young, I obviously hoped that one day I would understand what's going on, and I was in some way admiring the people who were older, because I thought they knew what they were talking about. Then all of a sudden I woke up and I was old myself, and wasn't a bit wiser, and saw that I don't understand much, or even some things less. And that's a bit depressing. And then I thought 'Well, but there must be something to old age after all, it cannot only be that there is less in it.'

I saw one possibility in old age which has been depicted in images too, is that when you're old you don't have to care so much any more – as a young man, when you are thirty, you have to make your career, and you have to see that you're judged as clever and intelligent and decent – when you can say: 'What the hell, what does it matter if people think I'm an idiot or if I'm an old fool?' So the archetype of the old fool is really a fuller archetype than the old wise man – who is a one-sided propaganda gimmick of older people to dominate the younger ones.

There is an irony in the fact that the first-generation of Jungian analysts, of whom so many have survived well into their eighties, embody both an image of wisdom and an intellectual vigour which could be envied by many younger people. Many of them appear far younger than their years. Dr Guggenbuhl-Craig objects:

That's a kind of tremendous pressure on these poor old people. They have not only to look younger, they even have to be more experienced and more clever and so on. I think it's an insult if you say to an old person: 'You look very young.'

Aniela Jaffe considers that age itself should be respected, and that a supposed youthfulness in old age is irrelevant:

Today old age is not appreciated very much. There are too many old people, so sometimes I'm ashamed to still be here with my eighty-five years. And the value which people give to old age is how young they feel, how youthful. You see, that is the value of old age now. But that's a tragedy, I should say. In his seventies, Jung mentioned his old age without any hesitation. He was very ironic if people pretended to be so young. You see, old age is a very important chapter or period of life. It is a limitation and a concentration, and for Jung the second part of life played an enormous role.

I must add something: life is not always good. If people are sick, you see this terrible illness of Alzheimer's disease, then old age is a curse.

Therefore we asked Aniela Jaffe how, at eighty-five, she wished to feel.

I wish to feel as I do feel. I'm quite satisfied. I don't want to be different. No. I don't look very much forward and I don't look backwards.

Jung himself, in acknowledging both the reality and the importance of old age, surprised some of those who were close to him in his later years; while they seemed to believe he was indestructible, he began to withdraw. Baroness von der Heydt, born in 1899, is a woman whose luminous beauty is seemingly unaffected by age. Until she suffered a severe fall and an enforced change of pace, she had overlooked the necessity of adaptation to old age – which she had seen Jung do himself.

I'm very old and for a very long time I didn't feel old, and I thought that I could and would do – or that one just did go on doing – the same things when one was eighty-five or eighty-six or so, as when one was sixty or seventy. And I did not heed Jung at the time. Because I was very surprised sometimes when Jung, when he was about at the end of his sixties, into his seventies, didn't do this or didn't do that because he said he was too old. And I couldn't understand it.

One finds evidence of Jung's determined withdrawal from the world not only in the recollections of his pupils and friends; in his published letters, he politely refuses requests from friends and acquaintances to visit him – as he did for example when his former pupil and old friend Professor Gustav Schmaltz, asked to come to see him at Bollingen in 1957.

I am now getting on for eighty-two and feel not only the weight of my years and the tiredness this brings, but, even more strongly, the need to live in harmony with the inner demands of my old age. Solitude is for me a fount of healing which makes my life worth living. Talking is often a torment for me, and I need many days of silence to recover from the futility of words. I have got my marching orders and only look back when there's nothing else to do. This journey is a great adventure in itself, but not one that can be talked about at great length. [30 May 1957]

Vera von der Heydt observes that Jung had set an excellent example, which she failed to follow:

Jung used to say: if you can't take a hint from life, then life will hit you. And that I think is true. There were hints, which I could have taken, and I didn't. And last year when I had my accident and I fell and broke my femur, I suddenly realized that it happened in order to help me to recognize that I should not go on going quite so fast, that I had to stop. So I had to break my leg before I was ready or willing or able to understand what it really was about. Particularly I felt some kind of relief almost that I could be old, that I was permitted to be old. It's the most extraordinary experience. And through that experience I realized how wise Jung was. He knew, he was unhappy, he didn't like being old either, not at all. I'm not that keen either, but nevertheless, one lives.

Dr von Franz, who has written a book *On Dreams and Dying* which considers the unconscious commentary on ageing and facing death, is herself very ill and before very long will be facing the end of her life. Age and illness have of course changed her life dramatically:

It needs a lot of readaptation, it poses a lot of outer problems, and reorganization of my life, because one gets invalid. Then it poses inner problems – 'Why do I have that illness? What for?' and so on. Naturally I look at the dreams for an answer, because all my friends and enemies suggest a lot of answers but I don't know which one to choose. I've dreamed that I saw a company of soldiers, dead tired – dusty and exhausted, trailing their feet in complete fatigue. And a voice said: 'One has kept those poor fellows in active service much too long.' That's probably the reason for my illness. I've overworked all my life, my illness is an exhaustion illness.

The question of old age and senility has given rise to a new Jungian approach – dealing with the difficulties of aged parents, whose ability to function in their social role – and even their conscious mental processes – are failing. Dr Jeffrey Satinover's clinic in Stamford, for example, is specializing in these problems, offering therapy and counselling not only to the Alzheimer's patients themselves, but to other members of the family who have to become increasingly responsible for them. By giving a greater appreciation to the unconscious mind, the psychological world of the elderly – as the ego's domination within the psyche slips away – may be given greater value. Dr Satinover:

In older adults who are facing death for any one of a number of reasons, most frequently just medical reasons, the unconscious is in effect something that rises up and demands attention, as individuals begin the process – usually reluctantly and often at times kicking and screaming – of reviewing what their life has meant; where it's gone, where it's going, coming to terms with questions of faith: do they have faith? do they not? do they believe in life after death? The big questions of life begin to press in and to demand some – if not answers – at least some consideration, as part of the process of adjusting to the transition out of this existence.

We see a great many people who, as they age, frequently as a consequence of Alzheimer's disease or other disorders, have begun to lose a lot of their faculties and abilities and knowledge that they have acquired over a lifetime. And then you see the unconscious emerging in a very different way. You see it emerging in the form of the reappearance of earlier, more primitive, childlike behaviours, and not in a way that is integrable – an individual who is losing his higher capacities cannot integrate these more primitive capacities, or more primitive methods of functioning and ways of life that come from childhood and that ultimately have their origin in the archetypal world. However, sometimes you'll see people in the early stages of Alzheimer's disease turn to their dreams. Frequently these are people who have developed an introspective capacity from the beginning, and so the inner world is a refuge for them to begin with. And as they become progressively less capable of handling the demands of the outside world, the turn toward the inner world is a natural one.

For almost everyone connected with cases of Alzheimer's disease, the affliction appears to be a pitiful tragedy; the strong parent can become as dependent on her/his adult children as if she/he had been wrenched out of mature adulthood into infancy. But some Jungian analysts – and their point of view is beyond proof, and highly arguable – believe that within the inner life of that senile person, a kind of serenity can replace the rage of the conscious phase in which faculties and abilities are being lost. Dr Guggenbuhl-Craig considers that the psychological state of the old fool can be a happy one.

The psyche changes in many different ways and everybody again is different. But discovering that your faculties slowly disappear, might have the effect, or it's nice if it has the effect that you are not caring so much any more, in the sense that you say: 'Well, why should I be so over-attached to everything? Why should it be so important to me to have these faculties?' I can sit here and enjoy a good meal or enjoy the sun, or love my grandchild, although I don't even know his name any more – you know, I still might come down to the more essential things, and my emotions might slowly turn to the more central things of life, and be less concerned with details.

Even in the more extreme case of Alzheimer's disease, or outright senile dementia, Dr Satinover argues that there is at least hope that the inner world offers some compensation or comfort when the conscious life collapses.

At the beginning of the disease, when function is being lost, and when the individual perceives that function is being lost, and suffering from the loss, mostly what you see is the individual's ego going through the pain of diminished capacity. But later on in the disease, when capacity even to recognize that something has been lost has itself been lost, what sometimes emerges – sometimes, not always – is a kind of childlike beneficence and a kind of calm, quiet happiness.

Just as the approach of death faces the conscious mind with questions of meaning, faith, and life-after-death, so the unconscious makes its own contribution. The analysts quoted here seem to offer a living example of Jung's view that dying is as much a part of life as growing old, that it is integral to life. Dreams of dying people have been studied by Dr von Franz, and she has observed that the evidence, such as it is, indicates some sense of life outliving death in some way.

We can only say that the dreams of dying people never refer to an end but they refer to a mysterious, very difficult to grasp, continuation of life. I cannot say that this is certainly true, but the unconscious psyche certainly wants us to believe it. One old woman was dying in the hospital and she told the nurse at eight o'clock in the morning that she had dreamt that she was afraid, because she saw a little candle burning on the windowsill and she thought it was burning down. She was afraid and thought: 'Now the great darkness is coming.' And suddenly there was a change of scene and she saw that the candle was on the other side of the window, outside, big and burning vigorously. Four hours after that dream she died. I think the dream is clear. It says there is a threshold and on this side of the threshold the candle of life goes out, but in another sphere it goes on burning.

From birth to death Jung's thought spanned human life. To him, life was meaningless without a search for meaning in the individual's life. In the course of his life, the world changed rapidly, throwing up ever-deeper symptoms of the absence of meaning for vast numbers of people whose lives are directed towards material ends alone. To Jung, and to his followers, life is meaningless if lived only at the level of the ego, the persona, the function, the job done and the bills paid.

Humankind has gone to the immense psychological trouble of preserving myths and legends, telling stories, and dreaming involuntarily the history of the human psyche – and in our state of ultimate knowledge and enlightenment, we consistently disregard it all.

By the end of his own life, Jung had come to embody the '*senex* archetype' – of the old wise man. But he resisted being mistaken for that impossible role. He had the humane commonsense to reject it. Jung himself told one of his pupils 'I am also an old fool' and 'I have also written a lot of nonsense.' In a letter to Aniela Jaffe, when he was almost eighty, he insisted upon his lack of certainty, which perhaps above all else preserves our sense today of the deep-rooted humanity of this extraordinary man.

> I observe myself in the stillness of Bollingen and with all my experience of nearly eight decades must admit that I have found no rounded answer to myself. I am just as much in doubt about myself as before, the more so the more I try to say something definite. It is as though familiarity with oneself alienated one from oneself still further.
> Cordially,
> Yours ever,
> C.G.   [Bollingen, 6 April 1954]

Graceful in her own old age, Aniela Jaffe told us, as she reluctantly agreed to be interviewed: 'When one grows old, one is relieved of the burden of remembering.' If further evidence were needed of the generosity of spirit that accompanied that inquisitive, doubting humility, it can be found in another letter, written to Charles H. Tobias – a man Jung had never met – on 27 October 1958. Tobias's son, also unknown to Jung, asked him to write a congratulatory letter for his father's seventieth birthday, since Jung was 'one of the famous men and women whose accomplishments he has always admired.'

> Dear Sir,
> A bird has whistled to me and told me that you have reached your seventieth year of life. Although I do not know you, I assume you are quite satisfied with this achievement. It is something. I can talk with some authority, as I am in my eighty-fourth and still in passably good form and – looking back, as you probably do on this day of celebration and congratulation – I see following behind

myself the long chain of five children, nineteen grandchildren, and about eight or nine great-grandchildren. (The latter number is not quite safe as at frequent intervals a new one drops from heaven.) Mature youth begins, as one says, at seventy and it is in certain respects not so nice and in others more beautiful than childhood. Let us hope that in your case the latter part of the sentence will confirm itself.

My best wishes,

Yours cordially,

C. G. Jung

Reflections on Film

'There are some aspects of human life that can only be
faithfully represented through poetry. ... All too often
dreams are made into a collection of old fashioned filmic
tricks, and cease to be a phenomenon of life.'
[Andrey Tarkovsky, *Sculpting in Time, Reflections on the Cinema*, Bodley
Head, 1986]

It is sometimes said that analysis is a 'work against nature' the *opus
contra naturam* in which the alchemists engaged. One is tempted to
plead that film-making, particularly making a documentary series
about the inner life of the psyche, the unconscious, and dreams – is a
work against nature too. There is not much that is natural or organic
in the process. The many individual components, of research, inter-
viewing, scripting, editing both words and pictures, and post-
production work, are peculiarly separate, yet entirely interconnected.

We have had to discard absorbing themes which seemed to us to be
important, but which none of our interviewees felt able to articulate;
sometimes they were determined to lead off in directions which were
not anticipated at all. One cannot order scholars to utter the words in
a programme outline; one cannot make them all think in the same
order.

Approaching this project in professional tandem, for the first time,
it gradually dawned on us how alike film-making and analysis are: in
interviews, one has to wait for the best material to emerge, often from
an unforeseen stimulus, just like the dream. Only then can you work
with it. The material doesn't come to order, or on cue; the images
which illustrate the ideas rarely work because of logic, or conscious

intent. The film-maker (like the analyst) has to organize whatever material does arise, and help to make sense of it and express it faithfully. As each unconscious has unique ways of summoning symbols and images in dreams to express psychological truths, so each film-maker has an individual imagination which produces a means of conveying the story.

In the preparatory stages of our work, we went to see Sir Laurens van der Post, to ask for his advice. As the maker of a film series about Jung for the BBC, in the early 1970s, and as a distinguished author and thinker whose name has become closely associated with Jung, Sir Laurens seemed to be a required participant in our work. But his advice was clear, and generous. 'You must make your own film,' he said. 'Do what you think is best, and don't do anything which you feel is imposed upon you. If you make your own film, it will be fine.'

But why on earth do people agree to give television interviews? Why, above all, would they agree to discuss matters which are highly complex and personal in a medium renowned for its triviality? While we should like to believe that it was because of our skill, and integrity, or of the reputation of British documentary film, Jung's own terminology provides a more honest explanation. Films and television are the primary myth-making mediums of today's world, and we all have a burning desire to participate in the myth. There is a widespread projection on to the film-making process and the film-maker. Everyone owns a television, and everyone consumes its products; there is a sense of public ownership of the television process, such that it is a constant occurrence, and often a real disruption of the work, when passers-by interrogate a film crew about what they are filming, why, and when it will be on.

For example, when we filmed James Hillman, in his little home-town of Thompson, Connecticut, the local librarian and other townspeople wanted to know all the details of our project – and to make sure we filmed all the best parts of their town. Filming in Arizona supermarkets, Swiss mountain railways, or St James's Park in London, the answer 'We're making a documentary series about psychology' evoked a mixture of surprise and a quite exaggerated respectfulness for the people engaged in this magical, mythical process.

Among the analysts and scholars we needed and hoped to involve in the films, we encountered an almost unanimous willingness to participate – some overcoming genuine reluctance for reasons of ill-health or time-pressures, yet agreeing; others, who had never been filmed before, clearly intrigued, or flattered, or romanticizing the idea of being 'on-screen'. It is worth confessing that through experience one learns to identify, and sometimes manipulate in the interests of the film, these 'transference' feelings with which people project all sorts of mythical powers and authority on to the role of Director.

Even though we are in the film business, we are not immune from this intense desire and joy at being part of the film myth. We were thrilled to see the building which houses our own new office used as a location in a recent feature film. It is no surprise then that the film-maker is well-placed to receive people's transferences. Like analysis, people are willing to be uncomfortable, to risk and to be honest and revealing, because of the faith and trust that they project on to the Director.

In many cases it was quite clearly understood – sometimes openly discussed – that a first meeting 'for research' amounted to an audition. Two analysts told us of dreams they had in which the unconscious seemed to be preparing for an interview. Dr von Franz, who had been asked to speak to an Italian interviewer on the psychology of love, told us how she had agreed to discuss this big subject in a brief, possibly superficial interview. She then dreamed that she went into a bathroom, where, instead of a normal toilet, she found a tiny receptacle – 'far too small for my needs' as she explained to us.

Jane Wheelwright had two dreams before we interviewed her in California:

> I had a dream about being with a crowd of people going down a spiral stairway, and going down this stairway with me was what I'd call an ageless young woman, dressed in grey. She was dark, she was obviously an introvert. And I was talking my head off, and I thought to myself 'I hope I can do that when Thursday comes around.' But then the following dream was of a very miserable situation, things were in a kind of shambles, and I was trying to pack, and things were out in the dirt and the dust, and there was a young woman, who was dressed in colours, and was blonde, so I figured she must be the extrovert. But the place was a shambles, and I thought 'Oh God, I hope that doesn't happen first.' I had to somehow get those two things together. In a way the dreams have perpared me for the interview. One can be extroverted and the other can be introverted and they come together. An introverted conversation in an extroverted setting.

The transference on to the film-making process allows reservations to be overcome, and often privacy is sacrificed when people admit the camera into their lives. As one learns rapidly in making television programmes and documentary films, the command of a camera is a great privilege – it opens doors and admits the film crew into private lives. What the camera requires of people in making television programmes, they undertake very differently in their analysis or therapy – sacrificing and sharing their secrets, but out of need and often desperation. The analyst or therapist is privileged too, and has a deep responsibility to honour those secrets.

Film-making and analysis do have their differences, of course – the most dramatic one being the question of audience. Psychotherapy is a very private affair, whereas the film is wholly for public consumption. Here our individual perspectives often clashed, as the introverted feeling/intuitive psychotherapist met head on with the extroverted thinking/sensation type film-maker. One could almost hear C.G. himself saying, in his distinctive Schwitzer-Deutsch accent, 'Well, you know, it's a hell of a business!'

And a hell of a business it was too. What could have been the destruction of not only a working partnership but also a marriage, became a vehicle for growth and renewed dedication to one another. It was a difficult time, but such is the nature of the long process of individuation.

The film-maker, who could so easily take advantage of the position that the myth of TV and film gives him, also has a responsibility – of honesty to his participants, and objectivity towards the material. In journalistic television, there can be, within limits, an objective stance. But we quickly learned to discard all pretensions to making the 'definitive' series on the work of Carl Gustav Jung. He has a personal impact on everyone who encounters him. We, who wrote this book, are a marriage of different cultures and nations – so his travels, and his cultural investigations attract us. To others, in different circumstances, nothing will seem more important than alchemy, or his religious ideas. But Jung ranged so far across the fields of human knowledge that almost everyone can be satisfied and stimulated by his work.

His breadth of intelligence and depth of intense self-examination can rarely have been equalled in human history. In another age he, and his no doubt different achievements, would have been recognized as extraordinary – or dangerous. Most of the great Renaissance scholars, especially those who combined an interest in scientific progress with religious and spiritual experience, paid a heavy price for their quest. In today's materialistic and suspicious intellectual climate, Jung's deep and unsettling insight into the human condition – which also offers such profound hope for humane understanding – evokes doubt, anxiety and embarrassment. Every individual with an open and curious mind, can find her/his own 'definitive Jung'. It is our hope – and conviction – that the privilege we have enjoyed of attempting to communicate a Jung, possibly *our* Jung, to a wide audience of viewers and readers will encourage them to set about their own journey and discover their own Jung, too.

Jung's life, eighty-five years long, was devoted to the reality of the psyche, and the play of his imagination. No one can doubt the impact he has had on our age. What we have attempted in this book, and the film series that accompanies it, is to indicate Jung's responsibility for so much of the psychological literacy which does exist today, in the use of language which he originated, and the presence in contemporary culture of themes which he essentially introduced. Considering the speed of scientific development and social breakdown, the legacy of a man born in 1875 could seem negligible. Yet Jung's psychology is current, relevant, and necessary; and it overshadows most academic and medical psychology as a means of truly gaining an understanding of ourselves, our fears, our troubles and our joys.

It does so, perhaps above all, because of the courage and integrity with which Jung faced himself and his discoveries. While this book was intended to be about Jung's work, not his life, his presence has in some ways overwhelmed us, for his identity is vividly present in his work. A few days after the main part of this manuscript was completed, we received, after a long wait, some tape-recordings. They were copies made from original wire-recordings, which we found in a dusty corner of the Jung Institute in Zurich, together with an antiquated wire-recorder. It was marked in German 'Bequest of C. G. Jung'.

There is no way of telling when the recordings were made, or how many other wires have been lost. But in what is apparently a seminar for his pupils, conducted in both German and English, the unmistakeable voice of Jung boomed out of the tape-recorder – speaking of the necessity for honesty between analyst and patient, the importance of who the analyst is rather than what she/he says, the unarguable facts of dreams, and many more familiar themes. He repeatedly made his audience laugh out loud.

The tapes, which no doubt one day can be published, are a small treasure in the legacy of C. G. Jung. At the end of our efforts, he returned to address us, and it is hard to imagine his voice fading away or the value of his message being lost, now. If today the unconscious is more than a mere abstraction, and the psyche has become a reality, we owe that largely to the scientist and doctor who listened to the wisdom of the dream: Carl Gustav Jung.

Selected Further Reading

G. Adler (ed.), *C. G. Jung Letters*, vols. 1 & 2 (Routledge & Kegan Paul, London 1973-4).

These two volumes are absolute gems. One gets a three-dimensional view of Jung the man and doctor as the reader traces his correspondence through his long life. Equally interesting are his letters to family and friends as well as the good and the great. A wonderful two volumes for dipping into.

I. Claremont de Castillejo, *Knowing Woman: A Feminine Psychology* (Harper & Row, New York 1973).

One of the books frequently recommended to women in the early stages of their Jungian psychotherapy or analysis. A down to earth and interesting view of the problems and challenges of the feminine psyche.

E. Edinger, *Anatomy of the Psyche* (Open Court, La Salle, Illinois 1985).

A look at the alchemical symbolism present in the process of psychotherapy.

R. Evans, *Jung on Elementary Psychology* (Routledge & Kegan Paul, London 1979).

The transcript of Dr Evans' four hour interview with Jung in 1957. Portions of this interview appeared in the film series *The Wisdom of the Dream* – for those who want to read all of what Jung said to Evans.

M. Fordham, *Children as Individuals* (Hodder & Stoughton, London, 1969; Putnam, New York, 1970).

Michael Fordham has taken Jungian psychology and integrated it with his own ideas which came out of his extensive clinical experience working analytically with children. A book mostly for clinicians, but also appropriate for those interested in the world of childhood and the practice of child analysis.

A. Guggenbuhl-Craig, *Power in the Helping Professions* (Spring, New York 1971).

Dr Guggenbuhl-Craig wastes few words and has a talent for turning concepts on their head and thereby revealing their true significance. An important book for all doctors, therapists, and patients.

A. Guggenbuhl-Craig, *Marriage – Dead or Alive* (Spring, Zurich 1977).

A good hard look at the institution of marriage and what actually happens to the psyches of those involved. Dr Guggenbuhl's direct and clear style make it a good book for all who have an interest in love and relationship. Read it to find out if his verdict is dead or alive.

C. S. Hall and V. J. Nordby, *A Primer of Jungian Psychology* (New English Library, London 1973).

A good introductory text to the nuances of the Jungian model of the psyche.

J. A. Hall, *Jungian Dream Interpretation* (Inner City Books, Toronto 1983).

As the title suggests, this is about the Jungian method of dream interpretation. A good book for clinicians and enthusiasts.

E. Harding, *The Way of All Women* (Harper & Row, New York, 1975).

This book is still relevant to the problems of women and their psychology. Along with the de Castillejo book one of the volumes frequently given to those beginning or contemplating Jungian psychotherapy.

J. Hillman, *Interior and Design of the City: Ceilings*, in *Stirrings of Culture*, R. Sardello and G. Thomas eds. (Dallas Institute Publications 1986).

There are many intriguing and thought-provoking essays by architects and thinkers – including Ivan Illich – in the volume which contains Hillman's observations on ceilings. A good resource for those interested in the inner world of the outer world.

Eli Humbert, *C. G. Jung.* (Chiron Publications, Wilmette, Ill 1988).

The most recent of the Jung biographies.

A. Jaffe, *The Myth of Meaning* (Putnam, New York 1971; paperback by Daimon, Switzerland).

This book is simply and profoundly about what gives life its meaning. Mrs Jaffe begins her book with a quotation from Camus: 'I have seen many people die because life for them was not worth living. From this I conclude that the question of life's meaning is the most urgent question of all.'

A. Jaffe (ed.), *C. G. Jung: Word and Image* (Princeton University Press 1979).

An illustrated volume, including photographs of Jung at different stages of life, his surroundings at Kusnacht and Bollingen, artwork produced during his period of confrontation with the unconscious, alchemical texts and the apparatus used in the association test experiments. A rich and accessible volume.

A. Jaffe, *Jung's Last Years and Other Essays* (Spring Publications, Dallas 1984).

Important and clearly written essays on a number of important topics in Jung's life and work, including parapsychology, alchemy, and the accusation that Jung was an anti-Semite or Nazi sympathiser.

R. A. Johnson, *He* (Harper & Row, New York 1974).

Robert Johnson is a gifted author, who has sold over 100,000 copies of his 'little' books, *He, She* and *We*. In just 81 pages Johnson discusses masculine psychology through the legend of Parsifal and his search for the grail.

R. A. Johnson, *She* (Harper & Row, New York 1976).

In 76 pages Johnson presents an interpretation of feminine psychology based on the myth of Amor and Psyche.

R. A. Johnson, *We* (Harper & Row, New York 1983).

Tristan and Isolde provide the mythic narrative for Johnson's wise words about the problems and power of romantic love in today's world.

R. A. Johnson, *Inner Work* (Harper & Row, New York 1986).

A book about the Jungian method of active imagination. A good how-to book for valuing one's creative impulses and fantasy thinking.

R. A. Johnson, *Ecstasy* (Harper & Row, New York 1987).

Using the Myth of Dionysos, the Greek god of wine, Johnson traces the rise and fall of this ancient cult to dramatize the loss of ecstasy in Western culture, and man's deep need for the experience of joy.

C. G. Jung, *Collected Works*, 2nd ed., ed. H. Read, M. Fordham, G. Adler and W. McGuire; translated in the main by R. Hull (Routledge & Kegan Paul, London; Princeton University Press 1975).

The complete edition of all Jung's published work, from clinical research reports to religious and philosophical speculation. A total of nineteen main volumes, with a supplementary volume of 'Dream Seminars' and a separate volume containing the general index.

C. G. Jung, *Memories, Dreams, Reflections* (Collins and Routledge & Kegan Paul, London 1963).

Jung's unique account of his own life as told to his then secretary and assistant, Aniela Jaffe.

C. G. Jung (ed.), *Man and His Symbols* (Aldus Books, London 1964).

A compilation of essays by Jung and some of his followers. It was Jung's only effort to bring his psychology to a mass audience. Its scope is selective in terms of Jungian psychology as a whole, but nevertheless it's an enjoyable and accessible book, now a classic.

E. Jung, *Animus and Anima* (Spring, New York 1957).

Although this book is somewhat dated, Emma Jung's description of the animus remains one of the best. It is also interesting to read the work of the woman who raised her family and worked as an analyst herself in the shadow of the great man.

D. Kalff, *Sandplay: A Psychotherapeutic Approach to the Psyche* (Sigo, Santa Monica 1980).

Dora Kalff's explanation of her development of the Lowenfeld Word Test into a unique Jungian psychotherapeutic technique. Excellent case material and view into the world of childhood.

R. A. Lockhart, *Words as Eggs* (Spring, Dallas 1983).

A series of essays by a poetic and insightful analyst/author. This collection contains excellent pieces on the hidden psychological significance in the etymology of words, the Jungian method of valuing and interpreting the hallucinatory content of psychosis, cancer in myth and dream, and other topics. An accessible book.

W. McGuire and R. F. C. Hull (eds.), *C. G. Jung Speaking* (Picador, London 1980).

A colourful and anecdotal assortment of journal entries by people who met and talked to Jung, reports of lectures he gave, as well as magazine, newspaper and radio interviews with him.

C. A. Meier, *Ancient Incubation and Modern Psychotherapy* (Northwestern University Press, Evanston, Ill 1967; Damion, Switzerland, 1989).

An interesting study of the cult of Asclepius and the Greek roots of modern medicine and the Jungian psychotherapeutic method.

C. A. Meier (and others), *A Testament to the Wilderness* (Daimon Verlag Zurich, and Lapis Press, Santa Monica 1985).

A volume prepared in honour of Professor Meier's eightieth birthday. Ten people (Sir Laurens van der Post, Jane Wheelwright, Sam Francis, Joe Henderson and others) wrote essays on an address delivered by Meier to the World Wilderness Congress in 1983. It is recommended for all concerned with the future of our troubled world and endangered wilderness.

A. Samuels, *Jung and the Post Jungians* (Routledge & Kegan Paul, London 1985).

An advanced book mainly for clinicians and those interested in the theoretical strands which now make up the world of Jungian psychology. Samuels presents a scholarly bird's-eye view.

Donald Sandner, *Navajo Symbols of Healing* (Harcourt Brace Jovanovich, London 1979).

For those readers interested in the culture and practices of south-western American Indians, this book explores ancient Indian rituals and their application to modern medicine and the practice of analytical psychology.

B. Shorter, *An Image Darkly Forming* (Routledge & Kegan Paul, London 1987).

Bani Shorter uses the stories of five women who, at important transitional stages in their life instinctively and spontaneously created rituals to mark their journey toward maturation. A book which honours the archetypal needs of women and the presence of the collective unconscious in women's lives.

J. M. Spiegelman (ed.), *Jungian Analysts: Their Visions and Vulnerabilities* (Falcon Press, Phoenix 1988).

An ingenious book in which the author has compiled and commented on the responses of twelve analysts to the question, 'How do you do it?.' An interesting view into the consulting-rooms of analysts around the world. Several analysts quoted in *The Wisdom of the Dream* are amongst Spiegelman's twelve respondents.

M. Stein (ed.), *Jungian Analysis* (Shambhala, London 1984).

An excellent and comprehensive reference book for clinicians, There are excellent chapters on transference and counter-transference; dream interpretation; play, group, and movement therapies; the issues unique to the treatment of children and the aged, as well as other topics.

A. Storr, *Jung: Selected Writings* (Fontana, London 1983).

If you want to read Jung in his own words, but find the thought of tackling the twenty or so volumes of the *Collected Works* overwhelming, this book is for you.

Count Nikolai Tolstoi, *The Quest for Merlin* (Hamish Hamilton, London 1985).

A scholarly book about this evocative and archetypal character at the crux of British mythology.

Sir Laurens van der Post, *Jung and the Story of our Time* (Penguin, London 1976).

A very personal account of Jung and his ideas and how they influenced the life and thinking of Sir Laurens.

V. von der Heydt, *Prospects for the Soul* (Darton, Longman & Todd, London 1976).

The Baroness von der Heydt was one of the most gracious, insightful and welcoming people we have ever met. Her Roman Catholic background, unusual in the Jungian world, informs her views on a number of topics addressed in this book, of which the most important is religion itself.

M-L. von Franz, *Interpretation of Fairy-tales* (Spring, Dallas 1970).

A classic of the Jungian world. A lucid description of how Jungians 'read' the psychological significance of fairy-tales. Marie-Louise von Franz reminds us that only in recent years have fairy-tales been relegated to the nursery.

M-L. von Franz, *Puer Aeternus* (Sigo, Santa Monica 1970).

Using the story of the Little Prince by Saint-Exupery, von Franz discusses the psychology of the man who is afraid of maturity and reluctant to leave the paradise of childhood. A thoughtful and detailed discussion of the 'Peter Pan' syndrome.

M-L. von Franz and J. Hillman, *Jung's Typology* (Spring, Dallas 1979).

These two giants of the Jungian world get together to describe Jung's theory of typology. A very practical book, it talks about the problem of the inferior function (von Franz) and the feeling function (Hillman).

M-L. von Franz, *Alchemy* (Inner City Books, Toronto 1980).

A volume taken from a lecture series von Franz delivered at the Jung Institute, Zurich. A complicated subject which von Franz makes vivid and comprehensible to the general reader.

M-L. von Franz, *On Dreams and Death* (Shambhala, London 1987).

A profound volume in which Dr von Franz looks at evidence drawn from a wide variety of sources about what the psyche has to say about death and the possibility of an after-life.

G. Wehr, *Jung: A Biography* (Shambhala, London 1987).

One of the two most recent biographies of Jung, it received a positive response from Jung's son, Franz Jung.

J. H. Wheelwright, *The Ranch Papers* (Lapis Press, Santa Monica 1988).

Jane Wheelwright's beautiful account of her life-long relationship with the wilderness on her ranch in Santa Barbara, California. The book seems hardly to have been written at all, but rather to have grown from the landscape. An impressionistic work from an extraordinary woman.

F. Wickes, *The Inner World of Childhood* (Appleton, New York 1966).

A classical Jungian view of the world of the child. A different view to that expressed by Fordham. For those with a committed interest in childhood, both volumes are recommended.

H. A. Wilmer, *Practical Jung: Nuts and Bolts of Jungian Psychotherapy* (Chiron Publications, Wilmette, Ill 1987)

A highly original and useful clinical manual, it came out of Harry Wilmer's years of teaching Jung to trainee psychiatrists. A down to earth and humorous volume, rooted in the common conversation of everyday life, it has something to teach all clinicians, regardless of philosophical orientation.

Index

Other C. G. Jung Foundation Books
from Shambhala Publications

A Guided Tour of the Collected Works of C. G. Jung, by Robert H. Hopcke.

In Her Image: The Unhealed Daughter's Search for Her Mother, by Kathie Carlson.

Power and Politics: The Psychology of Soviet-American Part-nership, by Jerome S. Bernstein. Forewords by Senator Claiborne Pell and Edward C. Whitmont, M.D.